# Time Shadows

## a prison memoir

by

Laurence McKeown

illustrated by Gabrielle Williams

First published 2021

Beyond the Pale Books
Teach Basil
2 Hannahstown Hill
Belfast BT17 0LT

www.beyondthepalebooks.com



ISBN 978-1-914318-11-5 (paperback)

Printed in Ireland.

Cover design: a collaborative effort between Gabrielle, Laurence, Mike and Gerry (Morrison). The cover photograph of Laurence comes from a Northern Ireland Office 'fact file' published during the 1981 hunger strike (see photographs, page H).When Laurence requested the photo from the prison authorities early in 2021, they said they had no record of it.

# Contents

# Acknowledgements

AS WITH MY WALK through life, there are a number of people who helped me along the way in writing this book; putting me in touch with others, confirming some detail that I was unsure about, or providing me with specific information. My deepest thanks to you all:

Benny McElwee, Geraldo McDaid, Jenny Meegan,
John Hunter, Kevin Lappin, Louise Purbrick,
Martin Mallon, Mick McVeigh, Mike Ritchie,
Richard ('Junior') May, Seán McGuigan, Seán Osborne,
Séanna Walsh, Róisín Kelly, and Teddy Crane.

A special thanks to Gabrielle who spent many days proofing – several times throughout the course of the writing. Her keen eye and skilful command of the English language improved the text immensely, as did her encouragement of me to go deeper into my personal journey through the story.

And to Mike Tomlinson, Bill Rolston, and Robbie McVeigh of Beyond the Pale Books who have once again provided me with the opportunity to add to our understanding of what took place during those prison protest years 1976-1981.

# Illustrator's Foreword

I AM ONE OF OVER TWO MILLION Australians of Irish heritage, albeit many generations ago. However, that fact alone doesn't come close to explaining my connection to Ireland, or more specifically my connection to the north of Ireland. In 2004, at 22 years of age, I travelled to Belfast to conduct some fieldwork for a thesis I was completing as part of my university studies. I was writing about the conflict and in particular about what motivated individuals to engage in violence. As part of this, I was eager to meet and speak to former prisoners, and hear their stories. The very first person I interviewed was Laurence McKeown. I learned a little about the man in the few hours I spent with him over two or three wet, wintery Belfast days. I've learned much more in the 16 years since, especially in the last year or so, as the idea for this project – and my contribution to it – unfolded.

One thing must be made clear. I am not an illustrator, nor am I an artist. Well, not by profession anyway. I am a politician, which some might claim involves its own special kind of creativity! But it's not a role that allows much time for hobbies, which is perhaps why this project is so special to me.

I hadn't painted or sketched for well over ten years when, a couple of years ago, I set up an easel in an effort to see if my fingers could create what my mind could see. They never can, but the work was passable. And most of all, I enjoyed it. In that time, I've shared some of my work with Laurence, which is when he suggested that I might like to do the illustrations for this book. Just as I have here, I reminded him that I am not an artist or an illustrator. This didn't deter him. And so, I sketched.

The illustrations are deliberately scratchy, attempting to capture an essence of the rough conditions they depict, but I've tried to make them visually interesting. Often, they serve a functional purpose, to demonstrate to readers unfamiliar with the topic what the Long Kesh prison hospital looked like, for example, or how tobacco was distributed along an H-Block wing. I've grown in my own knowledge in the process, gently tutored, of course, by Laurence.

Participation in the project has been an honour and a source of great joy. It has felt important, because any account of history is important. We must keep sharing these stories in whatever way we can, and I'm so very pleased that I could contribute to their telling on this occasion.

*Gabrielle Williams*
State of Victoria
Australia

# Preface

ONE OF MY FAVOURITE FILMS is *Burn After Reading* (2008), written, directed, edited and produced by that highly-talented duo, Joel and Ethan Coen. In the film, the main character, Osbourne 'Ozzie' Cox (played brilliantly by John Malkovich) quits his job as a CIA analyst after he is accused of having a problem with alcohol. Later that evening, in their bedroom, he informs his wife Katie (played by Tilda Swinton) about his loss of employment. Katie is seated at a dressing table, looking into a mirror and removing her makeup. Ozzie is seated behind her on the bed. Katie is not amused that he has walked out of his job, resulting in no income and no pension. She asks him what he intends to do now. In a close-up shot of Ozzie, he replies haltingly, "I've been thinking of writing a book … or … you know … a sort of … memoir". He pretentiously pronounces 'memoir' as it would sound in its original French. Kate continues to stare at him for a moment and then let's out a contemptuous laugh. Ozzie is crestfallen.

It's a great scene, in a film of great scenes, but forever after I cannot think of or say the word 'memoir', without thinking of how Ozzie pronounced it in such a grand, sophisticated (and pretentious) manner. And now that I've come to write a memoir myself, the word is all the more troubling! Pronounce it as you will; this is a memoir.

A memoir is different from a diary. The latter is written contemporaneously and may simply note what the author is doing on a daily, or fairly regular basis; what appointments s/he has and with whom, but it may also include thoughts and notes on how the author is feeling and thinking about events on that day. A memoir or autobiography, on the other hand, is written after the events have taken place. It could be many years later or even decades later. In my case, it is over four decades later.

There is no reason why the factual elements should differ whether they be in either a diary or a memoir. Dates, places, people. Certain things happened to certain people on certain dates at a certain time. They are a constant and can often be checked or verified by using other sources, conducting research, or seeking confirmation from others who were involved in the same events. But looking back on something many years later, with the benefit of hindsight and having lived a life in between, can change how we fully recall and understand moments. It doesn't necessarily mean that our memory is inaccurate, though that may well be the case. It's simply that we now view those events, and the duration of the time period over which they occurred, within the context of a longer life span.

When I was sentenced to life imprisonment in April 1977 and went onto the blanket protest, I didn't know how long it would last. I didn't know there would be a hunger strike. I didn't know I would take part in that hunger strike for 70 days but ultimately survive. I didn't know how long I would serve in prison. But I know all of that now. And knowing these things impacts on how I recall those five years and all that happened during them. It also puts those five years in context.

When you are living through a difficult period, be it in prison or on the outside, what makes it more difficult to deal with is not knowing how long that situation will last and what the outcome will eventually be. Maybe it is unemployment and poverty; maybe it is a serious illness; maybe a difficult time in a relationship; but the uncertainty over both the length of time it will continue and what the ultimate conclusion will be, adds greatly to the anxiety and pain felt at the time. During the blanket protest, for example, living through particular instances of brutality, I never knew if it was to be a short-lived event, something initiated by a particular guard or group of guards that would fizzle out after a few days, or something that heralded a more permanent development. What if the brutality experienced today was just a foretaste of what was to come? Uncertainty compounds the brutality of the moment. Once the period has ended you can look back and say it lasted for x number of minutes, hours, days, or weeks and you can identify the worst moment of it because it is now in the past. It is history. It may be repeated at some later time, and may then be worse than what happened previously, but at least that specific time period and brutality can be quantified both in terms of how long it lasted and its severity.

So, looking back, when writing this account of what happened, writing this memoir, I can recall the moments, good and bad, but I know I'll never be able to fully capture the strength of emotions as I felt them in those moments, despite the fact that I can still break into tears or laughter, or feel rage or pride, at their recollection.

And it reminds us that everything does come to an end, at some point. It is beautifully and simply summed up in the adage that is believed to originate in the writings of medieval poet Jalal ad-Din Muhammed Rumi (1207–73), a Sufi mystic born in Balkh in present-day Afghanistan – "This too shall pass". The human condition, and all that we experience, is temporary.

Apart from what I now know about the blanket protest and hunger strike, I now know many other things. I know that both my mother and father would die while I was still in prison. I know that I was eventually released in 1992, having served a total of sixteen years. I know that I went on to write, through a doctoral thesis, prose, poetry, a feature film, and plays, about the history of republican prisoners in the H-Blocks.

And apart from what I've written, I now know that I would become a father and experience what it is like to see my daughters grow up. I now know that I would travel to many countries and meet many people and would discover that I really enjoy travelling. I also now know that I would engage with many of those who were once sworn enemies or political opponents (not people I would previously have had much contact with) and would actually come to regard several of them as close friends.

I know all of that now and that undoubtedly shapes, consciously or unconsciously, how I look back on that period between 1976 and 1981.

This, then, is my memoir.

"*Patience is waiting. Not passively waiting. That is laziness. But to keep going when the going is hard and slow – that is patience. The two most powerful warriors are patience and time.*"

Leo Tolstoy

# Prologue

I WAS BORN on 19 September, 1956, and grew up outside the village of Randalstown, Co. Antrim, in the townland of Carngranny. I was the second of three children born to George and Margaret McKeown. My sister, Mary, was three years older than me and my brother, Eugene, three years younger.

We lived in a house, situated half-way up a long lane, that had no electricity, no running water and no indoor sanitation. We had a well and a pump at the end of the house, and the toilet was in an outside shed and consisted of an enamel bucket set below a board with a hole in it, and a pile of newspapers placed beside it.

Our family's experience wasn't an exception. Those were pretty much the conditions every working-class person lived in then, especially if your house was not close to main roads with direct access to water and electricity supplies.

Carngranny was a mixed religious area so Protestants weren't 'alien' beings to me, the way they may have been to those who grew up in mainly nationalist areas. In fact, our most immediate neighbours up until I was aged twelve were Protestants – the Warwicks and the Millars. I learned to drive a tractor at age ten while helping the Warwicks (Davy and son, David) on their farm during haymaking. I can remember the moment vividly. David and I were collecting bales of hay late one evening in a field. David had to drive the tractor and trailer to each hay stack, then get off and lift the bales onto the trailer. He eventually said to me, "Jump on there and drive it. You know how to do it. You've watched me often enough." He gave a laugh as he said it. I was both thrilled and terrified. But I got on the tractor and David told me to put my left foot on the clutch and press down and to move the gear stick into first gear, then let the clutch out slowly. It wasn't the smoothest take off I've ever made but it felt amazing. It wasn't just the fact that I was driving a tractor and trailer but that an adult had total trust and confidence in me to do it. An unforgettable moment.

My abiding memory of Davy, the father, is that he never smoked a full cigarette – Embassy, red packet – but would 'nick' it with thumb and forefinger when it was half-way smoked and put the butt in the breast pocket of his denim dungarees; the type that many men, including my father, wore in those days.

Davy's sister Mary, and brothers Sammy and Willie, lived at the top of our lane whilst Davy had his own home and additional farmland a couple of miles away. Neither Mary nor Sammy ever married; Willie became engaged to a woman apparently after courting her for about twelve years, and married her about ten years later. Willie was not the type to rush into anything! Mary was always very kind to me and had a very pleasant manner. Sammy worked as a labourer in the forestry service close to Antrim town and cycled to work each day. On a Sunday evening he would come into our house and read the Sunday newspapers. 'Our' Sunday newspapers were published in the south of Ireland and therefore reflected a Catholic ethos and I always wondered, in later years, what interested Sammy in reading them. It certainly showed that he was open-minded in his choice of reading materials.

The Warwicks were wonderful neighbours and very different from the Millars who lived at the bottom of the lane and who were regarded as more than a little 'odd', even by their co-religionists. They always had an Alsatian dog in the front yard of their large house. It had a chain on it attached to a heavy metal weight but sometimes the dog would break free of the chain and run out into the lane to bite whoever happened to be passing. My father was bitten once. I was always nervous when walking past their house.

Life was idyllic, and innocent. I walked or cycled to the local two-classroom primary school in the townland of Farinflough. Other than that, I spent my time making go-carts, tinkering with old bikes to create some mongrel version that combined my grandfather's old frame with racing handlebars, or I went fishing for sticklebacks with a jam jar in a nearby stream. For many years the stream was the border of my world. On the other side existed another universe, an unexplored world. It was home to an abandoned cottage that was said to be haunted. I remember the day I ventured to the other side. And to the cottage. I was really scared as I moved closer to it, slowly circling it first before I actually stepped onto the yard in front of it. I didn't enter the cottage but, nevertheless, felt an exhilaration at having conquered my fear of even approaching it. My world had greatly expanded.

That life came to an abrupt end when I was twelve. A new motorway, the M2, was being constructed and its path went right through our house. Why anyone would wish to build a motorway from Belfast to Randalstown is beyond me. Randalstown is a village; not an important village and definitely not the seat of commerce. What Randalstown does have, however, is the O'Neill family, or rather, the Lord O'Neill family whose huge estate (Shanes castle) runs from Antrim town to Randalstown. Perhaps the Lord needed a proper and speedy road to connect his residence to Belfast, so our home, and many others, were demolished to make way for it. My father built a new house beside my grandmother's, closer to Randalstown.

One afternoon, in early January 1969, as the outside of the house was being plastered, a number of cars and minibuses began to arrive at the small Ancient Order of Hibernians' (AOH) hall which sat at the corner of the field we were building our house on. I didn't know what was happening. The people I saw in this crowd were not the type I was accustomed to seeing at the hall. These ones were young, and mixed, men and women, whereas those who usually frequented the AOH hall were older, and all men. Later that evening our family passed the hall in our car – a Ford Anglia. I still recall its registration: AIA 3605. I think we were going to Mass so it may have been the 6th of January, the Feast of the Epiphany. Some of those who had arrived at the hall that afternoon were now standing outside it. Some had beards, others long hair, and one person was wearing what I later learned was an Afghan coat, trendy at the time, especially amongst the student fraternity. And that's who these people were: students from Queen's University, Belfast. They were taking part in a civil rights march from Belfast to Derry organised by People's Democracy. The march was modelled on the 1965 voting-rights march from Selma to Montgomery, Alabama in the USA. Arriving at Antrim town from Belfast, the marchers had their way blocked by Protestant, unionist protestors and it was then they were ferried to the AOH hall to spend the night there.

I didn't know any of this at the time, though. It was only in later years that I became aware of it all. It's strange to think back, however, and realise that I was living through a very historic period and that part of it was happening right on my doorstep. The other thing I couldn't understand at the time was why one of the Millar sons, our former neighbours, had apparently driven into the marchers in Randalstown the following morning when they were again stopped by unionist protestors. I was only twelve-years old at the time so it didn't make any sense to me.

We moved into our new home, a small bungalow, later that year. We now had electricity which meant we also had a TV – as well as running water, and a bathroom! I remember switching the light switch on and off, intrigued at the instant illumination, until my father told me to stop or I'd blow the bulb.

My parents were not politically-minded and would never have expressed a political opinion, either inside or outside the house. However, my father often got really excited when listening to nationalist politicians and Civil Rights activists on the TV; people like Bernadette Devlin (later McAliskey), Gerry Fitt, Paddy Devlin, and others. In later life I realised that his excitement when listening to these speakers was due to the fact that he was hearing, for the first time on mainstream media, an articulation of all the injustices and humiliations he had experienced growing up as a Catholic in the north of Ireland. He knew that he, and his co-religionists, were regarded as second-class citizens, despised and discriminated against by the Protestant, unionist government at Stormont. My parents' generation, and the generations before them, had largely kept their heads down, realising all too well the implications of raising them. Now, my generation was refusing to keep their heads down any longer.

Up until the advent of the Northern Ireland Civil Rights Campaign in '68/'69 the Stormont unionist regime had been able to rule with a veneer of democracy, albeit thin, that attempted to cloak the discriminatory and sectarian nature of the regime. With the advent of the Civil Rights campaign and the regime's brutal response to the very moderate demands for 'one man, one vote' and an 'end to discrimination in housing and employment', that regime was exposed for what it really was. It was as if the blindfold had been pulled from people's eyes. A new generation of Catholics, more confident than their parents or grandparents before them, and now more educated with access to third-level education, refused to be treated as second-class citizens any longer.

The unionist regime rejected any and all calls for reform (even from many liberal-minded Protestants) and instead initiated punitive measures and coercive tactics such as internment-without-trial,[1] curfews of republican areas, and house searches and arrests by the British Army. This marked a significant shift for my generation. It was no longer about 1916 or what politics your parents or grandparents had. It was no longer about being steeped in republican ideology or even being knowledgeable about Irish history – which I certainly wasn't. It was about the now and what was happening to us on the streets. It was about a new generation of republicans, or a new generation of activists drawn to the republican struggle in response to a now very visible, very oppressive, and openly brutal regime. That, in turn, led to a new republicanism.

As I grew into my early teens I began to take more of an interest in political debates in the media and took more notice of what was going on around me. I vaguely knew the families of some people who were interned-without-trial and later knew of some who had been at the same school as me who ended up in prison for IRA activities. This led me more and more to the conclusion that I too wanted to play my part. In the end, the factor that most influenced my decision to join the IRA was the behaviour of the Ulster Defence Regiment (UDR) towards me and other Catholic friends.[2]

---

[1] Introduced on 9 August,1971, internment-without-trial applied initially only to nationalists. Many hundreds were arrested in dawn raids. It is now widely regarded as having been largely ineffective (regardless of how its use may be regarded in both moral and legal terms). The information and intelligence reports upon which the British based their arrests were grossly outdated and often inaccurate.

[2] The Ulster Defence Regiment (UDR) was a regiment of the British Army, established in 1970 to replace the infamous 'B Specials'. It was the largest infantry regiment in the British Army and consisted mainly of part-time volunteers until 1976, when full-time members were added. Whilst initially, Catholic recruits accounted for 18% of its soldiers, by the end of 1972, following the introduction of internment-without-trial, Catholics accounted for just 3%. Many members of the UDR were also simultaneously members of illegal, loyalist paramilitary groups. 18 UDR soldiers were convicted of murder and 11 for

Although I lived a few miles outside Randalstown, I would regularly be in the village. Along with Vincent Kelly from Farinflough and the McNallys – Martin, Emmet, George, and Kevin, from the 'Ballymena line' – we'd walk to Randalstown and hang around the streets or play football with other young and/or slightly older Catholics and Protestants. There was no real hassle and relationships were amicable. We were probably all too young to recognise the potential for tension and even though the conflict had been going on for several years by then it had not impacted any of us personally. Then, one night, we were stopped by the Ulster Defence Regiment in the centre of Randalstown as we were returning home from a local dance in Toomebridge. Vincent Kelly could drive by that stage and he had an old Volkswagen Beetle that we'd all pile into. The UDR told us to get out of the car while it was searched. We were then asked for our names, where we were coming from, and where we were going to. Several of those in uniform were people we knew well – Protestants from the village, people we had chatted with outside the pubs, people we had played football with. The one who questioned me was embarrassed and awkward when asking me my name. He knew me. He knew me well. But when we were stopped for the second and third time, and regularly after that, the embarrassment disappeared and in its place was hostility. We were often held at checkpoints for up to an hour or more. On one occasion, returning home from a dance in the middle of the night, we were stopped in Randalstown and then taken to Antrim police station six miles away. There was no reason for it. There was nothing suspicious about us; just a bunch of sleepy guys returning home from a late night out. From memory, when we arrived at the police station the RUC[3] were even curious as to why we had been taken there and we were immediately released.

The checkpoints, with their inevitable delays, became much more frequent; and not just in Randalstown. Now that we had a car and were travelling further afield, to Moneyglass outside Toomebridge, County

---

manslaughter. Between 1970 and 1985, 99 were convicted of assault, whilst others were convicted of armed robbery, weapons offences, bombing, intimidation and attacks on Catholics, kidnapping, and membership of the UVF.

[3] Royal Ulster Constabulary, the police in the north of Ireland at the time. Following the signing of the Good Friday Agreement in 1998 the RUC was reformed to become the Police Service of Northern Ireland.

Antrim and eventually to Ardboe, a popular dance venue in County Tyrone, we were more liable to run into checkpoints. We were held for long periods at them, verbally abused, and generally harassed. It was at that point, then aged 16, that I realised that there were indeed two communities but they were not identified by what Church their members attended on a Sunday but by the fact that one community had uniforms and weapons – and could do basically whatever they wished to against their neighbours – and the other had neither. It was at that point, in early 1973, that I decided to join the IRA.

That wasn't a simple thing to do. I didn't know anyone in the organisation and anyone who was in it didn't go around advertising that fact. However, through a convoluted process, somewhat more accidental than planned, I did end up getting in touch with the IRA. I was dissuaded from joining; not from my family or friends but from the IRA. After my initial contact it took several months before I met two senior members of the organisation in the area. They were several years older than me. One was a man; the other a woman. They told me I'd end up in prison, or dead, and that I should rethink my decision to join. I didn't, or at least what they had said to me didn't deter me and I continued to pester my original contact any time I saw him.

Eventually, by the end of that year I was sworn into the IRA and became an active volunteer. The following year, before I had reached my eighteenth birthday, I had to leave home and go 'on the run'. I spent the next two years staying in billets (safe houses) in various parts of the north, in Monaghan, and for a brief while, in Dublin.

In December of 1974 talks between the IRA and Protestant clergymen, followed by talks between the British government and republican leaders, led to an extended ceasefire which continued into January 1976.[4] Many people who had been 'on the run' began to move around more openly during that period. Things became much more relaxed. More importantly, internment which had been initially introduced on 9 August 1971 was ended and those interned released to return to their homes. There was talk that Britain was withdrawing from the north of Ireland.

---

[4] What became known as the 'Feakle' talks as they took place in the small town of Feakle in County Clare. See: https://cain.ulster.ac.uk/events/truce/chron.htm

It was a very confusing time for me. Some people who had been active volunteers with me drifted away. There were no meetings to brief us on what was happening. Nothing seemed to have really changed, bar the end of internment. Loyalists were carrying out attacks on the Catholic community. On Friday 2 July, 1976, the loyalist Ulster Volunteer Force attacked the Ramble Inn just a few miles from my home. They killed six people but although the owner of the pub was a Catholic the clientele was mixed and of the six killed, five were Protestants, including Ernie Moore who I knew well.

The ceasefire was, by then, long dead and buried and the IRA slowly becoming more active as we moved through 1976. On 2 August, 1976, at 6.30 a.m. the RUC raided my home and I was arrested. I shouldn't have been at home, and rarely was by that stage, but had gone there that night after being out at a pub and later attending a dance in Moneyglass. I hadn't arranged a billet and it was late at night. I thought it would be safe to spend a night at home. It was lackadaisical of me – no doubt another impact of the lengthy ceasefire. There was still that uncertainty about what was really happening. Nothing appeared black and white, the way it had appeared to me just over two years previously when I'd joined the IRA.

I awoke as an RUC man entered my bedroom. I had only been asleep a few hours. I was told to get dressed. I put on the same clothes I had worn the previous night.

The RUC took me in the back of a Landrover to Castlereagh Interrogation Centre in Belfast.[5] On the initial part of the journey they had the back windows of the Landrover open. I could watch familiar places go past. It felt as if I was watching a movie. I wasn't part of this. But I was.

I had never been arrested before and had never been interrogated. When I arrived at Castlereagh I was medically examined by a doctor. My belt and shoe laces were then removed and I was placed in a cell. I was offered breakfast soon afterwards but refused it, vaguely recalling

[5] Castlereagh Interrogation Centre was a new centre developed in the mid-1970s and soon became infamous with many allegations made about the use of ill-treatment and torture during interrogations. It was the subject of several Amnesty International complaints, one government commission of inquiry and at least one secret internal police investigation.
https://www.theguardian.com/uk/2010/oct/11/inside-castlereagh-confessionstorture

something I'd heard once about how they might attempt to drug you. A myth, no doubt. Shortly afterwards the interrogations began, usually lasting about two hours each with a break in between. There were threats of physical violence and a lot of slapping tables hard and shouting in my face but no direct blows. The interrogation continued throughout the day. I continued to refuse meals when offered.

When I joined the IRA, the extent of my anti-interrogation 'training' consisted of simply, "Say nothing if arrested". That was the totality of it. There were no examples given of how an interrogation would be carried out or the tactics that would be employed. It was only in later years that the IRA developed a more sophisticated approach to anti-interrogation training – in response to the RUC successes in Castlereagh and other interrogation centres, such as the Strand Road Barracks in Derry or Gough barracks in Armagh. But this was 1976 and those developments were some years off.

In the afternoon of my second day in Castlereagh, those conducting the interrogations changed, as did the tactics employed. They became more psychologically manipulative than aggressive. I was told that my parents would be arrested and that word would get out to loyalists that my father was involved with the IRA (which he wasn't, of course) and that, given that he worked in mixed areas, he would become an easy target. Looking back, with the benefit of hindsight, I realise now it was highly unlikely they were ever going to arrest my parents. But at the time, in an interrogation room in Castlereagh, it felt very real and I made a brief verbal statement admitting my role in the IRA.[6]

It's always intrigued me ever since, how a day, an hour, a moment, can change the course of your entire life. You don't get a chance to rewind the clock. All you can do is to learn from mistakes. Looking back on it now I'm much more philosophical about it than I was then. I realise that if I'd been released from Castlereagh I would have been back active in the IRA and would either have ended up in prison at

---

[6] In a study conducted by academics, Kevin Boyle, Tom Hadden, and Paddy Hillyard, published in 1980, they found that; "...in almost all of the cases covered in our survey (86%) the defendant had made a confession. In a third of the cases (30%) this was supplemented by additional forensic or identification evidence which pointed to the guilt of the accused, but this additional evidence would often not have been sufficient to justify a conviction on its own." *Ten years on in Northern Ireland : the legal control of political violence*, London: Cobden Trust.

some later date, or maybe I'd be dead. At the time, though, I felt I had failed.

That evening I was taken to a special sitting of Antrim Court and formally charged with the attempted murder of an RUC man following a gun attack upon a mobile patrol. The attack had taken place just over a week after the attack on the Ramble Inn. I was also charged with causing explosions in Randalstown and Antrim. I don't recall much about it other than that my mother was at the court. I was remanded to Belfast's Crumlin Road Prison (the 'Crum', as it was generally referred to).

I was escorted there, handcuffed, in the back of an RUC car, rather than a closed-in Landrover, so I could clearly see the building as I arrived. The prison was an old Victorian-era prison designed and built in the 1840s. Today it is a museum. The building looked dark and dreary, with an air of foreboding and yet it also seemed somehow quiet and peaceful. I don't recall feeling afraid, though I was anxious about what lay ahead. However, after my experience in Castlereagh the thought of prison was almost welcome. Little did I know then that it would be 16 years later before I would be released.

# 1
# The Back Table

1976 WAS A YEAR fraught with difficulties for Irish republicans. During the lengthy ceasefire of 1975 the British security and intelligence services had built up a lot of information on the republican community, and on IRA volunteers, and that was now being used to arrest people in vast numbers. Changes to the powers of arrest, interrogation, and the admissibility of evidence (most notably verbal and written statements by the accused), led to the conviction of many before the new specially-created, non-jury, single-judge Diplock Courts; named after Lord Diplock who submitted a report to the British Government in December 1972 which recommended that jury trials be suspended.

In terms of those sentenced in the courts (for offences arising out of the conflict), prior to 1 March 1976 they were regarded as political prisoners, or, as the prison authorities categorised them, 'special category prisoners'. Male prisoners were held in Long Kesh Prison outside Lisburn, County Antrim or at Magilligan Prison, outside Derry. Female prisoners were held in Armagh Gaol. Long Kesh, a former World War II Royal Air Force camp, complete with runways, was where thousands had been interned without trial between August 1971 to December 1975. Whilst it was in operation, internment caused grave embarrassment for England in the eyes of the world and especially within Europe. Britain had joined the European Community (forerunner to the European Union) on 1 January, 1973, and a referendum on 5 June, 1975, had confirmed widespread support for their affiliation. The fact that Britain, at the latter part of the 20th century, was interning its own citizens without trial for up to four years, jarred with their claim that the country was the 'Mother of parliaments' and the role model for modern, democratic societies.[7] It is somewhat ironic now, at the time of writing, that Brexit has recently ended Britain's place in the European Union.

Those who were interned, and subsequently those who were convicted in the courts ('special category prisoners'), did not wear a prison uniform or carry out prison work. They were held in the 'Cages' of Long Kesh – as republicans referred to them – or Compounds as the prison authorities referred to them. The Cages consisted of several Nissen huts surrounded by high barbed-wire fences.[8] There were 22 Cages in total, Cage 1 being reception.[9] The area that held the Cages was then surrounded by additional fences and watch towers manned by armed British soldiers. The Cages housed republican and loyalist prisoners according to their particular faction, that is, Provisional IRA, Official IRA, Ulster Volunteer Force, Ulster Defence Association, etc. Each Cage appointed its own Officer Commanding (OC) who liaised with the prison authorities regarding matters that concerned their affiliated prisoners, including food, visits, handicrafts, and so forth. Other prisoners had little or no interaction with prison guards unless going to and from visits or attending the prison hospital.

To any observer from the outside, Long Kesh resembled exactly what it was – a Prisoner of War camp. It looked similar to what people had viewed in documentary or feature films about the Second World War. This was an image the British did not want to maintain. It gave legitimacy to the republican position that the IRA was waging a guerrilla war against an occupying colonial power. So, there was a change in tactics and the policy of 'criminalisation' was devised. From 1 March, 1976, anyone convicted of any offence in the North, whether it was claimed to be politically-motivated or otherwise, would be regarded as a common criminal and housed in a new section of Long Kesh which was specifically built to deal with the practical outcomes of the new policy. This new section became known as the H-Blocks.

---

[7] "England is the mother of parliaments" was a phrase coined by British politician and reformer John Bright in a speech at Birmingham on 18 January 1865.

[8] Named after their inventor, Major Peter Norman Nissen, the huts were made from a half-cylindrical skin of corrugated iron on a prefabricated steel structure. They were designed for military use, especially as a barracks, during World War I, and extensively used during World War II.

[9] One Cage, initially Cage 8, was later renamed Cage 23.

The prison name was also changed in 1976 and henceforth Long Kesh became officially referred to as Her Majesty's Prison (HMP) Maze. This was further broken down into HMP Maze (Cellular) – the H-Blocks – and HMP Maze (Compounds) which still held those (political) prisoners who had been sentenced prior to 1 March, 1976 and who still retained their 'special category status'.

The 'criminalisation' policy was part of a very comprehensive counter-insurgency strategy (including 'normalisation' and 'Ulsterisation') devised by the British to defeat the guerrilla war being waged by the IRA. British General, Sir Frank Kitson, masterminded the strategy. Kitson had previous experience of Britain's other anti-colonial struggles in Kenya, Malaysia, and elsewhere. Kitson argued that state institutions such as the political system, the legal system, academia and the media should be regarded as mere tools to be used in the war against the insurgents. And thus, in the North of Ireland, that's exactly what they became; mere tools to be used in the oppression and suppression of the nationalist community.

The operation of the media is one of the most obvious examples of Kitson's approach in action, easily recognisable by any comparative examination of news reporting about the North pre- and post-1976.[10] Coinciding with the advent of Kitson's counter-insurgency strategy was another 'social' development totally unconnected with British colonial rule in Ireland; the arrival of 'independent radio'. Independent radio challenged what, up until then, had been the hegemony of the British Broadcasting Corporation (BBC). Several off-shore pirate radio stations, such as Radio Caroline, had been broadcasting (mainly pop and rock music) since the early 1960s and the development led to a demand for more land-based, independent, commercial radio stations. Downtown Radio, which began broadcasting from Newtownards in the north of Ireland on 16 March, 1976, was, interestingly, one of the

---

[10] Many years later I had that discussion with a female reporter from the BBC based in London. In a pre-interview chat with her I challenged the terminology she was using and we got into a bit of an argument over it. I asked her to check out the BBC's own archives and see if there was a change in policy in the mid-1970s in terms of their reporting on the conflict. To her credit, she phoned me several days later to say how flabbergasted she was with what she had discovered and how embarrassed she felt that she had passively and unquestioningly accepted the terminology she was used to.

first of such stations to be established in 'Britain'. Especially interesting is that it began broadcasting on the same day that British Prime Minister Harold Wilson resigned and Downtown Radio got the scoop, breaking the news to the public over an hour before the official announcement of his resignation featured on the mainstream BBC Radio Ulster. Unlike the BBC at that time, Downtown Radio broadcast news bulletins not only every hour on the hour but also news summaries every 20 minutes. Suddenly we were getting a barrage of news and getting it in a new vocabulary. Prior to 1976, it was common for print, radio, and television media to refer to 'IRA volunteers', 'active service units' etc. Post-1976 and the introduction of 'criminalisation', the language used to report on the conflict changed dramatically, being replaced with terminology that had never been used before in the context of conflict in Ireland; 'Mafia-style shoot-outs', 'God-fathers', 'men of violence', 'sectarian gangs', and 'tit-for-tat' shootings/killings/bombings – to name but a few.

The new terminology had a very clear purpose – to present the conflict not as a centuries-old anti-colonial struggle but as a sectarian one between Catholics and Protestants, inspired by criminals who were out for their own ends and had no regard for the community. The RUC and British Army were portrayed as peace-keepers, bringing order to the chaos caused by two warring factions. The British government was presented as the 'neutral broker'.

How we 'name the world' is a reflection of how we understand the world and is therefore very important in framing how we think of other people who occupy that world with us, and how we behave towards them and interact with them. Often the first tool in the suppression of a people, community, or ethnic minority is to demonise them and make them the 'other': people to be wary of, suspicious of, or afraid of. Once you have made them the 'other' you are free to carry out whatever harsh measures you argue are necessary to 'deal' with them. To that end, new legislation is introduced, amended, or applied discriminately. New coercive restrictions and powers follow. Often there is blood on the streets and the prison populations swell in numbers.

That was the political/security backdrop to my arrest in August 1976.

* * *

When I arrived at Crumlin Road Prison there was no particular animosity or anger expressed by the prison guards. Looking back on it, they were well-used to political prisoners arriving at the jail and the new policy of criminalisation had not really kicked in yet, at least not in their consciousness, despite the fact that it was already being reflected in terms of the changed prison regime.

I was taken to the Reception area and, as is the routine when first admitted to the prison, was initially put into a small cubicle that had a wooden seat and held just one person. I would grow familiar with this cubicle over subsequent weeks as it was also where we were held when awaiting transportation to remand court hearings each week. On that first evening in the prison the door to my cubicle opened a number of times and various questions were asked of me to confirm my identity. I was then taken out, finger-printed and photographed, and then told to take a bath. The prison guards were matter of fact, perhaps unsurprisingly, given this process was monotonously routine for them. One elderly guard, however, was particularly friendly – or maybe he just appeared to me to be friendly as I was possibly expecting a different type of behaviour from guards. In later years, on 17 December, 1979, while we were on the 'blanket protest' that guard was shot dead by the IRA as he walked from the Crumlin Road Prison to a local club for lunch. He had been a prison officer for over 30 years. The target of the attack was any prison guard. He was not specifically targeted. I discovered later that his name was William (Tug) Wilson. His son was an Assistant Governor in the H-Blocks – Ronnie Wilson. I had various interactions with Ronnie Wilson in later years when I was OC (Officer Commanding) in various H-Blocks and had reason to see him from time to time regarding a range of issues. I often wondered how he felt, dealing with people like me who belonged to an organisation that had killed his father. To his credit, he never showed me any overt hostility; quite the opposite, in fact.

After I had gone through the process at reception I was taken to a cell on the ground floor of B wing, where newly-remanded prisoners were held until they were allocated to either C wing or A wing. The cells were about 10 ft long by 8 ft wide and had high ceilings. There was a window at the top of one wall with metal bars attached from the outside. The window looked out onto C wing exercise yard and those walking the yard would try to make contact with any new arrival in B wing, having heard on the news that someone had been charged and remanded. That's how I 'met' with some republicans from South Derry the following morning. I heard my name being called and got up onto the top bunk to see out into the exercise yard. I didn't immediately recognise the faces I saw there though gradually some became familiar; Kieran McKenna, Seamus McElhone, Martin Heaney and others. They had all been arrested sometime earlier that summer. We exchanged a few words and I learned from them that I would be seeing a Governor later that day and he would assign me to a wing. I was hoping it would be C wing now that I had met these ones. And that's what happened. I was called out to see a Governor that morning. His office was at the top of B wing. It was a very brief affair and I can't even recall what was said but it was just by way of an official 'introduction' to the prison. I was then moved to C wing and was put into a cell on the second landing. I believe it was Cell 24. There were three landings in the wing; ground, second, and third.

I soon settled into the way of life. Being imprisoned in a cell didn't cause me any problems, even when there were two others in what was meant to be a cell for one. It was the first time I was ever among such a mixture of people, of all ages and from different areas. I think it was the first time I had heard a Derry City accent. I had met people from Belfast before, during the very short period I had spent attending St Malachy's College, Belfast after I'd left primary school in 1968. And Thomas Crawford, a friend from Belfast's Ardoyne area, used to visit our home in Carngranny to camp out for a few nights. I remember sleeping in the tent with him. I was aged ten. It felt like a great adventure. And getting a smoke of his cigarette was even better, though it probably started me regularly smoking soon after. It was also Thomas who shaved the back of my neck for the first time at the bottom of my hairline, giving me a more 'modern' cut.

There was the inevitable urban/rural divide, or, culchie/city divide in the prison. Most of it was all good-natured banter though often the Belfast ones tried to 'pull a fly one' over those from the countryside. One day, not long after I'd arrived into prison, we were waiting to go in from the yard and 'Seando' Moore said to me, "Your turn to buy the baps tonight, big lad." I didn't even know what 'baps' were! I later discovered they are a type of white bread loaf peculiar to Belfast and sometimes referred to as 'Belfast baps'. Jackie

McMullan, who was on the same landing as me, C2, chipped in and said, "Yes, that's right. Your turn." I reckoned I was getting 'wound up' but wasn't totally sure if it was about buying this thing called 'the baps' or the fact of being able to buy something at all. We were allowed to buy various items in the prison shop but that was on a weekly and not daily basis. I just smiled and lived with the feeling of awkwardness until the grille opened and we left the exercise yard.

Another thing I was introduced to upon my arrival in the Crum was black Oxford shoes. I'd never seen anything like them before, or if I did they would have been worn by older men with a dress suit. Here they were being worn with denim jeans; largely Wranglers in those days. Belfast guys wore them and they'd be extremely shiny, such was the attention and care devoted to keeping them polished. It was then I learnt about the practice of 'spit and polish' to create that look on shoes. Finbar McKenna[11] and Tommy Cosgrave wore them as did 'Big Doc' (Kieran Doherty[12]), who was in a cell next door to me.

Life in the first few weeks on remand in the Crum was very leisurely. There was a routine to the day, which I suppose gave structure to my life – a structure that wasn't always there before my arrest.

Shortly after I arrived I was questioned by the wing's IRA Intelligence Officer (IO) about what I had been charged with and asked to write out details of my interrogation. All of this was conducted fairly informally. Then there was a change in the jail leadership and a new staff appointed. This staff took on a more formal, proactive role. Meetings in the yard and canteen became a regular feature as did the organisation of protests over the removal of political status. One development, which appeared more sinister, was the creation of a 'back table' in the canteen. Those who had given information under interrogation, such as the names of others in the IRA or the whereabouts of arms dumps, were now made to sit at the back table. Suddenly, familiar faces who had sat beside me or across from me at meal times, and whose backgrounds or cases I knew little

[11] Finbar McKenna was later sentenced, took part in the 'blanket protest' in the H-Blocks, and, less than a year after his release was killed while on active service with the IRA on 2 May 1987.

[12] Kieran Doherty later died on hunger strike on 2 August, 1981, after 73 days on hunger strike.

or nothing about, were physically positioned so as to let the rest of us know that they were in some way suspect and that we should be wary of them. We were encouraged not to associate with them, though that wasn't exactly an order. I felt totally conflicted at the time. These were people I knew and was friendly with. People I walked the yard with. Would there be personal implications for me, from the IRA staff, if I continued to show my friendship with them?

I'm glad to say that I did continue to associate with them though I must admit to having felt an overriding sense of relief that I was not one of them; not one of those sent to the back table. Something had shifted. We were not all the same. Some were less equal than others.

The system of the 'back table' continued for some time and was a reflection of a practice, that can only now be regarded as an inherently unjust practice, that was policy in the Cages of Long Kesh among the sentenced prisoners – the policy of 'cleared' and 'suspended' volunteers. 'Cleared' volunteers were those who had not given any information during interrogation and had not pleaded guilty at their trials. Only 'cleared' volunteers could attend certain meetings and be privy to certain information. 'Suspended' volunteers could not hold any rank within the prisoner command structures.

Some of those who introduced the 'back table' in the Crum in 1976 had come through the Cages and no doubt honestly believed these sorts of practices to be the norm in prison. However, others, some of whom had also previously been imprisoned, disagreed with the practice and more specifically with the humiliation it inflicted. Divided opinion prompted discussion on the issue and eventually led to the policy being discontinued. In an interview I conducted with Raymond McCartney years later for my doctoral thesis he recounts:

> People later asked how it (the back table) could have happened but a lot of it was that you had to be doing something, had to show, had to have punitive measures. People would be 'uncovering RUC agents' everywhere and I remember saying that from our own experiences in the barrack if you shake someone hard enough they will say what you want them to say. When Pearse McAleer was made OC and I was asked to be his adjutant Leo (Green) said that the first thing that should be done was to end the back table. That's what we did.[13]

[13] Laurence McKeown (2001), *Out of Time*, Belfast: Beyond the Pale Publications, p. 52.

In one sense, this was the first instance where the policy of criminalisation introduced by the British government had an (unintended) impact upon the social organisation of republican prisoners. The rupture from the already established 'social norms' in the Cages, and the air of uncertainty about our individual and collective futures, meant that, as republican prisoners, we were beginning to reflect upon our circumstances and actions, and question previous commonly-accepted practices. It was that questioning of the morality of the 'back table' that led to the policy in the Crumlin Road being abandoned. If political status had still been in place we would have had no real reason to question past practice and most likely would have retained the 'back table'.

We were all young, politically naïve, unaware of the enormity of the political events we were living through, and particularly the significance that the policy of criminalisation was going to have on our lives. We often relied on those who had been imprisoned previously, yet they too were ill-equipped to analyse what exactly was happening. It was a period of change; old 'certainties' had been removed and, in such a context, some clung to what they knew best.

Given the numbers arriving into the prison that summer, most cells contained three prisoners, or at a minimum, two. The cells contained a single bed and a bunk bed, with a narrow space between them.

I had a few different cellmates while in the Crum. Fergal McGuigan came from Belfast's Ardoyne area. Fergal was from a republican family. His brother Francis had been the first internee to escape from Long Kesh in February 1972, only days after Bloody Sunday. A group of priests had visited Long Kesh and as they left, Francis, dressed in black and wearing a clerical collar, mingled with them and walked out of the prison with them.

Unlike Fergal, however, most people I went on to meet in prison did not come from republican families, which was not surprising given that republicanism was not such a vibrant phenomenon in the North in the '50s and '60s. Republican families could be 'named' and counted, probably on the fingers of both hands. Those families had a tradition of republicanism stretching back over the decades but they were few in number in comparison to the thousands who eventually went through the prisons in the '70s, '80s, and '90s.

Another cellmate was Noel Quinn from Newry. Noel in later years would be nicknamed 'Noisy'. He was so named because he seldom, if ever, spoke.

We were allowed food parcels to be sent in to us while on remand: cooked meats, cigarettes, newspapers and suchlike. Noel's family would send him in stuffed pork loin. I had never tasted such before. My family would send me in sausages and vegetable roll. We'd heat the meat on the large central heating pipe that ran through the cell at floor level. I use 'heat' rather loosely in this instance as there was barely enough of it to melt any grease off the cold meat. But it was something to look forward to at night after lock-up at 8.30 p.m.

There were other cellmates over the period of nine months that I was held on remand but the one who I shared with longest was Niall McConville from Lurgan. His origins led him to being nicknamed 'Lurgan' by the South Derry ones. Niall was 17, just two years younger than me, but the age gap appeared significantly greater. Looking back on it, he was probably a very typical 17-year-old whereas perhaps I was not such a typical 19-year-old. I had been in the IRA from the age of 17 and had been 'on the run' for two years in various parts of the country. Not that it was obvious to me at the time but I'd seen more of life, or met a wider range of people, than many others my age had. Niall was charged with membership of Na Fianna Éireann, the youth wing of the IRA. You could be sentenced for up to three years for membership.

Niall's mother, Pauline, met my mother on visits and they became friends. I think his mother was glad he was sharing a cell with me, even though she didn't know me. I think she deduced from meeting my mother that I was probably 'OK'. She may have thought I could look after him. Niall's sister, Geraldine, then wrote to me and later we had a number of visits. I'm not sure if that was also motivated by a sense of care for her younger brother or out of an actual interest in me! Her letters continued until after I was sentenced and then had to stop because we were only entitled to one letter in and out per month and it was important to be in contact with my family. Niall was eventually sentenced. He got two years. His mother never wanted him to go on the protest and told him so and, in accordance with her wishes, he didn't. I never heard from Niall or his family after that until Niall's nephew, Antóin, a son of Geraldine's, made contact with me in 2009 and again later in 2016 when I produced a calendar as part of an artistic project called 'We Wore The Blanket' which commemorated the 40th anniversary of the start of the blanket protest.[14]

People come into our lives and move out of it again; or you move out of their world, either through accident or design. The interaction and communication during the time you're together can be pleasurable, intense, or mundane but if the circumstances of meeting them were accidental rather than planned then why would we necessarily maintain a connection in later years?

However, there are people from my past who I wish I had seen again, if only to thank them for their kindness and generosity; those who opened their homes to me while I was still a teenager. The people who were like parents or siblings to me, who welcomed me to share whatever it was they had and yet in most instances had never known me before I walked in their door. At the time of writing this particular section it is the anniversary, to the day, of Kieran Doherty's election as a TD for the constituency of Cavan/Monaghan.[15] Kieran was on hunger strike when he was elected. It didn't save his life but it did reveal how people regarded him. And yet he had never ever set foot in either Cavan or Monaghan. Good people. Decent people. Maybe it's an old-fashioned word these days: decency. But it's the most appropriate word to sum up some people. Those who you know will always treat you properly. Those who will never do you any harm. People who live by core values and respect for others, even those who may disagree profoundly with your social or political outlook. My father had a saying that always resonated with me, particularly in later years; "If you can't do someone a good turn, at least never do them a bad one". There's a very simple philosophy, and very good lesson for life, summed up in those few words.

Before entering prison, I had very little knowledge of what actually went on in them except that republican prisoners lived in open Cages in Long Kesh or Magilligan, wore their own clothes, and made handicrafts. I could recall hearing something about the change in government policy in relation to political status but didn't really know what it all meant. I was 19 and, like most others my age, I was pretty naïve in terms of the broader political developments. If it wasn't

---

[14] https://www.bobbysandstrust.com/we-wore-the-blanket/

[15] Kieran Doherty was elected on 11 June, 1981.

happening on our street or in our area it wasn't important. Arriving into prison I soon discovered what the immediate impact of the new policy of criminalisation was; all remand prisoners, loyalist and republican, were now held together on the same wings whereas before they had been segregated from one another, republicans in A wing and loyalists in C wing. Republicans and loyalists were now coming into regular contact with one another at meal times, during association time in the evening, and at exercise periods in the yard. Tension had arisen over the summer of '76 (before I was imprisoned) as numbers on both sides quickly built up following mass arrests. That tension eventually came to a head in C wing on 12 July when a row erupted in the canteen over televised Orange marches. Following that, loyalists confined themselves full-time in their cells. Their OC at the time was Lenny Murphy, leader of the 'Shankill Butchers'[16] and perhaps he held concerns that if there was to be any serious fighting he might be specifically targeted by republicans. Loyalists, for the next several months ate their food in their cells and did not go out to the yard for exercise. This meant that republicans had the freedom of the canteen for meals and association in the evenings, plus access to the exercise yard twice a day. That was the situation when I arrived onto C wing in August '76.

When Lenny Murphy was eventually sentenced and moved to the H-Blocks, a new loyalist OC took over and reversed the order Murphy had put in place. Loyalists made it known to the prison authorities that they would once again leave their cells to eat in the canteen and have association there in the evening, and would go out to the yard for exercise. This meant an inevitable clash with republicans. When the guards opened both loyalist and republican cells to allow prisoners out for exercise, fighting erupted. This happened on the ground floor, C1, as the various landings were let out one at a time, beginning with C1. Only when the landing below had been cleared were the cells on upper landings opened. The guards intervened and restored order by getting prisoners back into their cells. No one in C wing got out for

[16] The Shankill Butchers were members of the loyalist Ulster Volunteer Force (UVF). They were based in the Shankill area of Belfast and were responsible for an estimated 23 killings. They were notorious for kidnapping, torturing, and murdering random Catholics. The gang used butchers' knives and meat cleavers to torture and kill their victims, hence their name.

exercise that day. In one sense, it was fortunate that the fighting occurred on the ground floor as it would have been much more dangerous had it occurred on an upper landing with the possibility that a prisoner could have been thrown down the metal stairwell, incurring much more serious injuries.

Outbursts of fighting continued on the ground floor for several days, any time both loyalists and republicans were let out of their cells together. The guards began to let out few prisoners at any one time – and usually in fairly equal numbers – but on one occasion the guards let out a very limited number of republicans and when they were at the locked gate to the exercise yard, held in a type of airlock system, the guards released a greater number of loyalists from their cells. The loyalists piled into the airlock and attempted to make the most of their numerical superiority, raining blows upon the republican prisoners. Unfortunately for the loyalists, the republicans there – and there may have only been the two of them, Brendan McKenna and Martin Heaney, both from South Derry – immediately fought them out of the airlock and back into the wing where the guards had to intervene and lock everyone up again. Brendan was a very stocky guy and Martin knew how to handle himself so despite being vastly outnumbered they had not been overcome – in fact, quite the opposite. Shortly afterwards, a day-in-day-out system was agreed between us and the loyalists.[17] We would get exercise in the morning and the loyalists would get theirs in the afternoon, or vice versa; we would have association in the canteen one evening and them the next evening; and we would alternate who ate their meals in the canteen. If we ate breakfast in the canteen, they ate dinner there, and so on. The visiting area was a neutral space which we shared.

It was strange being so close to loyalists; people whose attacks upon Catholics and Nationalists I had read about in the newspapers. Growing up in Randalstown I had seen some young Protestants wear particular tartan scarves which, in the early 1970s, were popular amongst loyalist working-class youth. But that was something different and not particularly threatening. I regarded the scarf as more

[17] The system remained in place for several years but on 24 November, 1991, a bomb exploded in the prison canteen when loyalists were there eating their evening meal. Two loyalists were killed in the explosion and this led soon afterwards to the segregation of republicans and loyalists.

about self-identifying rather than posing a threat to Catholics/Nationalists. But here I was now amongst people who regarded me as the enemy and who had already carried out attacks and killings against my community. It was a surreal situation, especially when going to and from the visits with them.

One of them, who arrived into prison shortly after me, was a guy by the name of Garfield Beattie from County Armagh who was charged with the murder of several Catholics. Beattie was a member of what later became identified as the notorious Glenanne Gang,[18] though, back then, no one knew the extent of the murders that the gang had carried out. Beattie came onto our wing and onto my landing, and occupied a cell only a few doors down from me. Given the charges against him I had some image in my head (before I set eyes upon him) of what he might look like. Silly, I know, but that's how it was. When I came across him on the way to a visit I saw he was a sort of pudgy guy, not that tall, wearing glasses and a tweed jacket and grey trousers (rather than the customary jeans that practically everyone else in the prison wore). I was shocked. I shouldn't have been. Why does anyone have to look a particular way, as if to match our personal approval or disapproval of them? I imagine they must have had a similar image in their heads of republicans. On the visit he was in a cubicle across from me and his visitors (I don't know if they were his parents or not) had a Bible with them, which they appeared to read during the visit. A strange world; a challenge to stereotypes. As it turned out, during my time in the Crumlin Road Prison I never had any hassle with loyalists, thankfully.

In terms of the broader implications of the criminalisation policy, and what lay ahead for us, we were only vaguely aware of the building of the H-Blocks as a new part of Long Kesh Prison that would house us post-sentencing, rather than the Cages. Generally, we were fairly lackadaisical about the new policy, believing it to be yet another stupid idea the British government had come up with and that

[18] The Glenanne Gang, which included several members of the RUC and UDR, was centrally involved in the murder of over 120 innocent civilians across Counties Tyrone and Armagh and into the Irish Republic. Their campaign of killings lasted from July 1972 to the end of 1978. For detailed information on their activities see: Ann Cadwallader (2013), *Lethal Allies: British Collusion in Ireland,* Cork: Mercier Press, and *Unquiet Graves*, a documentary film directed by Seán Murray (2018).

it would all be over within six months. In fact, the concept of 'six months' became a very fixed measure in our thinking in regards to the protest for several years to come. Looking back on it now, it seems that six months was far enough away to allow for positive developments to take place regarding our situation, yet close enough that we were able to psychologically cope with the conditions we endured in the meantime.

The IRA OC for most of the time I was in the Crum was Barney McReynolds from the Markets area of Belfast. Barney had been previously interned so had some experience of prison. Barney was very small in stature and soft-spoken but he had a confidence that belied his age. He would call a meeting at times to give us any information or instructions to be carried out. There was usually little to give out by way of information. There wasn't a lot happening. One Sunday, Barney brought us together in the yard. Kieran Nugent, who was in our wing, was going to be sentenced the following week on a charge of IRA membership and he would thus be the first republican prisoner to be sentenced after the removal of special category status. Barney said only a few words that day, as was his wont. Kieran was going to be sentenced, republican prisoners would not wear the prison uniform or do prison work, and that was to be our position when all of us were sentenced and taken to the H-Blocks. It was as simple and as short as that. It was a warm summer's day (the summer of 1976 was one of the warmest on record) and when the meeting broke up people went back to strolling around the yard in their small groups and the football match in the yard (played with an old sock stuffed with papers) started up again. We were young and the H-Blocks were a million miles away.

The following week, on 14 September, Kieran was sentenced to three years imprisonment and taken to the H-Blocks of Long Kesh where he immediately refused to wear the prison uniform or do prison work. He is now famous for his remark, "You'll have to nail it [the prison uniform] to my back". He was beaten up and for three days was locked naked in a cell. Thereafter he was allowed to cover himself with a blanket. Thus began what became known as the 'blanket protest'.

Someone was always going to be the first person sentenced under the new regime and in hindsight there was no better person than

Kieran to confront the new policy. He was born on 4 May, 1958, (so, aged only 18 when sentenced) but had already personally experienced several traumatic events during the conflict and had served two previous periods of imprisonment. On 20 March, 1973, aged 15, loyalists carried out a gun attack on him and a friend, Bernard McErlean (aged 16), as they stood on the corner of Merrion Street and Grosvenor Road, Belfast. Bernard was killed and Kieran was shot eight times in the chest, arms, and back. Later, aged 16, Kieran was arrested and spent five months on remand in Crumlin Road Prison before the case against him was withdrawn and he was released. However, on 9 February, 1975, aged 17, he was re-arrested and this time interned without trial in Long Kesh for nine months, being released on 12 November that year. He was rearrested again on 12 May, 1976, following the hijacking of a bus.[19]

Kieran was joined on the protest shortly afterwards by Ned Flynn and Jackie McMullan, both of whom I knew from remand. Jackie was charged with attempted murder and at his trial was sentenced to life imprisonment – the first instance where a prisoner got a life sentence for attempted murder. It was a reflection of the draconian changes to the powers of arrest, interrogation, and the new and more cavalier approach of the Diplock courts. As the days and weeks passed and more republicans were sentenced, they too joined the others already in the H-Blocks and numbers on the protest began to grow.

All remand prisoners were taken to Chichester Street Court each week to be remanded in custody for another week. I went on a Monday. We travelled in Ford Transit vans that were fitted inside with a wooden box and benches, complete with a locked door separate from the outside door of the van itself which, of course, was also locked. The van held up to eight prisoners. Once the doors closed it was almost totally dark inside apart from a small light on the partition between us and the driver. There was also a small fan on the roof. The journey didn't trouble me at all but I wondered what it would be like for someone suffering from claustrophobia. The journey took about 15 minutes, depending on traffic. The vans were escorted by RUC Landrover patrols.

---

[19] If charged with IRA membership it is virtually impossible to prove your innocence as how do you prove you are *not* a member of an illegal organisation? The Diplock courts operated on the assumption of 'guilty until proven innocent'.

I usually travelled down to court with Kieran (Big Doc) Doherty, John (Pickles) Pickering,[20] Liam (Whitey) White, and Chris (Greek) Moran who had all been arrested together on an IRA operation. There would be several dozen prisoners taken down each morning. Loyalists were kept separate from republicans when travelling to and from the remand hearings. At the Court we were held underground in large cells. They were similar to the Punishment Block cells in the H-Blocks, though larger. They had a 'seat' in one corner made out of concrete and the 'bed' was a concrete slab on the floor with wooden slats on it. There could be up to six prisoners held in the cell at any one time, though generally it was less than that. We'd be called out one by one to go up and appear in the court. The 'appearance' took about two minutes; charges were read out and a remand in prison for another week handed down. Everything was carried out in a fairly civil manner, and there was generally no real tension with the RUC who were there in large numbers.

The thing that surprised me most was that the RUC facilitated our IRA command structures. At the time, we conducted various protests in the prison to highlight the plight of Kieran Nugent and the others already sentenced. Prior to any such protests in the court – and there were several over the period of months that I was on remand – the RUC would allow Pickles and Big Doc (who were on the prison IRA staff) to go around the cells and remind people of what they had to do when they appeared in court. It wasn't really that we had forgotten but I think Pickles liked the fact that the RUC facilitated his visits to the other holding cells!

One such protest took the form of attending remand hearings dressed only in our underpants, which was a laugh while all of us were together in the van being transported there, less so when I had to appear later in court, the first one to do so, and give a speech about our protest! Given that the dock we stood in came up to above waist level we could have been wearing trousers and no one in the court would have been any the wiser. I can't recall what I said that day but I do remember being very self-conscious of appearing in the dock almost naked.

There was never any doubt in my own mind that I would join the blanket protest when sentenced. The thought of not doing so would

[20] John Pickering who was on the 1981 hunger strike.

have been totally alien to me, not because I viewed myself as super-staunch but simply because I considered it the correct thing to do. I never heard anyone express doubt that we would ever get political status back; talk was about when, not if. As stated previously, 'within six months' seemed to be the longest period anyone predicted.

Reports started to filter back to us in the Crum about what was happening in the H-Blocks but it was very vague as those on protest were not taking visits. However, they were being held in wings that had conforming prisoners so some of those were passing word to the outside, via their own visitors. It was around this time that we heard a rumour that one of the H-Blocks was literally sinking. The rumour was regarded as believable as those in the Crum who had previously been interned or served a sentence in the Cages of Long Kesh reported that the soil was very sandy and prone to flooding. They knew this in particular from attempts to dig tunnels, of which there were several, as the tunnels would flood or collapse easily and had to be shored up with timbers. The 'news' that the Blocks were sinking added to our view that the whole policy of criminalisation had been hastily thought-out and was destined for failure. I recall feeling impatient – I wanted to be sentenced quickly and get up to the Blocks so as to be on the protest before it all ended and we once again had our political status. I thought it would be a relatively short-lived chapter in the history of imprisoned republicans and therefore one which it would be great to have participated in.

As it turned out, I got to experience the Blocks even before I was sentenced. In early 1977 prisoners 'awaiting trial' were moved to the Blocks. 'Awaiting trial' was when you had now received your 'depositions' (paperwork about the charges and date for trial) so you were no longer 'on remand' and didn't have to appear in the remand court every week. To reduce numbers in the Crum the prison authorities began to move prisoners 'awaiting trial' to the Blocks until just a few days before their trial was due to commence in the Belfast High Court, at which point they were returned to the Crum.

I was taken down to the H-Blocks – to H1 – around late February or early March. The Blocks were a shock to the system. Even though I was still a remand prisoner there was a really oppressive air to the regime imposed by the guards, unlike that in the Crum. The physical space was also different.[21] Instead of being held in a large space like C wing in the Crum with its three landings, I was now in the wing of a H-Block with low ceilings in both the cells and corridors (I could reach up and touch the ceiling in my cell). There was a higher guard-to-prisoner ratio as compared to the Crum. Four guards in a wing with maybe less than 30 prisoners. Everything was regimented with no organised segregation. In the Crum, on the loyalists' day to eat their dinner in the canteen we could go down and collect ours and return to our cells with it. This was not allowed in the H-Blocks. If you didn't go out for your dinner you didn't get your dinner. We could, however, refuse to go out for exercise when loyalists were out in the yard, and vice versa.

Davy Long was the Principal Officer (PO) in the Block. He was a short man with red hair and a reputation for brutality. He liked to go around the wings for inspections. My cell door opened once and he stepped into the doorway. I was sitting on the edge of the bottom bunk. He looked at me and shouted, "Key in the door, feet on the floor". In other words, I should have jumped to attention once I heard the key in the door. It took me a while though to actually comprehend what he was saying and in the meantime he turned and walked out of my cell again. I don't know what would have happened if he had remained. I would either have been dragged to my feet, or I would have stood up. This was something totally new to me. Even though by then I had already been in prison for six months this was unlike anything I'd previously experienced. Suddenly the Crum seemed like a very welcoming and even comfortable place in which to be held.

On 26 April, 1977, I was sentenced at the Belfast High Court to life imprisonment; actually, five counts of life imprisonment, plus a few hundred years thrown in for good measure. Whilst Jackie McMullan had been the first to get a life sentence for attempted murder, in the years that followed, life sentences became very common irrespective of whether the charge was murder, attempted murder, conspiracy to murder, or even possession of weapons or explosives. My trial lasted all of a day and a half. I refused to recognise the court, as was the IRA's position at that time. Despite this, and in line with state

[21] See photographs.

procedure, the state appointed a barrister to 'represent' me and a plea of 'not guilty' was submitted by the barrister on my behalf.

As it was a 'Diplock' court there was just the single judge and no jury. The judge heard the evidence presented, 'reminded himself to be impartial', then handed down the sentence. Very few people were ever found not-guilty in a Diplock court, especially not in those early days of their existence.

It was a tedious experience sitting through the procedure over the course of the one and a half days. At certain points I did challenge inconsistencies in the prosecution's claims but more by way of making a nuisance of myself, rather than out of any genuine belief that I could change the outcome. I was bemused by the whole affair; it seemed unreal to me. I felt that we were all merely going through a sham, the conclusion of which had been decided from the outset.

One memory that stays with me, is the vision of my mother sitting in the public gallery on her own. She looked so vulnerable in that space with so many uniformed RUC and prison guards surrounding her. When Judge Rolands pronounced me guilty he asked if there was anyone in the court who wanted to say anything on behalf of the 'defendant'. My mother, who would not have been prepared for this – it was her first time ever in a courtroom – stood up. She was a very quiet person, and very soft-spoken. A tall woman, she stood erect and uttered three simple, but very powerful words. Years later, I wrote in a poem about that day in court.

> You looked so vulnerable that day
> in the world of Diplock (courts);
> tired and sad, with an air of inevitability.
> I longed to go to you and hold you
> but the metal encasing my wrists held me to another.
> Stripped of the rhetoric
> our struggle was exemplified in that scene of
> the assembled might of Imperialist power
> aligned against one woman
> who stood before them and said, "He's my son".[22]

---

[22] From the poem titled 'Margaret', published in Laurence McKeown (2018), *Threads*, Clare, Ireland: Salmon Poetry, p. 31.

I had a visit later that afternoon in Crumlin Road Jail with my mother and brother, Eugene. I knew it would be the last visit for some time as those on protest were not accepting visits. I was cheerful, relieved that the trial was over, and eager to get down to the H-Blocks despite what may await me there. It wasn't simply a case of putting on a brave face for the sake of my mother, although that would certainly have been an element of it. Typically, prison visits did involve putting on a brave face. Besides, there was no time to talk through anything of any significance or of personal importance. And where would that take you anyhow? Into heartache? Sorrow? Best to keep the two worlds separate and keep conversation to banalities. For the visitor, that meant chatter about how friends, relations, and neighbours were; who was getting married, or who had another child. For the prisoner, it was often about keeping the conversation going by asking more questions.

In this instance, my mother had not only to take on board the fact that I just had been sentenced to life imprisonment – something that must have horrified her – but that I was also about to go on a protest that meant I would refuse to wear a prison uniform and that would mean no visits. She didn't know when she'd see me again. But this, of course, was left unspoken.

When you're young, you don't think of these things. At that age we were all caught up in our own worlds. We didn't consider what our parents must be thinking or feeling. Add to that the fact that I was engaged in a liberation struggle and was focused entirely upon what I needed to do – and wanted to do – as part of that struggle. I'm sure my way of conversing with my mother must have appeared flippant at times, probably even insensitive. Looking back on it now, it reminds me of the time when I left home to go 'on the run' in June of 1974, aged 17 and a half. I left suddenly. The decision to leave home was taken in response to reports that my security had been compromised. I had been informed that it was very likely the RUC knew of my activities. I didn't tell my mother I was leaving as she was not at home that evening. She was totally unaware of what I was involved with. I told a next-door neighbour, Peggy McKeown (no relative). Then I left. Some days later I was taken across the border to Monaghan where I stayed in safe houses. I was there about three weeks when I got news from a visitor from the north that my mother was inquiring about me. She had asked a breadman who delivered to houses in the area at the time if he could help get her any information. He lived in the Toomebridge area, which was regarded as a republican area, though this particular man would not have been viewed as a republican. However, he took the word to others who eventually got it to me and a meeting was arranged for a Sunday afternoon. My mother travelled down with the local parish priest, a young man, Fr McHugh. We met in the Hillgrove Hotel in

Monaghan, and, as with prison visits in later years, we didn't really talk about what was on our minds. Or, to be more accurate, we never expressed our feelings. This was my mother entering into a world that was totally foreign to her. It was most likely her first time ever across the border. Why would she ever have cause to cross the border? To go where? For what?

> I left hurriedly one night in '74
> without goodbyes.
> No doubt it was a shock to you
> though I wonder?
> For you knew me so well
> and soon inquiries led you
> across the border.
> But hotels are for lovers to meet in
> and our expressions had to speak
> the words we never uttered.[23]

Some parents find it difficult to 'let go' of their children as they get older. I say that as a father who hopes he has let go of his daughters. The best we can ever hope for is that we have passed on something that will help our children, now adults, walk their own path in life, wherever it takes them. I was blessed that way with my own mother. She showed me unconditional love – something I only realised in later years when I knew enough to compare different types of love and form some understanding of what love means. I broke my mother's heart with the life choices I made. Choices she could never understand. Choices that led to the deepest pain for her. But she never once used her love for me as a way to get me to make different life choices. She never once withheld her love for me, whatever the circumstances, no matter how deeply she was hurting, because she knew I never set out to deliberately hurt her. She accepted that I had to walk my own path in life and she was determined that she would give her love to me to fortify me on that path. An amazing, generous, selfless, unconditional love. And when I think back to that period in June 1974, when I left home suddenly without a word and then did not actively try to make contact with her, leaving her to track me down instead, I feel ashamed. I've never suffered from nightmares about anything in my life but

[23] Ibid. p. 30.

occasionally I'll dream that I'm in prison and have suddenly become aware that I haven't written to my mother in several weeks and I can't understand why I haven't written to her. How could I possibly not have written? It seems so bizarre; so thoughtless. So incomprehensible. And it is.

# 2

# Naked

As more and more republican prisoners were sentenced under the new legislation, they followed the example of Kieran Nugent and refused to wear the prison uniform or do prison work. In the early days, numbers were still small and those on protest felt very vulnerable. They were initially held in wings in H1 and H2, which also held those who were conforming to the prison system. A very strict regime was imposed on protesting prisoners in an attempt to break them. It was several months later before I was sentenced and joined the protest but I think it important to include here the accounts of others who were sentenced in the weeks immediately following Kieran Nugent, as they vividly capture both the conditions and mindset of those early days of the protest. The accounts are contained within a book I co-edited many years later while still in prison.[24]

> [Jackie McMullan] Hunger was a constant companion in those days. It's amazing; I had never known real hunger in my life before – at least not for any length of time. Now the days were filled by waiting from one meal to the next, seemingly always hungry. The ordinary prisoners could at least supplement the prison fare with extra bread and maybe some chocolate from the tuck shop. We could do neither and the hunger was made worse by our craving for cigarettes. To add to this, whenever the kitchen sent less food to the wing than it was supposed to, the shortage was shared by the blanketmen. We were at the bottom of the pile and if anything was short it was our loss.

---

[24] The accounts are taken from Brian Campbell, Laurence McKeown, and Felim O'Hagan (eds.) (1994), *Nor Meekly Serve My Time: The H-Block Struggle 1976-1981*, Belfast: Beyond the Pale. The book was clandestinely compiled in 1989/99 while I was still in prison.

But I think life was even worse for the ordinary prisoners. They could watch TV for a couple of hours each day and they had radios, reading material and tobacco but, as well as the humiliation of having to wear a monkey suit (prison uniform) and do prison work, they got a very bad time from the screws. They were out of their cells most of the day always under the eye of the screws who would lash out at them for any misdemeanour or for no reason at all. I saw screws hitting them for giving 'dirty looks', for not addressing them as 'Sir', for smoking in the wrong place and even for whistling. Most of these reasons of course were inventions and the real reason would be that the screw didn't think the prisoner cowed enough, or maybe he just felt like hitting someone.

They used to have cell inspections. These had to be seen to be believed. The screws would go into the cells at any time of the day and either search them or just look about to see if there was anything out of place, but cell inspections took place perhaps once every two or three weeks on a Saturday morning. When it was announced that one was to take place there was immediate and total panic. Men ran for brushes, mops and cloths and we could see the fear on their faces. All the furniture, beds included, was taken out of the cells onto the landing and dusted, scrubbed and polished, all at a frenzied pace.

The cell itself was subjected to the same process; every inch of it cleaned, all the surfaces, corners and spots you wouldn't even know existed made immaculate, walls washed, floor polished and made to shine, all within an amazingly short time. Then the furniture was put back and everything replaced exactly as it should be. 'Exactly' was the operative word. There were unbelievably precise directions for every single item in the cell. Shoes and boots had to be pointed in a particular way, books had to be ordered in a certain manner (only three books per prisoner), and a 'bedpack' of blankets, sheets, and pillow had to be made as if carved out of stone.

After an hour or so of this frantic activity word was sent down the wing that the SO (Senior Officer) was coming and the tension and fear rose to an incredible level. The men stood military fashion outside their doors and like a field marshal inspecting his troops, the SO looked them up and down, checked their uniforms and boots, and then entered their cell. Sometimes he wore a white glove and ran his finger along surfaces to check for dust. If he found nothing wrong in a cell he left and went to the next one. If there was the least thing out of place – a fag end or even ash in an ashtray – he went berserk, or pretended to. Bedpacks were flung out into the landing; books, chairs and everything else was overturned, and he came rushing out to scream abuse and threats at the terrified occupants of the cell. We were excluded from these cell inspections because we weren't conforming but we could see what was going on through the side of our cell doors. There was no greater incentive for us to stay on the protest.

[Ned Flynn] There was one screw in particular at this time given a free hand by the administration to do as he wished with us. He was very aptly named 'Jack The Maniac' (Jack Todd). He had the mentality of a child but physically he was very broadly built and his most outstanding feature was his hands; they were like shovels. The first night he ever came onto the wing, himself and two other screws came down to my cell. I had a fair idea what was coming. He asked me what I was in jail for and when I told him he slapped and punched me about the cell. The two screws with him thought this was hilarious. By no means was this a severe beating but I remember quite clearly when they left the cell I was shaking from head to foot. I was fortunate in a sense that my cell was the first he went to; my two comrades had heard quite clearly what happened and waiting for the inevitable was probably worse than the beating. When he went to each of their cells I could hear the usual noises that were associated with a beating; furniture being up-ended, keys rattling, moans and groans, walls being thumped – more than likely by one of my comrades who had been slammed against it.

Things just went from bad to worse. We were getting just enough food to keep us alive. Screws coming into the cell and slapping us about was becoming more regular and so the threat of violence was with us every minute of the day. With the lack of food, the beatings, the intimidation and harassment, we decided enough was enough, we'd go on hunger strike (we didn't seek clearance from the leadership or our camp staff). And so it was on a Sunday night at teatime we ate our last meal. Our demands were simple: 1) A substantial rise in the portions of food we were getting; 2) An end to the beatings.

On Monday morning when we refused our breakfast the Class Officer came to my cell and asked me why we were refusing our food. I told him we were on hunger strike and wouldn't be coming off it until we got an assurance that the brutality would stop and that we got the same amount of food as the other prisoners who weren't on the Blanket. He cursed at me, went out and slammed the door. I've no doubt that from the outset the screws were of the opinion that we'd last out until we got really hungry and that would be the end of it, so initially they weren't unduly worried.

Tuesday came and we were still refusing food. It was now plain to them that this wasn't a minor token protest. The food was being left in our cells and not surprisingly the portions were much bigger than usual. After mealtimes the screws came into our cells and said, "McMullan ate half his stew," or "Flynn ate one of his potatoes," or "Devine ate some of the vegetables," but we ignored them.

By Wednesday the administration was becoming very worried, most notable of all was the Class Officer who wasn't as cocky as he had been three days before. It was a hive of activity on the wing that day; SOs, POs, doctors, chiefs and even the Number One Governor, paid us a visit. The No. 1 was the same as all the Governors I'd come into contact with; surrounded by his foot soldiers he came into the cell with an air of superiority about him. He gave you a look which, if translated, would have said, "You are lower than the vermin in the sewers," and when he spoke his tone relayed the same message. It was he and his sidekicks who had introduced the policies which we were now on hunger strike against. He knew why we were taking this course of action, so when he started questioning me about it I refused to answer him and he just walked out of the cell.

Thursday was the fourth day and once again there was a lot of activity about the wing. The class officer was being called out to the Circle more than usual, which made me think that the administration was more worried than they were letting on to be. By this time the prison chaplain, Father Toner, was aware of the hunger strike and that night about 6 o'clock he paid us a visit. When I explained the reasons why we were on hunger strike he told me that the over 21s had sent a message with him telling us to stop the hunger strike. I told him that this was not possible and that it would just make our situation worse and my two comrades were of the same frame of mind. Fr Toner approached the class officer and that night we got a guarantee that the food would change dramatically and the brutality would stop. So we ended our hunger strike. We felt quite relieved but also quietly jubilant that we had got a moral victory over the regime. They had tried everything possible to break us but we were still there and we had now shown them that we wouldn't just lie back and take everything that they threw at us. For a while after that the food was brilliant and it was warm – it was the first time since I embarked on the blanket protest that I didn't feel hungry – and for a while the brutality also stopped.

It became obvious after this that the screws were growing anxious. There was no sign of our protest ending; we had established a solid base and our numbers were slowly but surely getting bigger. They had implemented a policy in H2 which was meant to break the back of the blanket protest but it was failing and they were running out of time. So they decided to intensify their efforts. The food got worse again and the harassment and intimidation intensified.

[Jackie] We weren't allowed to close the windows of the cells and I remember snow coming in. I was freezing but I didn't really care. By that time we were getting used to it and, to an extent, you soon learn to compensate for the hardship. We weren't allowed to talk; it would have resulted in a beating had we been caught, but we got to know the screws' routines and we talked to each other where the heating pipes ran through the walls between our cells. It was risky but there was a certain pleasure to be got out of taking the chance. We even laughed and joked about the ridiculousness of our situation. It was like something from a horror story; locked in a cell all day, starving, freezing, naked, terrified and watched over by a bunch of thugs who enjoyed making us suffer. Who would believe it? 'Sleepy' Devine was in the cell on one side of me and Kevin

Campbell on the other side. We had great craic talking about it all and swopping yarns. Then I'd get up from the pipes and pace the floor maybe smiling or laughing to myself about what had just been said.

The screws didn't let up any but with the increasing numbers we were starting to become more assertive and began challenging them on rules and conditions. According to their own rules we were entitled to one hour of exercise per day yet they had never offered it to us. We asked about this and they said that the exercise was available to us but we weren't prepared to wear the prison uniform in order to get it. Our argument was that this wasn't specified in the rules. This seemed to carry a bit of weight because next day they came to us and offered us exercise – in the nude. They thought we wouldn't take it but Sleepy and I went out and walked around the yard as if there was nothing unusual. There was sleet coming down and the gravel was sore on the feet but we knew we were being watched in the hope that we would give up; so we didn't. However, after about fifteen minutes they brought us back in. Next day and for a few days afterwards they offered us exercise inside an empty wing. We initially accepted this but then refused it on the grounds that we were entitled to fresh air.

[Kevin Campbell] On Sundays we were allowed to go to Mass as long as we wore the prison trousers. The Mass was in A wing canteen and we were escorted over two at a time. They had four rows of chairs specially for us to sit on: one at the back, one at the front and one at each of the walls. They then put the ordinary prisoners between us to avoid contact and around eight screws would gather at the back of the canteen creating an atmosphere of tension. Sunday was always a big day for us as we were able to count the numbers and exchange a few words with our friends.

As the weeks rolled by the numbers increased. After I was there two months the number of blanketmen rose to 30 and we knew that the numbers in H1 were probably the same. Our morale was climbing with the numbers. The harassment and degrading treatment continued. They introduced a system whereby men had to get washed in three minutes, saying they hadn't got the time to work with us. If anyone was still washing when the three minutes was up he was dragged back to his cell. They continued with the cell searching every day, even though we were always locked up and had no contact with anyone. We were forced to stand naked outside the cells while they conducted the search. We knew this was all geared to degrade us. During these raids someone was always knocked about creating an air of tension and fear in the wing.

When the number of blanketmen in the Block climbed above thirty we decided to take a stand on these issues, especially standing outside the cell naked, going to the canteen naked for our food, and slopping out naked. At Mass that Sunday word was spread about the Block that from Monday we would be refusing to leave the cells naked. We all keyed ourselves up for what would happen next morning.

The next day when we refused to leave the cells naked the screws were furious. They knew it was an organised effort for every Blanketman in the Block had refused to go naked to the canteen to get his breakfast. At first they refused to bring it down to our cells but come half-ten they relented. The breakfast had been put out at 8.00 a.m. and the tea and porridge were freezing. No one complained as we knew this would give them the excuse to tell us to go and collect it ourselves, naked.

That evening they started cell searching and they were very aggressive. When they told us to stand outside the cell door naked, we refused. Most of us were dragged from our cells by the hair and punched and slapped about. We were then thrown against the wall while they wrecked the cells. We knew that they were upping the harassment to try and get us to back down and go about naked. After about four days of this they broke and decided to give us towels to go about in. We viewed this as a major victory even though it was only to get a towel; it helped to break their efforts to degrade us.

[Jackie] The increase in our numbers meant greater contact with the ordinary prisoners, which led to more cigarettes and a greater flow of scéal. Our confidence also began to grow at this time and we spent more and more time talking to each other, down at the pipes and even out the doors. It was harder for the screws to handle the increased numbers, and the less committed among them became less diligent in enforcing the countless petty rules. But, for the most part, it was still a very fear-filled experience.

We weren't allowed any visits. We were entitled to one visit per month according to their rules but they insisted we wear the prison gear to get them. We refused. So we were very much cut off from the world outside that one H-Block. The only scéal we got was from the new men coming onto the protest and whatever bits and pieces we could elicit from the other lads in the wing. The screws at all times made a conscious effort to prevent us from getting any news, ensuring we heard no radio and that no newspapers were left about the wing while we were out of our cells. They hated us, either because they were bigots – and a lot of them were – or because they saw us spoiling their new jail. Before we came along they were having it their own way; they could dish out orders and slap people about when they felt like it. Now here we were threatening their power. We also hated them. I can honestly say that the screws in H2 taught me to hate. I had never hated anyone in my life before going there but I learned to hate them.

Throughout February and March there was a steady stream of men coming onto the protest. By the end of March it was clear that they were under pressure for space and would soon need to do something about it. All the other (conforming) prisoners were doubled up – two to a cell – but we were kept on our own. We were speculating that they would be forced to double us up too and when, just after Easter, on 12 April, they brought in bunk beds for our cells we thought we were about to acquire cellmates. When they opened our doors at two o'clock however, we were told we were moving to a new Block.

They took us naked out of the Block and put us into vans. It was all hustle and bustle; screws rushing around and dogs barking. It was disorientating. For the first time in four months some of us were out of the Block. We were very apprehensive and once again our nakedness added enormously to our sense of vulnerability. It only added to our confusion, therefore, when, on arrival at the door of the new Block, we heard men cheering and shouting out our names. I remember seeing a crutch waved from one of the cell windows; it was like some mad dream.

If we were going to get beaten – as we fully expected we would – it would happen just as we entered the Block before we went down the wings. We were made to face the wall. I stood like that for a while, then a screw touched me on the shoulder. I nearly jumped out of my skin, thinking, 'this is it'. But he told me not to worry, no one would touch us here. A friendly screw? I could hardly believe it.

From here we were allocated to different wings. I went to B wing and as I was walking down to the cell I heard men calling out my name from behind the cell doors. I couldn't take it all in, but as soon as the door was locked behind me I got talking to one of the men I knew and he filled me in on it all. We were in H5, which had only opened that day. All the prisoners in it were blanketmen; almost 100 of us. Two wings – A and D – were for those over 21 and the other two – B and C – were for the under 21s. My cell door was opened and a screw asked me if I wanted to brush my cell out – he actually asked me; I could hardly believe it. This was already like Butlins compared to the last place.

It immediately became apparent that this was going to be a completely different setup from the one we had just been through in H2. We could talk out the doors all day, we had singsongs at night and after those we talked to our neighbours into the small hours of the morning. On Sunday when we went to Mass all four wings of us were together and it was like a madhouse; almost every one of us with skinheads, wearing only prison trousers and all talking together, swopping scéal, renewing acquaintances and meeting new comrades. It was brilliant.

I arrived in the H-Blocks on 27 April, 1977 with three other republicans from North Belfast who also joined the protest – Mickey Loughlin, Gerard Doherty, and John Pearce. In the reception area of the prison we told the prison guards that we would not be wearing the prison uniform. They gave the uniforms to us anyhow and said we were to take them to the Block, which had become standard practice by then. Being in a group of four certainly gave me strength. I was anxious about what to expect. We had heard stories of new men arriving onto the protest getting beaten by guards, so I was expecting this to happen at any stage.

In the van taking us to the H-Blocks from reception we heard the guards in the front of the van saying that there was one for H-Block 2 and three for H-Block 5. I prayed that I was not the one for H2 and somehow imagined that it would be John Pearce as he was the youngest of the four of us (as if that made any sense) – not that there was a big difference in age between any of us. It wasn't just that H2 had a bad reputation for beatings, but we had heard shortly before leaving the Crum that all blanketmen had been moved together into H5, so whoever went to H2 was potentially going to a Block with no blanketmen – which was puzzling in itself.

The van pulled up in the front yard of H2, the back doors opened and my name was called. My heart sank. The others wished me well as I stepped out holding my bundle of prison clothes. In the Circle of the Block I was told to face the wall. I did this. I could hear guards gathering and thought this was where the beating was going to happen. One guard then told me to remove my clothes and put them into a brown bag that he provided. I stripped off down to my underpants and he shouted, "I said, all your fucken clothes. Get the heap off!" I removed my underpants and put them in the bag. I was then told to turn round. I was certain that this was the point at which the blows would come – but they didn't. For several minutes I stood while they stared at me, laughed at me, and made jokes about 'streakers'. They took the term from the song made famous by Ray Stevens in 1974 called 'The Streak', about the then-popular craze of people stripping off their clothes in public, usually at sporting events, and then running/streaking across the pitch.

I stood and looked about me, feeling awkward in my nakedness. I didn't want to look at the guards. To make eye contact would mean either engaging in a stare that could be interpreted as a challenge, or eventually having to avert my gaze, which could be seen as surrendering. I waited on the blows to come. They didn't. Something I realised in the years that followed was that waiting for a beating is usually worse than the beating itself. You psychologically go through the trauma, you picture how it will happen, and you fear the worst. Usually, when it does actually happen, it's never as severe as you imagined it would be.

I was then taken to C wing, which, like all others in the Block, housed those who were conforming to the prison regime. This included some republicans who had either been on the protest and later left it, or who had never been on it at all. The walk took forever, although it was a relatively short distance. Given my height, I'm not the type of person to walk down a narrow low-ceilinged corridor without being noticed. All the more noticeable, however, when walking stark naked. It was a strange sensation. I particularly recall the awkwardness of not knowing what to do with my hands. I had no pockets to put them in. They felt clumsy. Should I put them over my privates in an ashamed, embarrassed posture (which I didn't feel)? Or swing them by my sides in a 'devil-may-care' attitude (which I certainly didn't feel)? I didn't come to any definitive decision. I let them hang loosely by my sides. They felt like dead weights.

It's difficult to remain dignified in such circumstances, which was precisely the point. The object of the exercise was to humiliate. In a sense I tried to shut myself off from my body. I walked erect but casually and looked everyone in the eye. Some of the prisoners glanced my way and silently empathised with me. Others looked elsewhere. I was taken to the last cell but one at the very bottom of the wing, on the right-hand side. Empty cells either side of it. No one to contact me, to knock on my wall, to whisper through the pipes to me, to pass me cigarettes – even if I dared smoke in such a situation.

The first three days in H2 were, without doubt, the loneliest days of my life. In a period of just 48 hours my whole life had changed utterly. I had been sentenced to life imprisonment, then stripped naked and placed in solitary confinement. I felt totally isolated – from my family on the outside and my comrades on the inside. I knew no one. Life was going on around me but I wasn't part of it. Those who had conformed to the prison regime carried out their chores in their blue striped shirts and black denim trousers. My naked flesh set me apart as a non-conformer – isolated under total lock-up. The future seemed bleak and all I could focus on was either a far-off situation where we once again had our clothes and lived in the Cages with political status, or reminisce about a previous life on the outside.

The cell had a blue bunk bed, table, chair, and grey metal locker; standard cell furniture. It also has a Bible, again, standard issue. I opened the Bible at a random page – it was the Book of Sirach – and the first words I read were, "Gold is tested in the fire, and acceptable men in the furnace of affliction". I no longer hold to any religion – unless you count paganism, a oneness with nature and all other living creatures – but at the time those words greatly comforted me. They affirmed for me that what I was doing was right. I was following my path in life. Today I believe even more in serendipity; words, people, things, coming into my life for a purpose, either to affirm my chosen path through life, or possibly to warn me that I've strayed from that path.

I got some hassle from the guards over the first few days in H2, but not a lot. Nor was I beaten. On my second day there I had to appear before the Governor. In the morning, my cell door had opened and a guard had demanded that I wear the prison uniform and do prison work. I had refused. I was then charged with refusing to abide by prison rules and regulations and therefore had to later appear before the Governor for 'adjudication' and subsequent 'sentence' (punishment).[25] To attend the adjudication meant walking out to the Circle naked. As I walked there I was once again very conscious of my body and felt that same clumsiness I had experienced the previous day. However, despite the occasional remarks that some guards made, I became aware that most of them also felt awkward about the situation. Maybe they felt uncomfortable looking at a naked man. Possibly they felt that their comments would only serve to reveal that they were scrutinising a male naked body, and feared any inferences that may be drawn from this. That wouldn't sit comfortably within the macho-cultural constructs of a conservative prison system.

I appeared before the Governor in his office and stood before his desk, naked. It was a totally surreal situation. The whole set up – his office, his title of Governor displayed on the door, him on the other side of a large table with his Principal Officer standing behind him, and me led in by a guard who stood behind me. It was all meant to display a hierarchy of command; a regime where everyone knew their place and held to it. He, with his shirt and tie and suit surrounded by his uniformed subordinates. He who was meant to be obeyed, not only by his subordinates but certainly by the prisoners. But here was one standing in front of him, naked. It

[25] The charges were brought under breaches of rule 30 (1) of the *Prison Rules (Northern Ireland) 1954, No. 7* which state that: 'A prisoner who is guilty of any act or omission contrary to the security or good order of the prison shall be guilty of an offence against discipline and on his offence being reported to the Governor shall be dealt with as here and after provided in these Rules.'

subverted the whole social situation. Someone was not playing their part in the farce and if you don't play by the rules then there is no game. The bubble has burst. It was like something out of a Monty Python skit.[26]

The practice of 'adjudication' was something that continued throughout the five years of the protest, although, after the initial one, all other adjudications took place in the wing (eventually at our cells), not in the Governor's office. After the Governor sentenced me I said my piece, as we had previously been instructed to do. I was a political prisoner, I would not wear the prison uniform, and I demanded to be regarded as a political prisoner. He looked at me, shuffled the papers on his desk, then 'sentenced' me for breaching the 'good order and discipline' of the prison. He then said, "Return this criminal to his cell". As I walked back to my cell I felt more confident. I had arrived

[26] Monty Python were a British surreal comedy troupe who created the sketch comedy television show, *Monty Python's Flying Circus*, which first aired on the BBC in 1969. Forty-five episodes were made over four series.

in the Blocks, had appeared in front of the Governor, had made my speech, and now it was about just getting on with it. I still didn't know why I was being held in H2 on my own, but now that didn't seem to matter as much. Things would work out.

The 'sentence' the governor had given me was: three days cellular confinement, 14 days loss of remission, 14 days loss of earnings, 14 days denial of leisure clothing, and 14 days loss of privileges, including visits, (additional) letters, access to the 'tuck-shop', access to association each evening in the canteen, daily exercise, books, magazines, radio, TV, tobacco or cigarettes, pen and paper, and so on and so on. It's actually much easier to itemise what I was left with rather than what was taken away from me. I would get food, be permitted to wash daily, be permitted one visit per month (but would have to wear the prison uniform to go on the visit), and could write and receive one letter per month.

When I got back to my cell I was told to remove my blankets, pillow, and mattress from the cell. Part of the punishment for not abiding by the prison rules was that for three days I did not have access to those items during the day. They would be removed first thing in the morning and placed back in the cell last thing at night. Usually a prisoner charged with breaking prison rules would be taken to the Punishment Block, or the 'Boards' as they were called, due to the fact that the bed consisted of planks of wood on top of a concrete slab. Given the number of prisoners on protest, however, it was obviously not practical to take us all to the Boards for three days so the rule was being implemented in the H-Blocks themselves. You could say that the H-Blocks became an enlarged Punishment Block.

Ten days after my arrival in H2 I was told I was being moved to H5. Arriving into H5 was a great morale booster. I could hear prisoners speaking out the windows of their cells and when I was taken onto B wing I saw a few familiar faces out in the corridor dressed in blankets, brushing and mopping out their cells. Gerard Hodgins, who I had been on remand with, was next door to me. Jackie McMullan was at the bottom of the wing. It was only then I discovered why I had initially been taken to H2. When I had first arrived at the prison, only three cells were vacant in H5. Those were taken by the others who arrived with me that day – Micky, Gerard, and John. I had just happened to pull the 'short straw' and ended up in H2. But someone on B wing H5 had left the protest that morning thus leaving an empty cell for me. I was elated to take his place!

# 3

# Swinging and Cheeking

B WING, H5, was a YP (Young Prisoner) wing – or Yippee wing as some older prisoners referred to it. All of us were aged 21 or under at the time of being sentenced. It was normal prison practice at the time to categorise prisoners according to their age. The regime in our wing was not as relaxed as in the wings holding older prisoners, or even in the other YP wing in the Block, C wing. I suspect we were also regarded as 'trouble-makers' by the older prisoners in A wing, the wing adjacent to us. We'd be shouting over to the OC there at night about some issue or other and seeking permission to do something about it, and would invariably be told to refrain from doing anything.

The Class Officer of B wing was called Dodds; a tall man, at least 6 ft 4 inches (though he may have appeared taller as we were barefooted whilst he wore boots). He had large lips, and he walked in a gangling sort of way. He was English, possibly a former soldier, but I'm not certain of that. We may have assumed military service based solely on his English accent. He was a strange sort of guy. He never really beat anyone, as I recall, but then those were the early days of the protest. The brutality became common-place and casual later, once the no-wash protest commenced.

My cell in H5 was identical to the one I had occupied in H2. In the corner, at the bottom of the bed, stood a tall grey aluminium locker. It had a full-length door on the front. Inside there was a shelf on the top where the prison uniform we had been given in Reception sat. Alongside it, or at the bottom of the locker, there was a pair of prison-issue black boots. The other furniture consisted of a small table with a chair, a pisspot, a dark brown metal waste bin, a small floor mat, and a gallon water container. And, oh yes, the Bible. Who could forget the Bible! King James version.

As numbers on the protest increased, we started to be 'doubled up' with other prisoners. Bunk beds were put into our cells. Like the single beds, they were made out of light square-shaped metal tubing. They were painted dark blue. I vividly recall how rickety they were. It was ok on the bottom bunk, but not the top one. You could stand on the floor, place your hand on the top bunk and move it several inches to the right or left without the legs moving on the floor. And the welded brackets that held the springs to the top and bottom ends of the bunk sometimes broke. I often wondered what you'd do if, lying on the bottom bunk, all the brackets of the top one broke during the night and your cellmate crashed down on top of you. For that reason, I always slept on the top bunk, if possible!

There were certain situations in which the ricketiness of the bunk beds became particularly pronounced. I had a cellmate at the time who masturbated at least four times a day – no exaggeration. He was a walking (well, lying) orgasm. I'd be on the top bunk, reading one of the religious magazines we were permitted,[27] and the frame of the bed would be shaking. I can tell you, it's very difficult to read in such circumstances. One line on the page blurs into another. Growing up, I'd heard the old myth, (probably peddled by priests, who would be well-placed to know) that masturbation could make you blind. This was a slightly amended version of that; someone else's masturbation was making me blind! I'd never been in such close proximity to a man before, or after for that matter, who openly masturbated the way he did. I knew he could sense my discomfort because he said to me, as if by way of explanation, "I need to get rid of the tension". I just nodded. Well, what could I say, really? "I'm reading about the construction of a new water supply to isolated villages in Nigeria whilst you're jerking off? And in broad daylight too, for fuck sake!" In the film, *Hunger*,[28]

---

[27] *The Word* magazine, for example, produced by the Irish Divine Word Missionaries wasn't that bad actually as it dealt much more with social issues rather than theological ones.

[28] *Hunger* is a historical drama about the 1981 Irish hunger strike. Written by Enda Walsh and Steve McQueen, and directed by McQueen, it starred Michael Fassbender, Liam Cunningham, and Liam McMahon. It premiered at the 2009 Cannes Film Festival, winning the prestigious Caméra d'Or award for first-time filmmakers.

there is a scene where a prisoner on the protest is masturbating. He takes great care not to make any sound or movement that might alert his cellmate to what he is doing. That would be my general experience of how people masturbated when sharing a cell with others.

In the early days of the protest in H5 we got out to shower twice a week – or were meant to, at least. Depending on the wing you were in – and the Class Officer in charge of it – that didn't always happen. There was also a difference in the number of prisoners allowed out at any one time to shower. Often the water was lukewarm, if not stone cold. Dodds, in our wing, also had the habit of leaning over the half door of the shower and staring in at us as we showered. He would stand there for some time before walking off.

We had blue bath towels that we would wrap around ourselves when going out to shower or to go to the toilet. On other days, basins of water were brought around the cells and we washed in our cells and the basins were collected later. To get out to the toilet you shouted out your cell number and waited on a guard to come to your door and open it. Sometimes they responded quickly enough and at other times not. There was also a button in each cell which rang an alarm out in the control room in the Circle of the Block, but we were 'warned' against ringing this for access to the toilet. It was meant to be for 'emergency-use' only. Usually when someone was leaving the protest they would push the bell rather than shout out their cell number, as that way others in the wing weren't alerted until a guard appeared at the cell door of whoever had rung the bell. They'd lift the metal viewing flap ('spy hole') of the door, look into the cell, see the prisoner now wearing the prison uniform and would understand what was happening. The guard would open the cell door and the prisoner would leave, usually with no words exchanged; the only sound being the squeaky noise the previously unworn boots made as the prisoner walked on the shiny polished surface of the wing corridor. Hence the terms, 'squeaky booter' and 'squeaky booting' – terms used to denote someone who had left the blanket protest.

As stated earlier, part of the punishment for refusing to wear the prison uniform or do prison work was that each fortnight we appeared before a Governor for adjudication and were sentenced to loss of all privileges and the bedding was removed from our cells for three days. For those who have never experienced life in a prison cell, having bedding removed may not sound like any big deal. At home, you get out of your bed in the morning and usually only go back to your bedroom at night. But what if your bedroom is also your living room, sitting room, kitchen, hallway, toilet, and back yard? When locked 24/7 in a cell 10 x 8 with a bed that takes up at least one third of that space, then your bedding gone from your cell is significant. If you've been endlessly pacing up and down the cell for hours then the bed is nice to sit or lie on for a break, rather than sitting on a hard plastic chair.

In the early days of the protest the guards did not allow anyone to lie on their beds during the day, regardless of whether or not bedding had been removed from the cell. This was normal prison regime rules. They had, by then, given up on trying to impose a 'silence' regime in the wing – as they did at the start of the protest. It was now impossible to do that, given the increased numbers of men on a wing. In order to catch anyone lying on their beds, the guards would try to sneak up the wings and randomly open the spyhole on a cell door but someone at the top end of the wing would usually hear them and shout out, "Bear in the air". The phrase came from the song popular at the time, *Convoy.*[29] Between 12.30 – 2.00 and 4.30 – 5.30 the guards left the wings for lunch and tea, respectively. These were known as 'lock-ups' in the conforming wings. We would know that during that time no guards were going to be on the wing so we would usually lie down and sleep during those periods. However, if you had no mattress or other blankets because you had just been adjudicated it was hard to lie on the bare springs. If you had a cellmate, and he had not been adjudicated at the same time as you, then happy days! You could borrow some of his blankets to put on the bare springs to make a crude mattress.[30]

We brushed out and mopped our cells each day. We would do this while wearing a blanket. The brush and mop would be left outside the first cell of the wing. The cell door would be opened, you brushed and mopped your cell and then you moved the brush and mop to the cell next to you. The cleaning was generally an opportunity to speak in the 'side of the door' to others and the guards were fairly relaxed about

---

[29] A trucker's protest song, released in 1976 by C.W. McCall, which celebrated citizens band radio, trucker lingo and rugged individualism.

[30] Sometime after the no-wash protest started, in March 1978, the practice of removing the bedding from the cells for three days ended. We were still adjudicated though and lost all privileges and remission.

it, depending on how long you took to brush and mop. The process went on all morning until every cell was finished. If it looked like all cells would not be brushed and mopped before dinner arrived at around noon, then several cells would be opened at the one time.

We 'slopped out' in the morning and again in the evening. This consisted of taking our pisspot up to a small closet inset into the wall at the top of the wing where there was what looked like a very large sink but which functioned in the way a toilet does with a cistern of water overhead and a chain to pull to flush. We poured our piss and any solids into the 'sink' and flushed it. We then went to the ablutions area (toilets, three showers, seven hand basins and a bath) and scrubbed our pisspots at another large sink there. We filled our water containers and returned to our cells and the next cell was let out. Although it only took a few minutes to complete the whole process it was an opportunity each day to get out of our cells. Some men prolonged the moment as long as they could, often to the ire of others who were eager to get out to the toilet.

When we got out to shower or slop out we could pass the religious magazines from cell to cell. When locked up we could ask a guard to deliver them, but sometimes, especially at night-time, we'd pass them up the side of our wing by 'swinging' them. To 'swing' we'd use the prison trousers that we had in our cells, tie a knot in the bottom of one leg, drop the magazine into the leg, drop that leg out the window whilst holding onto the bottom of the other leg and then swing it to the next-door cell where someone with their arm held out their window would grab it. They could then pass the trousers (and magazine) further up the wing by repeating the exercise. Sometimes a guard patrolling the yard would try to race down and grab the trousers but usually someone would spot him and shout out a warning. At other times, someone, out of devilment, would hold onto the trousers and not return them for a while. It was an 'offence' not to have the full uniform in your cell so if you got a cell search and the guards discovered that the trousers were missing you would be charged.

There were 'orderlies' in each wing. They were non-political prisoners who carried out the usual chores of cleaning the wing and distributing food. They were kept in Cell 26, a double-cell at the top of the wing. The cell had two sets of bunk beds so could hold four prisoners. Depending on who the orderlies were we could get some scéal (news) from them when they mopped and bumpered[31] the corridor of the wing, as long as they were far enough away from the guards to avoid being overheard talking to us. On a rare occasion, an orderly would slip the odd cigarette to a prisoner but generally they

[31] An electric machine with a circular disc for polishing the floors.

were very timid and afraid of being caught as it would have meant being sent to the Punishment Block, losing their position as orderly, being moved to another Block and assigned to a different, less-appealing, form of prison work. Being an orderly was regarded as a 'cushy number'. When the no-wash protest began in March '78 the orderlies were moved out of the wings and into the classrooms closer to the Circle of the Block. This was a huge room compared to cell 26. They also got awarded additional special privileges such as a TV and a record player in the classroom.

Upon arriving in H5, my memory is that we collected our food from the canteen and took it to our cells to eat but this procedure (assuming that my memory is correct in this instance) changed very shortly afterwards when the food was brought around the wing on a large aluminium trolley. It comprised of three shelves. Dinners sat on the top two shelves, and desserts on the bottom shelf. It could take up to five minutes for the food to be distributed to all cells, depending on the guards and orderlies. It seemed much longer than five minutes if you were in the last cell.

In the early days of the protest, by way of ensuring 'equality' – as is the Irish republican code – no one could start eating their meal until everyone in the wing had received their meal. Once the last cell had been served, the person in it would shout out '*Fuai*r' (got) and the wing OC would shout out. "*Leanaigí ar aghaidh*" (go ahead). For the person who got their meal first, waiting on the order from the OC, whilst looking at their food and smelling its aroma, was probably worse than being in the last cell. Someone got caught out one day when they had gone ahead and started to eat their meal before the OC of their wing – Kieran Nugent – gave the order to go ahead and eat. It turned out that not everyone had got their meal, or there was something missing from someone's meal, and Kieran gave the order for no one to eat. But when the guards came round to collect the plates (with dinners still on them) they discovered that someone had already half-eaten his and they made sure to make the rest of us aware of that by shouting out his name and telling us about it! Kieran later questioned the guy if it was true what the guards had claimed but he said no, and that they were trying to 'put the mix in' between us. However, days later his cell-mate confirmed that he had indeed ate half his dinner.

There was a long-established Irish republican tradition that prisoners refused prison food on Christmas Day – the best food of the year. There's masochism and then there's Irish republicanism. I don't know where this tradition originated. Maybe some OC in bygone days was a great admirer of Padre Pio and his proclivity to wearing hair shirts and self-flagellation, and thought it admirable that republicans, even though imprisoned and already denied the broad range of carnal pleasures available on the outside, should deny themselves such gastronomic pleasures attached to the celebration of Christ's birth. Regardless of the origins of the tradition its purpose was questionable, or certainly lacked depth, particularly for those republican prisoners in the Cages who enjoyed political status. It may have been a noble gesture to inform the heathen, materialistically-minded officials of the prison regime that Irish republican prisoners were refusing their food on Christmas Day – thus highlighting their commitment to global revolution and the establishment of a socialist society – but the fact that they had their 'food parcels' from home to fall back on, rendered the gesture more symbolic, at best. The (weekly) food parcels contained meat, chicken, sausages, bacon, cake, biscuits, cigarettes etc. At Christmas there was an additional allowance in terms of the quantity of the above items permitted in the parcel. Therefore, refusing the prison-cooked turkey and brussel sprouts wasn't such a huge sacrifice after all. Padre Pio would turn in his grave, or give himself another 50 lashes! Given that in the H-Blocks we did not receive food parcels from outside, the tradition of refusing Christmas dinner was thankfully confined to the dustbin of history, and from then on we looked forward to the prison-cooked turkey, brussel sprouts, roast potatoes, and plum pudding on Christmas Day. It was Heaven!

Another Christmas tradition involved the prisoners in the Cages sending us a 'Christmas message' of solidarity. They probably sent ones to others prisons too and we may well have sent them one. However, as our protest continued over the years, and intensified in severity, I recall how one particular Christmas message of solidarity from the Cages was received. The author of the message had obviously worked himself up into quite a state of patriotic fervour (or was a bit pissed on home-brewed poitín) as his message ended with something along the lines of, "and the day when we drive the Brits into the Irish Sea". All very rousing stuff and well-intended sentiments but when our wing OC read out the message it was greeted with laughter, the blowing of raspberries,[32] and shouts of 'fuck off!'. We became very irreverent in that regard. The old emotional 'wrap the green flag round me, boys' didn't really cut it any more for us; not in the conditions we existed in. We were slowly transitioning from romantic, idealistic, fanciful notions of victory to the cold reality of what we now believed would be a long drawn-out struggle both within the prison and on the outside.

In the early days of the protest I didn't go to Mass – which was held in the prison canteen – as we had to wear the prison trousers to do so. Or at least that was my rationale at the time. I've wondered since, though, was it just that I preferred the silence of the wing when others were at Mass rather than the bedlam that was the canteen when 80 or so blanketmen were brought together. Others loved being out of their cells for that extended period each Sunday.

The IRA policy at the time was that we didn't take visits because we had to wear the full uniform – though married men could take them if they wished. Some did and some didn't. It wasn't until 1978, after the start of the no-wash protest, that we were all encouraged by the IRA Camp OC to take visits for the purpose of communication – to let people on the outside know what was happening and to smuggle out written 'comms'.[33] It was then that I began to attend Mass as well as take visits. In 1977, however, Mass was the place to hear *scéal* (news). No one ever questioned where this *scéal* came from, which was strange given that visits were so rare, but after men returned from Mass each Sunday there was always *scéal*. It generally centred around the BB (Belfast Brigade, IRA) and somehow or other the BB, or someone involved in it, knew that political status was just around the corner. It was nothing more than wishful thinking but still, it gave us hope and maintained spirits.

As mentioned earlier, once the blanket protest began, prison guards referred to us as 'streakers' but officially we were categorised as 'non-conforming' prisoners to distinguish us from conforming prisoners or, as *they* began to be referred to, 'ODCs' – ordinary, decent criminals. I've often wondered how that term became so commonly used, within

---

[32] Making a noise similar to flatulence that signifies derision, real or feigned.

[33] 'Comms' (communications) were written on cigarette papers and wrapped in cling film so that they could be secretly carried in mouths and often passed across to a visitor via a kiss.

the prison and on the outside, by media commentators and academics. I wonder how they would respond if asked to define what or who makes for a 'decent' criminal? A dictionary definition of decent is, 'conforming with generally accepted standards of respectable or moral behaviour'. The inference, therefore, that republican prisoners on protest were 'indecent' and 'amoral', whereas a rapist, for instance, abiding by the prison regime, would be classified as an ODC – an ordinary decent criminal. It sort of stands the concept of decency and morality on its head a little. The term is still used today by commentators and/or academics and I often wonder if they are aware of its origin or *why* it was originally coined.

Because we had no visits at that time, tobacco or cigarettes were practically non-existent, unless a priest visiting on a Sunday carried some on him. When going out to wash or to 'slop out' we'd be on the lookout for large cigarette butts lying on the floor. Some people became very adept at being able to scoop up the butts, sometimes even grabbing them between their toes. Anyone going out to the Circle to see the doctor or MO (Medical Officer) had a greater opportunity to get their hands on butts as often there would be ash trays sitting between the grilles on the way to the Circle.[34]

Getting a light was another challenge. In prison, the lighters that were allowed were of the old petrol type; a long cylinder filled with cotton wool with a screw top on one end of it. You filled the cylinder with petrol and flicked the lid on the top of the lighter which moved a small metal wheel with a serrated rim across a flint causing a spark to hit the wick; the type of lighter you see in World War II films and later. Anyone reading this under the age of 40 has probably never seen one in real life, other than in an antique shop! Blanketmen were not allowed lighters, of course, as we were not allowed to smoke, but some of us had smuggled them onto the protest or later got them from an orderly or somewhere. Sometimes we shared responsibility for holding onto the lighter. To exchange it from person to person, the one who had it would go up to the toilet and hide it, possibly in the middle of the toilet roll, and then someone else would ask to get out to the toilet later and collect it. I held one at times.

---

[34] In *H3*, the feature film I co-wrote with Brian Campbell, there is a scene where 'Madra' lifts a fully lit cigarette sitting in an ash tray as he passes through the grilles without the guard noticing.

A lighter, like any sort of contraband on the protest, had to be hidden and the best place to hide it was on, or in, your body. At that stage of the protest we didn't hide contraband internally. That came later. We would 'cheek' it. To 'cheek' something, your first wrapped it (lighter, pen, tobacco, or whatever) in a piece of tissue, or toilet paper. This provided some 'grip' and then you placed it between your arse cheeks. To ensure that it was wedged as tightly as possible between your cheeks, you'd squat down so as to part your cheeks fully open, place the object, and stand up again. Unless the object was very big no one would be able to see it even if you were standing naked. That was important as sometimes the guards did cell searches and during them you would be asked to remove your blanket and shake it. It took a bit of practice to get used to cheeking but once you did, you could pace up and down the cell all day with something firmly cheeked, without it falling to the floor.

The problem we had with our lighters, though, was that we had no petrol for them. What use is a petrol lighter with no fuel for it? As it turned out, even without the petrol, you could still get a light with it. We would take out a very small piece of the cotton wool from the cylinder and gently pull it apart so that it was 'fluffed up'. If you then removed the cylinder from the lighter and held the end of this small piece of cotton wool at the top of the lighter and flicked the top, the spark from the flint would ignite the cotton and it would flare up for an instant. It took a pit of practice to accomplish this and even when you were successful you had to be very quick to get a light from it. To assist the process we were sometimes able to light a piece of tissue paper first, which provided a longer lasting flame from which to light your cigarette – if you were lucky enough to have a cigarette!

Numbers on the protest continued to grow and in October 1977 some men were moved from each of the wings in H5 to start a new Block, H3. It was around the same time, 7 October, 1977, that the IRA shot dead a guard who worked in the prison. Desmond Ernest Irvine, aged 38, was a Principal Officer. He must have worked in either the Cages or in the conforming Blocks because he wasn't known to any of us on the protest. We didn't even know about it at the time it happened. Irvine was Secretary of the Prison Officer's Association (POA) and was shot as he left a meeting of the POA. In those days, when we didn't take visits, news was very sparse and often couldn't be relied upon. However, when we heard of his death we also heard that he had recently spoken out in favour of our demands to be treated as political prisoners. We couldn't understand how the IRA went and killed a guard who was publicly arguing in favour of the return of political status. In conducting research for this book, however, I discovered that the story wasn't quite as we had heard at the time, though there were some key elements of truth. Peter Taylor, well-known journalist and documentary maker, had interviewed Irvine for a TV programme Taylor made in 1977 about the removal of political status and our protest in response to that change in policy. Forty years later, in 2017, in advance of a broadcast on BBC Radio 4 of Peter Taylor's documentary, *Fifty Years Behind the Headlines – Reflections on Terror*, Taylor wrote an article on the subject for the BBC website. In it, he said that the killing of Desmond Irvine in 1977, only a few days after his documentary had been broadcast, was the killing that affected him most personally above all others.

> The blanket protest by the IRA prisoners in the Maze started in 1977. They refused to wear prison uniform, insisting they were political prisoners and not criminals. The protesters resorted to wearing only a blanket to try and force the issue.
>
> To try and understand the situation from the other side of the cell doors, I met Desmond Irvine, the secretary of the Northern Ireland Prison Officers Association.
>
> As a unionist prison officer, what he said came as a surprise. He agreed to do an interview despite the Northern Ireland Office advising him against it. I felt he wanted to get his message across.
>
> I asked if he respected the prisoners for their protest. 'I don't think they just do it mainly for publicity but because it's their belief. I suppose one could say a person who believes sincerely in what he is doing, and is prepared to suffer for it, [deserves] a certain measure of respect which you give to him.'

So it wasn't the case that Desmond Irvine was arguing for the return of political status but he nevertheless recognised that we were struggling for what we believed in and he respected that. Many more prison guards were to be killed over the course of the protest and beyond.

# 4

# Eggy beggy seggy fucken weggy!

THE AVERAGE AGE OF PRISONERS being sentenced during 1976-78, and most likely thereafter, was about 19 years. Interests, besides what was happening in the struggle outside, were in football, pop music and girls (if anyone had an interest in boys they sadly wouldn't have felt able to voice it in those days), not necessarily in that order. Whole days were spent in long conversations out the side of the doors, out the windows, or at 'the pipes'.[35]

Political status, and its return, was often the topic of discussion; what we would do once we got it and what life would be like in the Cages once we were moved there. In those days we assumed a return of status meant a return to the Cages. The two were synonymous. Status equalled Cages. We assumed that the Blocks would be reserved for ordinary prisoners. Generally, the view was that we would have status restored in about six months – that eternal six months that never changed no matter when you posed the question. It was idealistic thinking, wishful thinking, involving no real analysis of the British Government's strategy in the North and the part that criminalisation played in that strategy.

There was some 'loose talk' in those early days and a degree of boasting amongst some. Plus there were some humorous exchanges. One particular incident I recall is where someone from Belfast (I'll not mention names), who to be blunt about it was a bit of a 'slabber',[36] was talking out the side of the door with a friend of his on the other side of the wing from him. He was putting it across that his area was

---

[35] The heating pipes that ran through the cells just above floor level. Prisoners would get down to the pipes and speak through to those in the cell next-door.

[36] Know-all, boastful, ignorant.

well-armed and had all the latest equipment. Another guy, from a rural area, joined in the conversation and after a few moments said, "I bet you never got your hands on a Massey Ferguson 165?" To which the 'slabber' replied, "For fuck sakes we had that many of them we were giving them away to you lads down the country." The response to that was, "Well we could put them to better use seeing as how the Massey Ferguson is a fucken tractor you idiot?" Most of the wing burst out laughing.

Other boasts were in regards to amorous conquests. Of course, most of the exploits recounted were patently unbelievable and grossly exaggerated. I often felt, however, that if they were all true then I had, by comparison, lived quite a sheltered existence.

In general, the days were boring. Extremely boring. I think it was largely psychological, however. We were in some sort of time warp. We weren't on the outside. We weren't on remand. We weren't in the Cages with political status. We were detached, adrift, floating free somewhere. Waiting on something to materialise.

Even the best conversationalist got bored with endless tales from bygone days or dreams for future ones. It filled a vacuum and helped cope with 24/7 incarceration in a small cell but more was required and it was here that the Irish language came to play an important role. It gave us something to focus our minds on and provided us with a means of communication which was unintelligible to the guards. Generations of imprisoned republicans held one thing in common – an interest in, or commitment to, learning the Irish language. Our circumstances in the H-Blocks made it difficult to do this. We were without grammar or exercise books, nor had we pens or pencils. But just as our conditions threw up obstacles, they also encouraged resourcefulness and ingenuity. The need to communicate covertly was a key motivator and perhaps the most compelling driver for the beginning of Irish language classes.

Before the classes started to develop there was, however, another language used to communicate without the guards understanding it, though when they heard it spoken, they thought it was Irish. It was, apparently, what was known as 'Showband' language. I haven't a clue why it was called that or why it was only people from Derry city who were aware of it, but it was very simple to use once you understood its structure. However, just hearing it spoken and not knowing how the words were formed, it sounded like gobbledegook. Basically, you inserted the word 'egg' in front of all vowels in any word. For example, if I wanted to shout over the wing to someone and ask, "Do you have any tobacco?" I'd say, "Deggo yeggou heggave eggany teggobeggacceggo." I know, it's a bit difficult to get your tongue around but once you knew how the words were formed you'd get the gist of what someone was saying. I remember Dodds, the guard, walking down the length of the wing one day as two Derry guys were having a very fluent conversation in the language. It obviously had been annoying him, hearing them speak and not knowing what was being said. He took out his baton and as he walked he beat it against the cell doors, shouting, "Eggy beggy seggy fucken weggy!"

I hated learning Irish at school (largely due to the teacher who taught it) and I knew only a couple of words when arrested but within a few months of being sentenced I understood the need to learn it and had the motivation. However, there were few who actually knew the language and it was obvious that from the limited classes conducted there was no coherent grasp or comprehension of the language by those who were trying to teach it. They were relying on memory, and often a distorted memory at that, rather than being fluent speakers. When asked questions, the 'teachers' often could not give any clear or definitive answers, or else gave a number of different answers when challenged by others. Listening to all of this I decided that whilst I did intend to learn the language I would wait until we had got political status – and sure, that was only six months away. No way was I going to spend time learning something that I would later have to un-learn.

However, shortly afterwards, I shared a cell with Paul Montgomery from Newington, North Belfast, and Paul had decided that he would be fluent in Irish by Christmas. Pacing up and down the cell for hours on end he would repeat the irregular verbs; *Ar chuala tú*? Did you hear?; *Chuala mé*. I heard; *Níor chuala me*. I did not hear. Despite efforts on my part to resist it I soon found myself mentally repeating, *Ar chuala tú, chuala me, níor chuala me*, and that was how I began to learn the Irish language. Later in the protest, the Irish language was as commonly heard as English and many people, including myself, became fluent speakers (even if with a limited vocabulary based around politics and imprisonment) and went on to teach others. We smuggled into the jail articles in Irish, largely from the *Irish Press*,[37] which was still published at that time. We also got pages from grammar books smuggled down to us from the Cages. But primarily, the advancement made in regards to the language – and the teaching of it – was down to a small handful of people who were already fluent in it; Séanna Walsh (who I learned practically all of my Irish from) and Bobby Sands. Coincidentally, Séanna and Bobby were good friends from a previous period of imprisonment in the Cages.

Paul Montgomery's family didn't want him on the protest. He told me about this and it was contained in the letters he received through the prison censor from his family, so the prison authorities were also aware of it. As we didn't take visits, letters were the only means of communication. It was only later, once we resumed visits, that we were able to develop a much more comprehensive system of covert (smuggled) communication, both personally and in terms of the movement, from inside to out and vice versa.

Paul got a letter one day, in late 1977, saying that some members of his family were going on a trip to the USA. It may have been his parents. At around that time we had heard, somehow or other, that miniature radios were easily available in the States. We thought that if we could secure such a radio it would provide a valuable source of information about events on the outside. We discussed the option of Paul taking a visit with his family to ask whether they could source one of the miniature radios. The family were due to fly out in a few days so we thought going through the usual channels of sending out a visit permit would take too long, given the prison authorities posted out the permits to visitors' home addresses. So Paul requested to see the Prison Chaplain. There weren't many, if any, requests at that time to see the Chaplain so he arrived that evening. Paul asked him if he would contact his family to arrange a visit before they went off to the States. Paul also requested to see the prison Governor to inform him that he was seeking a visit with his family and ask that they be allowed in, despite the short notice.

---

[37] *The Irish Press* daily newspaper was founded in 1931 and ceased printing in 1995. Eamonn de Valera, future Taoiseach and later President of Ireland, was behind the establishment of the paper.

Given some of what had been written to Paul in his family letters the prison administration likely thought that Paul was under some pressure to come off the protest and they granted the visit readily. Paul's family were probably disappointed to discover that he was not coming off the protest – and indeed had only requested to see them to ask them to get him something from the States. Nevertheless, they did get to see him and see that he was OK and I think that put their minds at ease.

Shortly after that I was moved from B wing to C wing. Jackie McMullan had been OC in B wing but was moved out of the wing precisely because he *was* the OC! On leaving, he asked me to take over. I agreed simply because I believed I couldn't refuse. My time in the role was short-lived, however, as I too was soon moved, to C wing – via the Punishment Block, charged with 'undermining the good order and discipline' of the prison. Dodds didn't like any challenge to his authority as Class Officer. However, the experience of being asked and then fulfilling the role, no matter how briefly, was important for me as it made me think more about how I was perceived by others. At that time I would never have thought of myself as leadership material. I suppose I just assumed that such a role was for others, though I realised that I was beginning to think more about the type of people who *did* occupy leadership positions and the qualities they did, or often did not, possess. It still came as a surprise though when Jackie asked me to take over as OC.

The wing structures in those days were very simple. There was the OC, who really had very little to do given that we were locked up full-time. The OC's role was basically about keeping some type of order in the wing and liaising with the Block OC, though again, there was very little to liaise about, especially in those early days. The OC had an Adjutant but the Adjutant's role really only came into operation if the OC was taken off to the Boards; the Adjutant would then fill in until the OC's return. If the OC didn't return, because he was moved to another Block after leaving the Boards, the Adjutant would take over permanently.

Generally, order in the wing was dependent upon the attitude and self-discipline of the men in it. But if someone did decide to make a nuisance of themselves there were really no sanctions that could be imposed upon them. On the rare occasion when someone *was* making an ass of themselves they would be put on a 'black out' for three days, which meant that no one was to speak to them. Of course, if they were the type who didn't really talk out the windows or doors it wasn't much of a punishment for them. And people in the cell next door to someone on a 'black out' would usually speak to them anyhow, unless they risked being overheard by the OC.

One particularly annoying thing that some prisoners occasionally engaged in during those early days was the 'rattling of the pipes'. Two large (about 5" diameter) metal heating pipes ran through each cell from wall to wall, below the window. If anyone was to 'tap' them with a metal object (or even their knuckles), no matter how lightly, the noise travelled the full length of the wing. It was very hard to detect who was doing it. Even if you were next door to the person doing it you couldn't really be sure if it was them or if the noise was travelling from further away. Of course, once it started, someone would get particularly annoyed and shout out to whoever was doing it to stop; which, of course, only encouraged them. That was the reason they were doing it in the first place: to wind someone up and get a response. The rattling didn't have to last too long to unsettle everyone in the wing because, even if it stopped for a time, you never knew when, or if, it would start again. If anyone was caught doing it they were definitely on a 'black out'! On one occasion, someone was caught by Kieran Nugent when he was OC of C wing. A prison guard let Kieran out of his cell once the rattling on the pipes began and Kieran was able to walk up the wing and determine the cell from which the noise originated. He then lifted the flap on the door and caught the prisoner red-handed.

It wasn't necessarily about badness; it was about boredom. We were locked up with little mental stimulation to pass the time other than chats we had with one another, or reading the religious magazines. Interestingly, it occurred only in the early days of the protest and disappeared after the no-wash protest began. That must say something about a shift in mentality or a growth in maturity; possibly a growing awareness or consciousness that we existed as a group, relied upon one another, looked out for one another, and therefore needed to be considerate and care for one another.

In C wing I shared a cell with Richard 'Junior' May from Turf Lodge. Junior's father was also called Richard but was called by the common abbreviation of, 'Dick', 'Dickie', or, given his height, 'Big Dickie'. As Junior grew up into his teens he was not amused about the way in which locals began to distinguish him from his father; Big

Dickie and 'Wee Dickie'. He feared the latter may be misunderstood, so he insisted on being called Junior instead. In the time I knew him, he was only ever known as 'Junior'. Some years later I had another cellmate, Paddy Molloy from Belfast. Paddy decided, at that stage in his life, that he too would give himself a nickname; '*Croí Mór*' (big heart). When anyone would shout up the wing to him "Paddy? Paddy Molloy?" Paddy would get up to the door and respond, "Hello, is someone looking for '*Croí Mór*'?"

Junior's mother was one of the founders of the local Relatives Action Committee in Turf Lodge; the organisation set up to campaign in support of our demands for the return of political status. His friend, Mickey Holden from Turf Lodge, was also in the wing and his mother too was a prominent activist in the Relatives Action Committee. In later years I met with Chris McArdle, again from Turf Lodge, whose mother was equally prominent in the campaign. The three women/mothers were regularly referred to in the Belfast vernacular of 'Ma'. 'Ma' McArdle, 'Ma' Holden, and 'Ma' May – the latter term always making me think of the Al Jolson song, 'Mammy'. It was these women, and many more like them across the North who first highlighted the jail situation and took our protest onto the streets. At a time when the Republican Movement had many other issues to deal with – transitioning out of the very difficult aftermath of a lengthy ceasefire followed by mass arrests – it was these women – mothers, wives, sisters, partners, relatives, neighbours – who became the bedrock of our campaign on the outside.

In the cell next door to Junior and me was Gerard Doherty from the New Lodge area of Belfast (who had travelled down to the jail with me that day after being sentenced) and Seány McVeigh[38] from the Short Strand area of Belfast. Seány was very good at drawing and sketched what I believe were the first images of blanketmen onto toilet paper which were then smuggled outside. Gerard was very quiet; Seány made up for him!

In those days you could buy cards (on the outside) for Birthdays, Christmas, Valentine's Day that were 'padded' on the front. I don't

[38] Seány died in 2016 and shortly afterwards his brother Mick established the Facebook group 'blanketmen/women 1976/81' to give a voice to former republican prisoners who had experienced the blanket protest.

know if they're still available to purchase today – which surely says something about my approach to card-buying. Basically, the padded cards had a thin fabric attached to the front cover of the card with foam between the fabric and the card itself. They were generally quite big – probably about a foot tall and eight inches wide. I don't recall how we came up with the idea, but we (Junior, Seány, Gerard, and I) conceived a plan to get such a card sent in which would have items hidden inside the foam. Seány sent a smuggled message out to his sister Rosie and shortly afterwards a padded card arrived in for him. I'm not sure if it was his birthday or it may have been close to Valentine's Day. In any case, the padded card secretly contained tobacco, some flints, some cigarette papers, and an article about our protest taken from the republican newspaper, *An Phoblacht/The Republican News*. A few days later another card with similar contents arrived, this time for Junior.

I always thought it particularly poetic that the card, with its smuggled contraband, was actually hand-delivered to Junior by a guard. The guard, in this instance, was Mike Trainor, the Assistant Class Officer in the wing. Trainor was a Catholic who ironically came from Turf Lodge, the same area as Junior. He handed the card to Junior and said, "Someone loves you, May". Trainor was a tall guy but wore high-heels to give himself a couple of extra inches in height. He was a good-looking guy, 'salt and pepper' hair, well-groomed, and had a bit of an air about him. He claimed the IRA had tried to kill him once when returning to Turf Lodge to visit his family. We never learned if that was true or not. I suspect that as a Catholic – and originally coming from a working-class republican area of Belfast – he wasn't sure how to behave when working as a prison guard with republicans. Other Catholic guards weren't burdened with that uncertainty; whatever they felt, it often translated into brutality against us. A classic case of the 'Castle Catholic'.[39]

In addition to the padded cards, we managed to slip items past the screws through the 'soap parcels' we could receive from our families. Before we began the 'no-wash' protest we were allowed one soap parcel per month. It consisted of one bar of soap, three sachets of

[39] The term, 'Castle Catholic' originated in early 20th century Ireland to describe those middle-class Catholics who were assimilated into the pro-British establishment at Dublin Castle, the seat of the British administration.

shampoo, and a small packet of tissues. My mother always kept a bar of Imperial Leather soap in cupboards at home to make the clothes smell fresh and I grew up associating clothes with that smell. The bars were unique as they had a small, red, metallic label stuck on them. Apparently it was meant to make the soap last longer by preventing the soap going mushy after use. You were meant to set the soap down with the label underneath, any excess water flowed off the soap, allowing it to dry. I only gained that knowledge when writing this memoir! I had previously thought the label was just decorative. Whatever its official purpose, the label proved very useful to us. It could be peeled off, and a small hole gouged out of the soap where flints could then be inserted. Soap could then be put back in on top, and the label set back in place. We continued getting flints in this way right up until the soap parcels were ended at the commencement of the no-wash protest.

Life in C wing continued much as it had in B wing, though things were much more relaxed there. Whilst Mike Trainor was Assistant Class Officer on the wing, the Class Officer was Jed McKnight, an older guy who had a nervous energy about him; not the worst – though in those days, prior to the start of the no-wash protest, relationships on the wing with most guards were generally, though not always, amicable enough. Kieran 'Header' Nugent, as OC of the wing, had a good relationship with both McKnight and Trainor. Both were smokers; Jed smoked *Park Drive* cigarettes and Trainor, *Benson and Hedges*. They'd occasionally slip you a cigarette and some guys would occasionally have the 'brass neck' to ask for one! Given Header's role as OC they were more inclined to keep him 'happy' by slipping him the odd cigarette, or sometimes more than the odd one.

Occasionally, when there was tension with the guards over something Header would call a 'red alert'. That meant we had to put on the prison trousers and boots and be ready for action. What that action was going to be was never spelled out. We couldn't *take* any action unless the guards opened the cell doors, which they were hardly going to do if they saw us wearing trousers and boots, ready for a battle. I don't believe that any of the other wings had such a system in operation. To his credit, it was rare that Header called a 'red alert' but when he did, Jed McKnight would be down to his cell to talk about the issue, cigarettes would be immediately produced, and the matter would eventually be resolved.

When the guards left the wings in the evening at 8.30 things became livelier. Although people spoke out the doors and windows during the day, conversation increased much more with the guards gone. It was also the time when various forms of entertainment took place. I use the term 'entertainment' fairly loosely. In the early days, the main form this took was sing-songs; years later it developed into story-telling. I found sing-songs a frightening experience. I can't sing for love nor money. There were others in the wing who also lacked any singing ability but that didn't deter them. One particular comrade who was especially horrendous would finish one song and then ask, in all seriousness, "Would youse like another one?" He had obviously never heard his voice recorded and played back to him.

You could simply refuse to sing but that prompted even more abuse than if you sang badly. On the few occasions I did sing (preferring to engage in my own self-degradation rather than take the abuse for not singing) I sang, 'A horse with no name' by the folk-rock band *America*.

> On the first part of the journey
> I was looking at all the life
> There were plants and birds and rocks and things
> There was sand and hills and rings
> The first thing I met was a fly with a buzz
> And the sky with no clouds
> The heat was hot and the ground was dry
> But the air was full of sound.

The song was released in 1971 and was a big hit, though I recently discovered it was banned by some US radio stations because of supposed references to heroin use. It turns out 'horse' is a common slang term for heroin. I didn't know that then, but I'm quietly impressed that my choice of song back then referred to drug use; very radical of me.

Another way we entertained ourselves was through quizzes. There would be a quizmaster who drew up the questions, sometimes with the help of comrades next door to him (who were then unable to participate in the quiz). In C wing the quizmaster was often 'Pidgey' – Paul Peter Pious Prigent – from the Short Strand area of Belfast. Pidgey was a character. There would be various categories of questions; sport, music, books etc. There was no choice given; each team had to answer in all categories. Team members conferred out the door and had an allocated amount of time before they had to finalise their answer. Often the allotted time was greatly extended, accompanied by shouts of disapproval from the other teams and allegations of bias on the part of the quizmaster. It also frequently happened that the quizmaster's answers were hotly disputed, which again led to much uproar. However, the quizmaster's decision was taken as final, which, in disputed circumstances, led to men 'blowing raspberries' out the door. Some would also respond in 'squeaky voices', disguising their voices so as to hurl insults. Pidgey, who was a bit hard of hearing, would retaliate by accusing them of cowardice. If they had courage, he would say, they'd make their remarks to his face at Sunday mass. This would prompt more squeaky voices. Often, in addition to this, Jake McHugh from Turf Lodge would get up to the door and call down to Pidgey in a South Derry accent, imitating Paul McGlinchey who was next door to Jake. Jake (in his put-on accent) would tell Pidgey that he hadn't a clue what he was talking about and that he should get away from the door and lie down on his bed and give everyone's head peace. Pidgey would respond in his own inimitable manner and then, by way of ignoring the abuse, would call out to Seány McVeigh about the "reprobates down the wing", some of whom were "lower than a snake's ballbag". Listening to Pidgey conversing in this manner was usually the best part of the night's entertainment.

We were allowed to write and receive one letter per month. We had to request a prison-issue letter page. The guards took 'requests' first thing in the morning when they did a head-count. All requests involved standing at your door as they opened it and requesting what it was you wanted – a letter page, to see the doctor or Governor or Chaplain, etc. They ignored your request if you were not at your door. Whenever the no-wash protest began we didn't get the letter pages as the guards would say, "Show me your pen and you'll get a letter page." Given that we were not allowed to have pens, we were denied letter pages.

At the top of the letter pages there was printed, 'When replying to this letter, address it to' and there then was, 'Number' – a space for the prisoner's prison number and then, 'Name' – the name of the prisoner. The guards filled in this detail themselves so, for instance, mine would read, NUMBER ... 454, NAME ... McKeown.[40] We were opposed to being referred to by a number rather than our names and I didn't want my family to write a letter to me addressed in the manner the guards wanted, so I smuggled out a comm to my mother to tell her to either leave off the number on any letter sent in or at least put it after my name, which is what she did from then on. Somewhat curiously, my mother always ended her letters with the phrase, "I hope you and your comrades are well", or a version of that. It was the word 'comrades' I found so strange. It wasn't a word my mother would commonly use. She would have more naturally referred to 'your friends'. I hadn't asked her to use the term 'comrades' when writing to me and I'm not sure what prompted her to use it. I regret that I never got around in later years to asking her why she did.

Some months after I moved into C wing, I noticed that very detailed and seemingly accurate news was being shouted over daily from B wing. I think we all assumed that some sympathetic prison orderly must have been passing on the news, but even then it seemed too accurate and too comprehensive. Then Paul (Montgomery), who was still in B wing, was moved across to the other side of his wing, which meant he now directly faced my wing, and it was Paul who now shouted over the news each evening. It was at that point that I had my Eureka moment – Paul must have got the radio.

In those days, if we had mates in the wing opposite us, we would communicate with them through 'writing' with our finger at the window pane. We would spell out the letters of a word, then raise an open hand to indicate a new word, and then continue. It was our form of today's 'texting'! Those who regularly communicated in this manner were able to develop their own shortcuts and abbreviations.

---

[40] See photgraphs for a letter I wrote to my mother just after being sentenced.

It sped up the communication but also ensured that no one else could make out what was being said. Many people became quite adept at it and a lot could be communicated in this manner over an hour or so. However, Paul was too far up the wing for me to be able to 'write' to him in this way. Because of the obstruction caused by the concrete bars on the window you had to be more or less opposite the person to get a clear view. At the time I still didn't attend Mass on a Sunday. Paul didn't either, so the following Sunday when everyone else was at Mass I shouted over to him and asked him if the American trip had been successful. He said it had been. It confirmed that Paul was in possession of the radio. I never got to see it and I never saw Paul after that. I don't think there was ever another purchased miniature radio smuggled into the Blocks, at least not that I'm aware of. Sometime after the start of the no-wash protest, however, the IRA started to manufacture their own radios to smuggle into us.[41] They operated by way of a crystal as a power source and had one wire which you had to earth to something metal in your cell and another wire with an earpiece at the end of it. There was a small screw to enable you to tune into channels. It was a bit like being a 'safe cracker' from those old movies where they put their ear to the safe and tweak the nobs on the outside until they get the right combination, and the door swings open. I often wondered why the 'RA didn't just get a shipment of miniature radios from the States, given the support we received from Irish-America. But you know the 'RA; they like to be self-sufficient even if the radios they produced were most likely much larger than those that could have been purchased across the counter.

It was in C wing, H5, that I first learned about Cuba, Fidel Castro, and Ché Guevara. Two guys who were originally housed in the Cages with political status, Thomas 'Ta' Power and Mickey Ferguson, arrived into our wing. Ta and Mickey were affiliated to the INLA (Irish National Liberation Army), a group that split away from the 'Official' IRA in late 1974 and were originally known as the 'People's Liberation Army'. However, in 1977 there was an internal row within the INLA in their Cage in Long Kesh and a group of them, possibly 10-12, walked out of the Cages and were moved

[41] See photographs.

to the Blocks by the prison authorities. Ta was very quiet and soft-spoken but politically well-educated and he wrote up (on sheets of toilet paper) a lengthy article about the Cuban revolution which was passed around the wing.

This was not toilet paper as you'd normally think of it – not your modern tissue-paper variety. This was squares of what resembled greaseproof paper which only those of a certain age will recall from public toilets. When you folded the paper, it creased, which made it rather unpleasant to wipe your arse with. It definitely wasn't your 3-ply tissue infused with aloe vera! But, as I say, we didn't always use it to clean our arses with but instead found it useful to write on. That also came with some challenges. The grease covering on the paper regularly clogged up the nib of the biro pen so you had to clean the nib by putting it in your mouth and licking the end of it, followed by some scribbling on a non-greasy page in your Bible which helped the ink to flow again.

The toilet paper had 'Property of HM Government' stamped on it at the end of each individual square. The mind boggles as to why some bureaucrat somewhere thought it important that toilet paper, of all things, should stipulate that ownership resided with HM Government. I remember being fascinated by the article on Cuba and the fact that it was on HM Government paper seemed to add to the thrill of it.

Ta was serving a relatively short prison sentence, and, with full remission was due for release within a matter of months. Remaining with us, on the protest, would have meant, however, regularly losing remission and he would have ended up serving several more years in prison. On account of that, he eventually left the protest. It was an unusual situation because when he left everyone was sad to see him go and wished him all the best. Due to his situation he wasn't regarded as 'squeaky-booting'.

I never saw Ta again. Tragically, he was shot dead on 20 January 1987, aged 33. The killing happened in the Rosnaree Hotel on the Dublin Road, outside Drogheda, County Louth. Another INLA member, John 'Jap' O'Reilly was also killed in the same incident and another member, Hugh Torney, injured. The three of them were there to help broker a truce with the IPLO (Irish People's Liberation Organisation), a splinter group which had split away from the INLA in 1986 resulting in a feud and a number of deaths. The IPLO were accused of the killings.

I also never again saw the prison guards from C wing – Mike Trainor or Jed McKnight. They remained on our wing for a short time following the commencement of the no-wash protest but thereafter disappeared. Throughout the no-wash protest, due to the harsher conditions, the guards who worked on the protesting Blocks had to volunteer to work there. It's possible the two of them decided against that. Those who *did* work in the protesting Blocks during the no-wash era got paid significant financial bonuses for doing so. Those who did the actual steam-hose cleaning of the cells got paid even more. It meant, of course, that the protesting Blocks often attracted the worst elements. Not only were the wages very lucrative but you got the chance to 'beat up Provies' with little or no scrutiny.

# 5
# Shit and Maggots

By early 1978, numbers on the blanket protest had increased to approximately 250. We were housed in H-Blocks 5 and 3. Despite the increase in numbers and the fact that the protest had already been ongoing for eighteen months, there was no sign that we were any nearer to having our demands met. Instead, the guards appeared to be intensifying harassment. Getting out to the toilet or to shower had become more difficult. More significantly, we became aware that newly-sentenced republicans were being more extremely brutalised upon arrival at the jail. It appeared that the prison authorities thought that once they, the new arrivals, were on our wings and on the protest there was little likelihood of them later leaving, therefore it was best to try and break them before they got onto the wings.

There wasn't a lot of discussion about how we could go forward. At the time, we thought that the issue was being highlighted, and would eventually be resolved, through the blanket protest itself, and by the supporting protests organised on the outside by the Relatives Action Committees. Beyond that, there didn't appear to be a lot that we could do to drive things forward. We would just sit and wait and hope, or believe, that things would somehow happen. However, as it turned out, some were thinking about how we could become more active. This was largely due to the arrival of Brendan ('The Dark') Hughes into the Blocks in January 1978. Brendan was transferred from the Cages of Long Kesh where he had been the OC. He, along with four others (Teddy Crane, Gerard Burns, and brothers, Terry and Séamus Clarke), had been charged with an incident in the Cages involving an alleged assault upon a prison guard. The case was taken to an outside court where they were sentenced to five years imprisonment. Given that the charge, and new sentence, was for an offence committed after 1 March 1976, their special category status was withdrawn and instead of being returned to the Cages after their court appearance they were brought to the Blocks. Some shock to the system. They left the Cages, with all its comforts, that morning and by evening they were naked in a cell in the H-Blocks.

The change in their conditions of imprisonment highlights in stark contrast the contradictions inherent in the criminalisation policy. On the morning of that particular day Brendan Hughes was the appointed representative of several hundred republican political prisoners. He was recognised as such by the prison authorities at the highest level and consulted with about issues that affected the prisoners. By the end of that same day he was deemed a 'common criminal', referred to by a number, not his name, and, officially, he represented no one.

However, it wasn't long before Brendan was again occupying a leadership position. Shortly after he arrived in the Blocks he assumed the position of Camp OC. Soon after, he 'sounded out' the proposal that we wear the prison uniform, enter the system, and attempt to undermine it from within. His proposal was met with a resounding 'no'. The idea of 'putting on the gear' (wearing the prison uniform) was anathema to us. Whether or not that was the right approach is neither here nor there. Hindsight is an exact science. Some could argue that, if we had gone into the system, over the years we may have been able to win some control over our lives. In later years, post the hunger strike, we did exactly that – went into the system – but in totally different circumstances, which therefore doesn't make for a fair comparison. We had six years of intense protest behind us by then. We had lived through two hunger strikes and witnessed ten comrades die. Through that struggle, our situation had been highlighted, not just in Ireland but around the world. In that sense, we were very clear about what we were about to do and how we would do it. We also had the discipline and the iron determination to achieve our goals. And we did. But back in March 1978, voluntarily going into the system just wasn't going to happen.

The OC of our Block, H5, was Seán McKenna. In 1970, when aged just 17, Seán was interned without trial for three years. His father, Seán Senior, was also interned and was one of the 14 men arrested at the very start of internment who later became known as the 'Hooded Men' due to the torture they received at the hands of the British Army.

The British government was later found guilty of 'inhumane and degrading treatment' (but not torture) by the European Court of Human Rights.[42] Seán Senior died aged 42, in June 1975, as a direct result of the injuries inflicted upon him during his interrogation. A year later, in 1976, Seán Junior was abducted by British Special Air Services (SAS) soldiers from his home in the south of Ireland and smuggled back across the border where he was charged with attempted murder and sentenced to 25 years in prison.

Following the rejection of Brendan Hughes's proposal, Seán contacted the wing OCs suggesting a discussion about what alternative options were open to us. Basically, those options were: to sit as we were, indefinitely, or to intensify our protest in some way to highlight our conditions with the aim of bringing about a resolution to the situation. There could only be one outcome to such a choice: we would take action. We had been sitting around long enough and once the choice was put to us as starkly as that, the consensus was to up the ante.

One Sunday, Séanna Walsh, then OC of C wing, returned from Mass and gave me a comm he had got from Seán. I held the position of Adjutant in the wing. It outlined how we would increasingly, over several weeks, withdraw co-operation from the regime by firstly refusing to brush out our cells, then refusing to wash in our cells, instead demanding access to proper washing facilities, and so on. I was excited by the prospect of us taking action. It was moving from a passive position to a proactive one. We were no longer going to be adrift at sea, hoping for some ship to rescue us. We were going to act. Make our own decisions. Those boring days of 1977 were beginning to recede.

I believe that excitement was felt by all when we did act on 10 March. It was a very minor action, nothing dramatic. We simply refused to brush out our cells but in that small act of defiance there was an air about the place. We were active and we had agency. We felt as though we were setting out on a course of action that would move us much more quickly towards our objectives.

---

[42] The case of the Hooded Men is still ongoing in 2020. In September 2019 the Court of Appeal in Belfast ruled that "Interrogation techniques used against the so-called Hooded Men during internment in Northern Ireland would be torture if deployed today." https://www.irishtimes.com/news/crime-and-law/hooded-men-court-rules-treatment-of-men-would-be-torture-if-deployed-today-1.4024773

I don't know if anyone ever seriously considered how the administration would respond to our intensification, but we didn't have to wait long to find out. The reaction was as swift as it was 'over the top'. Tom McFeeley and another prisoner, Seán Campbell, were put on the Boards and charged under an ancient prison rule about treason or sedition that would allow the administration to keep them in isolation for at least 40 days. Both of them went on hunger and thirst strike immediately. After several days without food, and more particularly water, their condition became grave and news of it hit the media outside – one of the first occasions that the media gave any attention to our protest, other than to churn out the NIO statistics about how many prisoners were conforming and how wonderful the prison regime in HMP Maze was. Tom and Seán were returned to the Blocks right away. We viewed this as a huge victory and, with it, we realised the importance of getting our message out to the media.

The evening they were brought back, an old English guard commented to me, "Everything should go back to normal now". How wrong he was. Things were never going back to where they once had been. There had been a shift and it was a shift that buoyed us – made us feel more alive, more active, more empowered.

On the following Monday, as planned, we went ahead with our next phase of action; we refused to wash ourselves in basins brought to our cells and demanded to be allowed out to wash in the sinks and showers. Again the response from the prison authorities was way out of proportion to our actions. We didn't get out to wash and nor did we get to slop out. Our pisspots soon filled up and overflowed. We tried initially to pour the urine out the window but the concrete bars prevented us from being able to position the pots at the opening of the window. We tried to create makeshift funnels, using pages from religious magazines to pour the urine through the gaps, but they soon became saturated and collapsed, leaving the urine running down the inside of the window, into our cells. We then began to pour the urine out under the doors and throw excrement out the windows. The guards' reaction was to pour very powerful undiluted disinfectant under the doors, making the occupants of the cells violently sick. Some had to smash the windows for ventilation. Soon the order came from the Block OC for all to smash their windows so that the few could not be victimised.

In the days that followed, the protest escalated rapidly. The cells began to stink and the prison authorities removed all the cell furniture. As the guards started the process of furniture removal, an order came from the OC to smash the furniture and throw it out the window before the guards could remove it.

We went to the task eagerly. It was like releasing the past years' pent-up frustration in a few short minutes. Junior and I smashed the chairs, the table, the small wall-shelf and threw them out the window. We dismantled the beds and the frames went out the window also. We were considering how we could squash the heavy metal locker to get it out between the bars of the window when the guards came into the wing in force and began opening the cells.

They were enraged at what we had done and responded with violence, inflicting many bad beatings. Kevin Campbell (Derry) and Drew Forbes (Strabane) in my wing got a particularly bad beating. When the guards first went into their cell one of them punched Drew in the face a few times. Kevin, knowing what was in store for him, attacked one of the other guards. More guards ran in and beat both Kevin and Drew. They then left but a larger group of them returned shortly afterwards and ordered Drew to leave the cell as he was being taken to the punishment block. As Drew walked out of his cell the guards again attacked him and severely beat him. I watched out the side of my door as Drew was dragged past my cell. He was barely conscious. Two guards held him by the ankles and dragged him along over the broken furniture and metal bed springs. Kevin was then taken out of his cell and severely beaten too, but he resisted being dragged by the ankles. They eventually grabbed him by the hair and arms and ran him up the wing until they reached the ablutions area at the top of the wing, where they stopped and beat him again. He was then taken to the Circle to join Drew and both were transported to the Boards. A doctor examined them there but refused to listen when they told him what had happened. That night Drew was removed to the prison hospital with a suspected broken jaw. Kevin had a black eye, swollen nose and was bruised all over.

Kevin and Drew were held on the Boards for the next 14 days on remand, charged with 'assaulting' the guards. Apparently the guards were 'off sick' as a result of the 'assault' and only when they returned to work did Drew and Kevin appear in front of the Governor to be sentenced for the assault. An alternative interpretation would be that the Governor was reluctant to have them appear before him when clearly displaying injuries from the assault they allegedly carried out.

The outcome of the disciplinary process was that Kevin and Drew were sentenced to three days solitary confinement, fourteen days loss of remission, and three days on the Number 1 diet[43]. The latter consisted of two rounds of dry bread (no margarine) for breakfast, a bowl of soup and four rounds of dry bread for dinner, and four rounds of dry bread and a cup of black tea for supper. In all, they spent 17 days on the Boards before being returned to the Block.

I had been on the Boards before being moved onto C wing so I knew what the experience was like, though I was held there for only three days. The Boards were freezing. The heating utility in the cells on the Boards was a metal contraption attached to the ceiling. It was a rectangular metal box about three foot square and about six inches deep. Anyone with a basic understanding of physics knows that heat rises so a metal box on the ceiling heats the ceiling, not the space below. To be there, practically naked, barefoot on the concrete floor without blankets (the mattress and blankets were removed from the cell during the day), made it all the colder. At least in the Blocks we had blankets to wrap ourselves in. The days spent on the Boards were very long and as soon as the bedding was returned in the evening I made my bed, and got into it immediately – as much to get warm as anything else. Sleep came quickly.

I ended up on the Boards again, a couple of years later, and whilst I was there a conforming prisoner was admitted. I don't know what he was charged with but he was denying it. I could hear a Governor arrive at his cell across from mine and speak to the prisoner. The Governor wanted him to admit to whatever it was he was being accused of. The prisoner refused. I then heard the Governor speak to the guards, "See if you can refresh his memory", and then he walked off. I next heard the sounds that became all too familiar in those years; the groans and gasps, the heavy-breathing and curses, as the guards beat the prisoner in his cell. A few moments later the Governor returned and asked, "Maybe your thoughts are clearer now?"

---

[43] In a legal case taken by Tom McFeeley and Kieran Nugent to the European Commission of Human Rights – *161 McFeeley v United Kingdom Application 8317/78 – the British Government stated that from October 1978 the No. 1 diet was no longer employed as a disciplinary award.

By that stage of the protest, I had already personally experienced many instances of brutality in the Blocks, inflicted by guards upon me or others. However, this incident on the Boards always stood out for me. Maybe it was because it was such a blatant display of how power really works; the bit we don't usually see. The command from the top for the underlings to abuse others. Usually those at the top of the hierarchy can remain invisible from the actual assault, a step removed from the consequence of their orders, but in this instance I witnessed it all. It was the might of the system bearing down on one individual. It was the abuse of power. It was physical coercion. It was assault upon the person. It was all the crimes you could be charged with in an outside court if you were to carry out the same acts on a member of the public. But this wasn't a member of the public. This was a prisoner. This was a person with no rights, a nobody. And no one other than me, another prisoner, was there to witness the brutality, and nothing was going to be done about it because the reality was that, in this context, in this place, this brutality was commonplace and acceptable. It would happen again tomorrow and next week and the following month, just as it had happened each day, week, month, and year up until then. This was 'the system' exposed in all its savagery. At least in the case of protesting republican prisoners the authorities could make some (granted, illegitimate) argument that they were forced to try and crush organised resistance to the 'good order and discipline of the prison', but not in this instance. This was a prisoner who believed he had done nothing wrong but was being told he had to admit he was guilty of some crime so the system could function 'properly'.

Back in the Blocks, guards in overalls now began to clean the yard outside our cells and with the windows smashed would throw excrement back into our cells. It was as a result of this that the order was given to smear our excrement on the walls of the cells. The idea of covering the cell walls in our own shit was not something we had envisaged when we stepped up the protest. It simply evolved – and rapidly, at that – over the course of the action and reaction by the prison authorities. Like the blanket protest itself, there was no clearly thought-out, long-term strategy. We were simply responding to the conditions and circumstances we found ourselves in. Ironically, in protesting to get better access to toilet and washing facilities, we ended up being totally denied the minimal access we originally had.

Smearing the walls of a small room (cell) you live in 24/7, with shite, must seem horrific to anyone who has never experienced it. And let's be honest, not many have. But in the context of this new phase of struggle, of becoming active as opposed to being passive, the act wasn't as offensive as you might expect. I recall only one prisoner voicing any reservations about doing it. At the time we probably thought it would be short-lived. We could never have imagined that the 'no-wash' protest, as it became known, would continue for the next three years.

While we referred to it as the 'no-wash' protest, the authorities labelled it the 'dirty protest'. Some could say that it is only a case of semantics but it is a deliberate manipulation of language to achieve a political purpose. A 'dirty protest' implies that we deliberately set out to smear our cells with excrement by way of waging a protest (which also suggests a certain mentality or moral depravity on our part) whereas our original (passive) protest – refusing to wash ourselves in basins in our cells – was an attempt to get better access to washing facilities. It shows the role that labelling and language plays – just as the policy of criminalisation brought with it a whole new vocabulary. It's interesting to see just how readily the label of 'dirty protest' is used by many commentators and/or academics who never question its origins. Unfortunately, some republicans, equally unaware of its origins, often refer to the 'dirty protest' rather than the 'no-wash' protest.

As the dirt from decaying food and excreta built up in our cells the prison authorities removed prisoners from one wing in H5 and H3 and started a new Block in H4. It now meant there was an empty wing in H5 and H3. The guards then cleaned the empty wings. They wore protective clothing and headgear and used high-powered steam hoses. Once a wing was cleaned, prisoners from another wing were moved into it and the wing they had vacated was then cleaned and another wing of prisoners moved into that. And so the cycle continued. In this way each wing was cleaned every 2-3 weeks. During wing shifts we walked across to the new wing wearing a small white towel. Mattresses and blankets were moved over later by the prison orderlies.

Wing shifts were feared. We were vulnerable to assault, especially during search procedures. Initially these consisted of a quick frisk but shortly afterwards the 'mirror search' was introduced. The mirror search was meant to discover anything hidden between our hips in the process of 'cheeking', which (up until then) was the securest

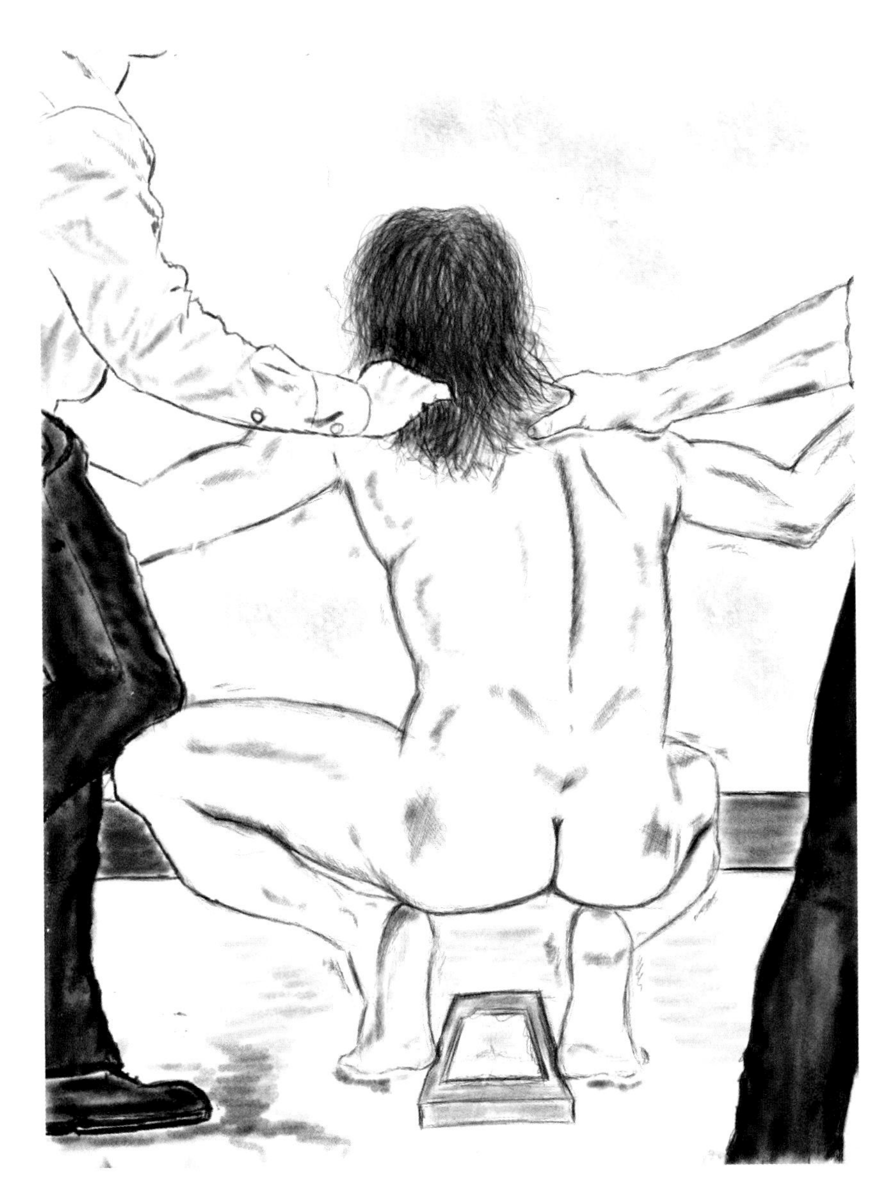

place for hiding contraband items. With the introduction of the mirror search, however, we were forced to hide such items inside our bodies. We wrapped them securely in cling film (smuggled in from outside) or sometimes plain paper if we didn't have cling film, and then put them up inside our anuses. The practice of hiding items in this manner became known as 'bangling'. The prison authorities became aware of this practice and, as such, became aware that the mirror search no longer served any practical purpose. It could only detect if you had something between your hips. It could not detect if you had something hidden in your anal cavity. Despite this, the prison authorities continued using mirror searches, revealing that their true purpose was to intimidate, degrade, and brutalise.

It was amazing how quickly you could get used to the practice of bangling and yet when I first heard of it I was shocked. John Thomas (JT), in one of the other wings, had been caught with a lighter bangled. It was one of the first wing shifts since the no-wash protest had begun and the guards used a metal detector on him. It registered that he was carrying something metal within his body. Thomas Loughlin, who was in the same wing as JT at the time, gives a very comical account of it in *Nor Meekly Serve My Time*:

> During the move they put the metal detector between JT's legs and the thing went berserk "He's got something up his rear end!", squealed the screws. At that he was taken into the MO's room. "Right, what is it?", the screws asked. "Fuck away off", said JT, "There's nothing up my arse". "Right, get him up to the prison hospital and we'll use the tongs to get it out". JT's heart nearly stopped. He shouted that he had a metal pin in his leg, there was nothing up his arse. But they took him up to the hospital where the good doctor asked him what he had hidden. JT kept saying "nothing" and that no one was sticking tongs up his arse. "OK," said the doctor, "in that case we'll have to take you to the outside hospital". Again JT nearly collapsed. "I'm not going to any hospital", he said. For a second there was a Mexican stand-off until JT said he had a lighter but it wouldn't come down. The doctor told him to sit on the table, pull his legs up to his chest, and don't worry. Within seconds the doctor had the lighter out. The next day he was up in front of the Governor who seemed slightly bemused by it all. Sitting on the desk was a wee plastic bag and in it was the lighter covered in shite. "Listen, Thomas," said the Governor, "Yesterday you were a nobody, today you are the talk of the camp and because of that I'm not going to sentence you. Now go on back to your cell". At that, the Governor burst out laughing.

When I heard about what had happened with JT I wondered how you could put something the size of a lighter up your anus. I thought it practically impossible. There was no moral objection to the act, it was just the anticipation of pain that I associated with it. And what happened to it once you inserted it into your anus? Where did it go to? And more importantly, how could you be sure you'd ever get it out again? The only way to get an answer to those questions was going to be through direct experience. We certainly weren't going to find any answers in the King James version of the Bible; not even in the Old Testament.

As time wore on, a lighter seemed such a small item to bangle in comparison to some of the other materials we hid. We also came to realise that there was really no need for a lighter. All we needed to get a spark (and flame) was a flint and something to strike it with; the wheel from an old lighter or a blade from a pencil sharpener – which some got smuggled in. I kept the wheel from my lighter and disposed of the rest of it. I put a flint into the end of a pen refill cut to about an inch in length. You had to apply pressure to get the flint into the end of the refill but it meant that it then held tight when you struck the wheel across the flint to get the spark. We didn't even need the cotton wool from a lighter as someone discovered that the small coarse cotton towels we now had for wing shifts (rather than the previous blue bath towels) were the perfect source for cotton. You just had to pull a short strand of the cotton out of the towel and then lightly pull it apart – 'fluff' it out – and it would work perfectly. During wing shifts over a three-year period I carried the wheel in my belly button and it was never found.

The summer months of 1978 were 'good' ones for us. The numbers on protest rose to around 300 and morale was sky high as reports reached us from outside that our protest was now receiving heightened coverage in the media. Commentators were referring to the need for some form of 'emergency (political) status' as fears were expressed about the dangers of all sorts of serious skin diseases breaking out, especially given the hot summer weather we were experiencing. The diseases never occurred, thankfully, and given that we had orders from the Camp OC not to request to see the doctor or dentist unless in extreme or emergency situations, it was just as well that there were no serious health issues. We discovered later, that apparently because we were not washing, our bodies' own natural oils gave us protection from the germs we lived with. In fact, we also began to notice that those who suffered from bad acne actually saw an improvement in their skin once they stopped washing.

Thanks to the radio Paul had smuggled in, we were able to get up-to-the-minute and accurate accounts of these debates. A further major boost to the media coverage occurred when Tomás Ó Fiaich, Catholic

Arch Bishop of Ireland (later, Cardinal), visited the prison on the 31 July. In a statement he made to the media immediately upon leaving the prison, he said;

> "Having spent the whole of Sunday in the prison, I was shocked at the inhuman conditions prevailing in H-Blocks 3, 4 and 5 where over 300 prisoners were incarcerated. One would hardly allow an animal to remain in such conditions, let alone a human being. The nearest approach to it that I have seen was the spectacle of hundreds of homeless people living in sewer pipes in the slums of Calcutta. The stench and filth in some cells, with the remains of rotten food and human excreta scattered around the walls, was almost unbelievable. In two of them I was unable to speak for the fear of vomiting. The prisoners' cells are without beds, chairs or tables. They sleep on mattresses on the floor, and in some cases I noticed they were quite wet. They have no covering except towel or blanket, no books, newspapers or reading material except the Bible (even religious magazines have been banned since my last visit), no pens or writing material, or TV, or radio, no hobbies or handcrafts, no exercise or recreation."

To have someone so prominent in the Catholic hierarchy speak out in such a colourful and emotive manner gave us the feeling that there would soon be movement on the issue.

Although the intensification of our protest (and the media attention it was now receiving) did not, ultimately, result in any concessions to our demands, it did have a huge impact. It pushed into the public gaze the issue of how those convicted of offences related to the conflict should be regarded (and subsequently treated) – either as political prisoners or criminals. It thus raised a whole debate about the conflict itself and its history up to that point – internment without trial, Bloody Sunday, the granting of special category status in 1972, and, in particular, the 'special' legal and judicial processes that led to our arrests, interrogations, and, finally, convictions in the one-judge, no-jury Diplock courts. Thus the public became more informed. Within the H-Blocks, we felt we had achieved a victory by creating a stir in the media. We also began to develop a growing awareness of the power of the media and the need to propagate our demands to a wider audience. By and large, however, we retained a belief that our refusal to conform to the prison regime would eventually move the government to concede to our demands.

Our daily routine of life had obviously changed significantly; no more 'slop outs', brushing cells, going for showers, or out to the toilet. We just went into the corner for the latter and then smeared it on the wall. It got rid of it, killed the smell fairly quickly as it dried out (or at least dried quicker than if it just lay in its natural state in the corner), and caused the guards some hassle in having to clean it off. In terms of the urine, we poured it out under the door. To get it out, and stop it coming back in again, we built a small 'dam'. To construct it we moulded slices of bread between the palms of our hands until it became like dough. Then we formed it into a thin line to lay across the doorway, about 3-4 inches back from the door itself. Depending on how generous you were with the bread the dam could be of a greater or lower height, but as long as it was higher than the bottom edge of the door you were then able to pour the urine into this dam and the only way out for it was under the door and into the wing corridor. I don't know who first thought of the idea of a dam and how to construct it but it was ingenious. At night, when the OC would give the order, we'd slop out under the doors. In the early days of the no-wash protest, some guards came around and tried to destroy the dams by pushing items such as metal coat hangers under the doors, but later they just accepted it. Their process each night entailed, firstly, pouring strong, undiluted disinfectant along the length of the corridor and then, using a very wide floor 'squeegee', pushing the urine to the bottom of the wing and out through a door to the yard on the outside. The procedure is very well shown in the film, *Hunger*.

Scraps of food that were thrown into the corner of the cell soon decayed and began to smell. Sometimes when we knew that officials were making a visit to the wing we'd disturb the pile of rotten food so as to intensify the smell. While it was indeed unpleasant for the officials to be greeted by such an aroma, it was arguably worse for us who had to live with it for the next few hours until it settled down again – long after they had left.

The decaying food soon produced maggots and when you disturbed the pile, the maggots would come crawling out. Some guys lifted them and pushed them out under the cell door to annoy the guards. Apparently some cellmates 'raced' maggots across their cell floor. When we had no glass in the windows others set the maggots between the concrete bars of the window to see if birds would pick them up.

Without beds or furniture of any sort, we now lay on mattresses on the floor. The mattresses consisted of a rectangular block of foam, about four inches deep, originally covered with a heavy cloth material, usually coloured red. As weeks passed, the covers were ripped off by the guards during cell searches, leaving the exposed foam. We used pieces of the foam mattress to smear our shite on the walls, so as a consequence, our beds became shorter and shorter. One piece of foam could suffice for quite a time but some guys felt the need to use a clean piece each time they went to decorate the wall. It made no sense and simply hastened the erosion of the mattress. This may have been OK for those who were not very tall but if you were, then your feet were soon resting on the bare concrete of the cell floor when you lay down. I remember once, the following year when I was in H6, I inherited Larry Marley's mattress following a wing shift. Larry was a lot shorter than me and he had totally cannibalised his mattress, both lengthwise and breadthwise. When I lay on it I was barely able to get both head and arse on it. The entire length of my legs were on the concrete floor.

Long Kesh was constructed on swampland – prone to flooding at times. As a consequence, the cell floors were always damp, especially in summer when the heating was switched off. When you woke in the morning and got out of bed, you'd discover that the underside of your mattress was soaking and you had to stand it up on its side, leaning it against the wall to dry out. Depending on the size of the food pile you had in the corner, you might also need to brush the maggots off the underside of your mattress. They seemed to be attracted to the body heat. Thankfully they confined themselves to the underside of the mattress, rather than climbing on top of it! I've often wondered if those years, sleeping on damp sponge mattresses, resulted in pains in limbs, especially legs and hips joints, in later life.

* * *

One result of covering the cell walls in excrement was that the cells became much darker; the white walls were no longer white. This inadvertently removed, what until then, had been a problem for several prisoners – the glare of the reflection of light off the walls which impacted their eyesight. Many had been experiencing headaches due to it. Given that we were contained 24/7 there was no escaping the glare. I had never had the headaches but what I had noticed in the early days of the protest was that when I got out of my cell, to slop out or shower, I momentarily had difficulty in focusing long-distance – to the top of the wing, for instance. Obviously that was due to regularly focusing on objects within the cell, all of which would be within a 4–6 foot radius. What I started to do, once I realised that, was to always take time throughout the day to regularly focus my gaze further away; out through the bars, to the fence and further afield. Maybe watch a bird in the air high up. And if there were no birds, then an imaginary one, or a cloud.

* * *

When the Governor came round to do his adjudications[44] everyone in the wing now made as much noise as possible by banging pisspots against the metal cell doors or the pipes or walls, or shouting out. Depending on what time the Governor did his rounds there could be either a muted response or a crescendo of noise. The Governor stood at the door in his suit and shirt and tie and we'd be standing naked but for a blanket, long hair unwashed, beards and banging our pisspots as hard as we could against the walls. The monkeys had taken over the zoo!

During the day, most of us paced up and down the cell to pass away the time though there were a few, the 'cabbages', who rarely got off their mattress and seldom appeared at their cell window. Some people folded one of their blankets length-wise and laid it on the floor to walk on. I never did that. It felt awkward, especially as the blanket did not stretch the full length of the cell so when you paced up and down you had to step on and off the blanket at each end of the cell. I'd walk for about ten hours a day; five paces forward, five paces back. They were small steps – it's a small cell, after all – but the blanket, which would be wrapped around your waist, came well down below your knees, thus restricting the length of your stride. If you think of a woman in a tight, ankle-length skirt, you'll get the picture.

Pacing up and down, my mind would be anywhere but in the H-Blocks. I could be back outside with friends and family, or off on some imaginary trip, or, more often than not, having imaginary conversations with people, often historical figures. It was pure escapism but it also fulfilled an important educational role as it allowed me to tease out my thoughts. In those imaginary

[44] From 19 October 1978 adjudications took place at 28-day intervals rather than 14-day and the punishments were extended to 28 days.

conversations others would be challenging my views and opinions and I'd have to argue my case, countering their challenge.

Following the intensification of the protest we looked afresh at our previous policy of refusing to take visits. The original decision had been made in accordance with our refusal to wear the prison uniform, a pre-requisite to being granted a visit. Now we were more concerned with getting our message out to the public about what was happening in the prison, and to do that we needed a communication system to the Republican Movement on the outside. The obvious communication channel was through visits, so we dropped the earlier policy and now encouraged men to take them. Besides facilitating communications, visits also relieved pressure on some prisoners whose families were concerned about not seeing them, particularly those who had children. The other important functional role of the visits, however, and the one which many regarded as the most important role, was the opportunity to obtain tobacco.

I recall preparing for my first visit which was in the middle of 1978. I was really looking forward to it and had sent out word to my family to smuggle me in an ounce of tobacco, tightly compressed and wrapped in cling film along with cigarette papers and the refill from a biro pen. I told them to bend the refill over in half so as to fit within the parcel of tobacco. This had to be passed across to me when the guard's attention was distracted and I'd then bangle it immediately. At that time the visiting rooms were in an old section of the prison, close to the Cages and the Boards. In fact they may have at one time been part of the visiting facilities for the Cages. They were prefab huts with individual visiting rooms leading off one side of a corridor.

I don't remember a lot about what was said on that first visit with my mother and brother, Eugene, but both were delighted to see me. I was anxious about getting the parcel and getting it bangled. This would be my first time bangling when not in my cell. I suppose you could call it bangling in public! At one point during the visit, when Eugene felt no guards were in sight, he passed the parcel over to me. I grabbed it quickly and as I did so I could feel that the refill stuck out from both ends of the parcel. What the fuck! There was also thread tied around the middle of the parcel, by way of holding it together better, even though the parcel was wrapped in cling film. There was nothing I could do about either the refill or thread; I was just going to have to be careful with where I aimed the pointed refill but speedily get the parcel bangled. To my deep satisfaction, I accomplished the mission quite easily. With my arse raised slightly above the chair, in one fluid movement of the wrist I soon had the parcel delivered to that place where the sun never shines.

However, there was one hiccup. Just as I was about to ease my arse onto the chair again I could feel a bit of thread that shouldn't be there. I tugged on it and could feel the parcel inside me move. There was no way I wanted to pull the parcel out again, even if that was possible, so I tried to snap the thread by chugging on it sharply. To no avail. I had visions of the mirror search upon my return to the Block and the guards spotting the thread dangling out of my arse. I was also aware that I didn't have a lot of time to play with as the visits only lasted for 30 minutes and we were already well into that time. Guards had begun to hang about the doorway of my visiting room. They were chatting with one another, not necessarily concerned with what I may or may not be doing, but still, they could at any time look in my direction.

The way I was sitting in the visiting box my right-hand side was towards the door. I had a cigarette in my right hand (we were allowed to smoke on the visits and occasionally some prisoners over-indulged, turning green with sickness because they had chain-smoked too many cigarettes) and I turned my body slightly to the left so that my left hand would be out of view of the guards. Then, using my right elbow on the top of the table to help me raise up from the chair a little, but not too far in case it would be noticeable, I used the thumb and first finger of my left hand to roll the thread up into a ball and then shove that up my arse too. That all sounds very simple and straightforward as I write it now, but if you take into account that I'm naturally right-handed this was not an easy operation to accomplish. However, I did get the business done and returned to the Block walking on air, supply of tobacco (and pen) safely secured.

In later months, visits became more arduous. A new visiting centre within the H-Blocks complex opened which contained small cubicles in a large room. The sides of the cubicles came up to a height of approximately four foot, which provided the guards with much more visibility of both prisoners and visitors. Stricter regulations were imposed and guards on patrol were more numerous and more vigilant. Nevertheless, we were able to keep supply lines of communication and contraband open, thanks to our visitors; family, friends, and even 'strangers' – those (women) who volunteered to regularly visit the prison specifically to keep the lines of communication open.

Throughout the protest, visits with family or friends were mostly uncomfortable, not in the sense that there were arguments – quite the opposite – but because it was difficult to know just what to say, especially with a guard present. There was never the opportunity to sit and talk freely. But even if there had been, would I have availed of it? What would I have said really? "I'm OK, food's not so bad and we're having good craic?" One look at me was enough to let visitors know we weren't getting it OK. Gaunt faces spoke volumes about the food and families had read and heard of the mirror searches and the beatings that regularly took place. Instead, I put across as good an impression as possible and demonstrated that I was in good form – which I was most of the time anyway regardless of the conditions.

* * *

Blanketmen often refer to 'the winter of '78'. It was the coldest winter we experienced on the protest. It was the winter when ice formed on the top of the water containers in our cells. We had no windows as we had broken the glass in them at the start of the no-wash protest and it was cold. Very cold. Extremely cold. Several former blanketmen mentioned 'the winter of '78' in their accounts for *Nor Meekly Serve My Time*[45] so before the book went to print, Mike Tomlinson (one of the publishers), out of curiosity or a concern for accuracy, contacted the Meteorological Office at Aldergrove. He inquired about the coldest winters on record in the north of Ireland in recent years and was told that 1978/79 was one of the coldest. When he asked what areas of the north were most affected, it turned out that the weather station at Down Royal Racecourse, next door to the prison site, recorded some of the lowest temperatures. *The Irish Times* also reported that, "Appreciable falls of snow between December 28 and 31, 1978, were followed by frosts of unusual severity".[46]

After we had smashed the glass in our windows shortly after the no-wash protest began, the authorities attempted to replace them. In one side of A wing in H5 they fitted a form of heavy Perspex to the windows

[45] The book we clandestinely compiled and edited within the prison many years later.

[46] https://www.irishtimes.com/news/ireland/irish-news/snowstorms-through-the-centuries-a-history-of-irish-cold-snaps-1.3406525

rather than glass. That night the lads set fire to the Perspex. Thick plumes of black smoke not only went up into the air but also into the cells, almost suffocating some of the occupants. The guards unrolled the heavy 'fire hose' in the yard and sprayed the cells with it, not only dousing the burning Perspex but totally soaking the occupants and their bedding. A later experiment to close off the windows consisted of a metal plate about a quarter inch thick with half-inch holes drilled throughout it to let in some light. This was placed across the bars of our windows but the holes didn't really let in light. The cells looked and felt like dungeons. It was some time before the authorities made another attempt to secure some covering for the windows and this one was more successful. Inside the cells they constructed a metal grille that covered the entire window then outside the cells they constructed boxes with clear flat Perspex at the top part of them and opaque corrugated Perspex at the bottom of them. The Perspex let light into the cell but also hindered us from shouting across the yard to the other wing and particularly shouting over to another Block. The metal grilles also stopped us from 'swinging' anything from cell to cell as we could no longer get our arms out between the bars. The upside to it all, however, was that the cells were about ten degrees warmer than they had been. The first time we had a wing-shift from a wing that had no windows into one that had windows was unbelievable. I think it was only then I realised how cold it had been.

Prior to the box-type windows being constructed some men would put a blanket up over the window at night to try and retain some of the heat in their cells. They held it in place by using the pisspot and water gallon to wedge either end of the blanket between the end concrete bars of the window. One problem with this was that often a guard patrolling in the yard during the night would pull the blanket down. However, the idea worked in that it conserved heat in the cells that would otherwise have disappeared out the window. The downside to it was that it meant having to sacrifice one blanket, leaving only two to wear or to wrap around you when sleeping. I recall telling my former wife, Mick, about this years later. She looked at me sort of puzzled and said, "If you had three blankets each, why not pull your mattresses together, and that way you'd have six blankets covering the both of you?" "Yes, dead on Mick!" While the logic of this suggestion cannot be disputed, it would have been unfathomable that two naked blanketmen would huddle together under shared blankets, even if it did mean being warmer. The irony was that we thought nothing of going into the corner of the cell, having a shite, then smearing it on the wall whilst simultaneously holding a conversation with our cellmate about some topic or other.

* * *

The Deputy-Governor of the prison at the time was Albert Miles. We'd see him occasionally come into the Block on his rounds. One day, in late 1978, as he walked out of our Block, some lads starting shouting abuse to him. He stopped, smiled, turned around and faced A wing, and with both arms reached high in the air he gave the 'fingers' to those in A wing. He then turned around and faced our wing, D wing, and repeated his actions. The two guards with him laughed and then all three of them walked out the front gate followed by shouts of abuse from all of us. It was the last time I saw Deputy-Governor Miles. A few weeks later, on 26 November, the IRA executed him. He was aged 50 and had been in the Prison Service for over twenty years.

* * *

At some time in late '78 I had a cell shift and was moved in with Adrian 'Foxy' Callan from Gobnascale, which is on the east side of the River Foyle in Derry City. It was the first time I shared a cell with anyone from Derry. Foxy was an SOSP (detained at the Secretary of State's Pleasure), which means he was serving a life sentence but as he was younger than 18 when the killing with which he was charged took place, he could not be given a life sentence and was given SOSP instead. I've always thought it a very peculiar term: at the Secretary of State's Pleasure. Did the Secretary of State really get a pleasure out of it? Does detaining someone for life give you a certain pleasure?

It was from Foxy that I first heard of Pink Floyd. He was a big fan of theirs and apparently his mother became one too (and now today his children Éimear and Odhrán also!). Foxy would pace up and down the cell and sing/hum 'Dark side of the moon' and 'Wish you were here'. Anyone who has ever heard those songs, or listened to any of Pink Floyd's music, will know that that was some achievement. To be honest, when I eventually did get to listen to an album of Pink Floyd's I was impressed with Foxy's renditions. And I became a fan too! My favourite track is *On the turning away*.

As with Junior, as with any other cellmate I had either before then or in the years to follow, Foxy and I got on well. In general, despite the horrible conditions we lived in 24/7, and all the pressures that continuous confinement created, the overwhelming majority of cellmates got on well with one another. That in itself was some achievement.

* * *

Besides adopting procedures to clean the cells on an ongoing basis the prison authorities also looked at measures to clean *us*. To this end, they involved medical staff within the prison and justified their actions by claiming they were for the health and medical benefit of the prisoners.[47] Before we could be charged with refusing to do prison work we first had to be pronounced fit for work. As such, prior to the Governor doing his adjudications, the prison doctor would do his rounds. In the early days of the protest the doctor actually came to our doors and asked if we had any illnesses. Later he merely walked down the wing and, without breaking his pace, took a glance into each cell as one guard rushed ahead of him opening the doors while another guard quickly closed them as the doctor passed on his way.

Around November, 1978, the doctor on his rounds ordered that certain men should be washed for 'health reasons'. This was not based on any close examination of the men. The result of his order, however, was that men were removed from the wing, taken to the Boards, and forcibly washed. I believe that the first ones in our Block were Joe Watson and Ned Flynn, though men were taken from other Blocks as well. As a policy, we would not resist an order to go to the Boards, which meant there was no brutality experienced in this instance. It was a new situation and those selected to be washed were told by our OC to show passive resistance to the wash on the Boards and not to wash themselves. My recollection is that the men taken to the Boards were washed but did not have their hair cut. This was a new development and we didn't know what it would lead to. Would they, for instance, make it the norm that every time someone was adjudicated that they would be washed? At the start, the selection of prisoners to be forcibly washed seemed to be random. Not everyone

[47] See photographs. See also, the *Report of the Independent Panel of Inquiry into the Circumstances of the H-Block and Armagh Prison Protests 1976-1981*, Coiste n nIarchimí, Belfast, 2020.

scheduled for adjudication was washed but if you were due for adjudication and you spotted the doctor arriving in the Block, you were filled with dread.

Looking back, it appears as if the prison authorities may have been doing a 'dry run' for what was soon to follow. Possibly they were testing our response to the forced washings; seeing what we would do before they would initiate a camp-wide programme of forced washing. That programme arrived on Monday morning, 4 December.

In H3, five men – Martin Hurson from Tyrone (later to die on hunger strike), Tomboy Loudon from Ardoyne, Joe McNulty from Tyrone, Tom 'Buck' Bradley from Ardoyne, and Jake Mc Manus from the Market, Belfast, were dragged from their cells. They were then beaten and kicked and dragged naked to the doctor's room in the Circle of the Block. There the doctor, Dr Emmerson, from a distance of around 15 feet, declared that the men had 'head lice'. They were then dragged to an empty wing and put into separate cells. Later, one by one, they were again dragged out, this time to the wing canteen, where they were held down on a chair while guards forcibly cut their hair and beards with scissors and shears. They were then dragged to the bath and forcibly washed with scrubbing brushes. Following the bath they were again placed on a chair in the ablutions area and had their heads and beards shaved. It was the most blatant, deliberate, organised and vicious assault that had yet been carried out on blanketmen.

That afternoon the Block PO, Paddy Joe Kerr, a Catholic from County Armagh, sent for the Block OC, Joe Barnes. Kerr told Joe that he had orders to wash everyone in the Block and that he would carry out those orders. He added that if prisoners offered only passive resistance the washes could be carried out with a minimum of trouble but that if anyone was so much as to breathe heavily on one of his officers then what had taken place that morning was an indication of what to expect.

Later that evening Martin Hurson was removed to the prison hospital where it was discovered that he had two fractured toes. Joe McNulty was taken to an outside hospital, the Royal Victoria, Belfast, where it was confirmed that he had a broken nose. Tomboy Loudon had a swollen nose and black eyes.

That night, men from H3 shouted over to us in H5 and told us what had happened to the five men and what was to take place in coming days. We were in A wing at the time and I relayed the message over to Jackie McMullan in D wing (across the front yard), who then shouted it across to C wing which was adjacent to them. Brendan Hughes, the OC, was in that wing. Sometime later that night Jackie shouted over the reply from Brendan that the men in H3 were to actively resist any attempt to forcibly wash them and that this should mean physically fighting with the guards. A silence went over the whole Block as Jackie shouted the message across the yard to me.

We tried for about an hour that night to forward the message to H3 without success. They kept replying, "*Abair sin arís*" (Say that again). This was eventually followed by, "Oíche mhaith" (Good night). We realised that they must in fact be receiving the message but didn't want to 'hear' it.

In H5 we spent the night discussing the implications of the OC's decision. It had come as a shock to us as our protest until then had been a passive one of non-cooperation. I recall wondering how I would feel if I was in H3 and felt almost sick with fear, followed by relief that I was in H5. The following year I learned from Willie 'Deek' Johnson about what exactly had happened that night. Willie had been in H3 and confirmed that they had received the message to actively resist, but were devastated by it. Morale was already low following the beatings that day and the brutal treatment they had been receiving for some time. The thought of actively fighting with the guards filled them with horror and dismay. There was a form of open rebellion. As the message was being repeatedly shouted over to them some men in the wing banged on the pipes to drown out the voices, so that the message could not be understood. But everyone had already heard it.

Joe Barnes, the Block OC, initially gave the order for the men to physically resist but early the following morning withdrew the order and told men to offer only passive resistance. In the days that followed, everyone in H3 was forcibly washed and had their hair and beards cut off.

The original order – to fight the guards during forced washes – still stood, however (regardless that it hadn't been carried out in H3), and we in H5 wondered if we would be next. They were anxious days, though after the initial dread I don't think the feeling was ever again so bad. As things developed, the random selection of men by the doctor ended and there was some comfort in the fact that if you were going to be forcibly washed then at least everyone else was going to endure the same; you weren't going to be on your own.

There was an interval of a few weeks between the completion of the forced washings in H3 and their commencement in H4. It's hard to say why this delay occurred. It may be that the policy was being evaluated at the highest level. It may just have been that other administrative duties took precedence for a time. Or it possibly could have been that the authorities waited to see our response or the effect the washings would have on our morale. Whatever the reasons, the washings eventually resumed. The men in H4 physically resisted the washes and were subsequently brutalised.[48]

I saw the results of the forced washings and shavings – from both H3 and H4 – when out on a visit. Tufts of roughly-shorn hair mingled with the scars from cuts. By then, the thought had started to formulate that if the administration could justify forced washings on the basis that men required them for health reasons, then they could repeat such washings on a regular basis. I suppose this had been the logic at the time the Camp OC had instructed men to physically resist. It wasn't going to be much of a no-wash protest if men were kept clean.

After weeks of fearing it, H5 never experienced forced washings. To this day I don't know why that was so. It may be that the adverse publicity the washings had received in the media was too much for the NIO to continue with the practice. Priests visiting the prison, especially H4, had been horrified at what they had witnessed and reported this to the outside, as did the families who visited and saw first-hand the results of the washings (and assaults) on their relatives. As for us in H5, we were not so much concerned why the forced washings did not continue; we were just relieved that we would not have to endure them. A few men had left the protest saying they could not carry out the order to resist the washings and tensions had been high for many weeks.

We wondered at the time if the Principal Officer of H5, Kevin Lappin, had anything to do with the forced washes not being

---

[48] For a detailed account of the forced washes in H3 and H4 see Brian Campbell, Laurence McKeown and Felim O'Hagan (eds.) (1994) *Nor Meekly Serve My Time: The H-Block Struggle 1976-1981*, Belfast: Beyond the Pale, pp. 58-66.

implemented there. Kevin, like Paddy Joe Kerr who was in charge of H3, was also a Catholic (a little ironic that the guards in charge of two out of the three protesting Blocks were Catholics), this time from Tyrone – but he was totally unlike Kerr. While he was in charge of the Block, and on duty, it was rare that any beatings ever took place. And all food that arrived in the Block was given out to the prisoners. They even got sugar and jam – unheard of in other Blocks. While writing this memoir I wondered if Kevin was still alive and made a quick inquiry from a former blanketman from Tyrone. Within minutes I had Kevin's phone number, supplied to me by another former republican prisoner (not a former blanketman) who had met Kevin once or twice. I contacted Kevin and he invited me to his home. I arrived there late one evening along with my youngest daughter, Órlaith. He met me at the foot of the steps to his house, took my hand in both of his in a very emotional gesture, and thanked me for coming to visit. We had a very broad-ranging conversation that evening and never really got down to the particular questions that I wanted to ask, though he *did* tell me that he was able to 'manage' the general situation in H5 at the time by having a secret communication channel with Brendan Hughes, our Camp OC, via an orderly, who, ironically was from my home town and known to me. Brendan would alert Kevin to various situations that had arisen, or about the behaviour of particular guards. Kevin and I planned to meet again for a more focused discussion and had arrangements made, but travel restrictions imposed by Covid-19 prevented that. A phone conversation did not seem sufficient, or appropriate, to cover the subject matter, so we never got around to delving further into our discussion.

Regardless of how they ended, the forced washings were introduced merely as a device by the prison authorities, cloaked in medical justification, to physically assault us on a sustained and mass scale; the purpose being to terrorise us into giving up the protest. There was no credible medical reason why we had to be washed and have our heads and beards shaved just a few months after we had stopped washing. If there had been, it would have been necessary to repeat the practice at regular intervals. That did not happen and we refused to wash for a further two and a half years, making it three years in total. During that entire period no one ever had head lice or any other illness directly attributable to us not washing.

Paddy Joe Kerr, the Principal Officer in charge of H3 and the prime instigator of the brutal attacks that took place there over a sustained period of time, continued in subsequent years to be to the fore in implementing any and all policies of the NIO and/or prison authorities. Even long after the protest and hunger strikes had ended, he still attempted to enforce coercive policies upon us – especially following the mass-escape of 38 IRA prisoners from H-Block 7 in September 1983.

One day, in early 1985, I was standing at the top of our wing with a senior member of the IRA camp staff when Paddy Joe arrived into our wing on one of his regular trips around the Blocks. He liked to make an appearance from time to time and would stride down the wings in a very authoritarian manner accompanied by two or three other guards. He was a tall man; at least 6 feet 2 inches, but could have been even taller. And he was well-built; resembling a rugby player.[49] The guards loved him. He was their hero.

He walked to the bottom of our wing that day and as he returned and was about to leave, the person standing next to me said to him, "Paddy Joe, this can't go on. There's only one way it's going to end". Paddy Joe looked at him and smiled. He recognised the thinly-veiled threat. He patted the left side of his chest with his right hand and said, "If anyone comes looking for me they'd better come prepared. I pack a .45 Magnum." He smiled again, the other guards with him laughed, and then they all walked out of the wing.

I don't know if Paddy Joe ever carried a .45 Magnum but if he did, he never got to use it. On 17 February, 1985 (his 37th birthday), as he left Mass in St Patrick's in Armagh city, two IRA volunteers walked up to him and executed him on the steps of the Cathedral.

---

[49] The character, 'Macken', in the feature film I co-wrote with Brian Campbell, *H3*, is based on Paddy Joe Kerr.

# 6
# Eleven Cornflakes

In early January 1979, 32 of us from H-Blocks 3, 4, and 5 were moved to H-Block 6. This included some of the camp leadership at the time, namely Brendan Hughes, the camp OC, and Bobby Sands, the camp PRO (Public Relations Officer). The rest of us were a mixed bag. Some had been in positions of command at a wing or Block level but others had not occupied leadership positions. And there were loads of others who could have been identified as leadership but who were not moved to H6, so the logic behind the move was lost on us. Myself and Séanna (Walsh) were moved from our wing.

It was all very sudden and unexpected. The guards just came and told me I was moving and I was taken immediately. It wasn't as if I had a lot of things to pack; maybe a couple of letters that I'd held onto. Nothing else. Didn't even really get time to say a proper goodbye to Foxy.

When I arrived in H6 I didn't know what lay in store for us. Davy Long was the Principal Officer in charge of the Block, the same Davy Long I first encountered back in 1977 when I was in the H-Blocks awaiting trial. The Davy Long who had stood in my doorway and barked, "Key in the door, feet on the floor". He had a reputation for brutality but had only been involved with the protest in its early days back in 1976 when he had been the PO in H-Block 1.

We were put into various cells upon our arrival. There was no overt brutality that I can recall. However, later that evening they decided, for some reason, to rearrange us. It was then we discovered what type of regime they wished to impose. In the other Blocks, when we left our cells for a wing shift, cell search, or to go to the big cell to put on the prison uniform in preparation for visits, we wore the short white towels we had in our cells. That first evening in H6 we were told we were not allowed to wear the towels outside our cells and must go naked. Blanketmen had a policy of not going anywhere naked so when told to move to another cell, and to do so naked, we refused. The guards then dragged men out by either the feet or arms and dumped them into the new cell. That's how I first met Gerry McDonald.[50] My cell door opened and this naked man was thrown into it. He gathered himself up and, whilst still bollock naked, stretched out his hand to me, smiled and said, "*Is mise* (I'm) Blute. Gerry McDonald".

Later that evening, as John ('Greener') Chillingworth was pacing up and down his cell, a much more favourable event occurred; a package was thrown through his window. It was dark at the time and John didn't see who threw it in. The package was wrapped in cling film and John discovered that it contained tobacco, cigarette papers, chewing gum, and some sweets. It turned out that a civilian prisoner from West Belfast, Emmanuel ('Mano') O'Hagan, who had been on remand with us in the Crumlin Road Prison, was actually Davy Long's personal orderly. Mano had the run of the place so had been able to access the back yard of the Block that evening with the parcel of goodies and he promised more was to come. Suddenly H6 didn't seem such a bad place to be in.

Being dragged, naked, from cell to cell is one thing. It's a matter of a few feet or yards in distance, but being dragged from your cell, down the wing and out to the Circle, is something else. In H6, Davy Long initiated a regime whereby, for the Governor's adjudication, we were dragged out to the Governor's office rather than the Governor coming around the wings, as was normal practice.

H6 had not previously held blanketmen. The floors were highly polished, just as they had once been in H3, 4, and 5 before we started pouring urine out the doors every night, which lifted the paint from the concrete. In H6, with the highly-polished floors, a body being dragged along it made a squeaky sound; not quite the same as the 'squeaky boot' sound but fairly similar. Naked flesh being dragged across a polished surface. The sound of naked flesh being brutalised.

During this time, the guards discovered that the easiest way for them to drag a prisoner was by the feet rather than by the arms. Those being

---

[50] Escaped in 1983 mass escape.

dragged out to the Governor in this fashion would try to put their hands under their hips or sometimes put their hands out on either side and press down on the floor so as to raise their body, if even for a second, just to ease the burning sensation on their bums or back. But that only eased the burn slightly. They were still left with abrasions on their backs and hips where flesh met polished concrete – with no lubrication between them.

Blute was dragged out in such a fashion to the Circle for adjudication. Knowing Blute, he probably relished it! Another opportunity to display non-conformity. From memory, there were four guards who came to our cell to take him. Blute sat down on the floor as they opened the door and their biggest difficulty was getting him out of the cell. We had been instructed by Bobby Sands (now the OC of the wing) to show only passive resistance. Thankfully! But the doorways were narrow and four men trying to pull a fairly large man out through the door, when he isn't assisting in any way, can be awkward. As well as trying to pull Blute out the door they had to, at the same time, take the blanket off him before he left the cell. This was very difficult given that Blute was sitting on the floor with the blanket wrapped tightly around his waist. However, the guards eventually got him out of the cell, one way or the other, and away he squeaked to the Circle. I could chart his journey by the variation of the sounds of the squeaks and the opening and closing of grilles. Bobby (Sands) had instructed us that, whilst we would refuse to walk out to the Circle, that we should walk back. Blute arrived back in my cell shortly afterwards and I could see the red marks and abrasions on his back and hips but before he even had his blanket back on he looked at me and laughed. That was Blute.

Over the following days, several others were dragged out to the Circle for adjudication. I was due to experience this naked 'floor skiing' later that week – but thankfully it never came. Davy Long was transferred from the Block, a new PO took over, and the Governor came down the wing again to do his adjudications. This revealed that it had been the personal policy of Davy Long, who had implemented the same regime back in H1 and had been intent on continuing that practice in H6, even for the few days he was to remain in charge of the Block. It goes to show the discretion a Block PO had to implement his own regime, even if it contradicted the usual practice of Governors.

With Davy Long gone from H6 we were once again able to wear a towel whenever we had to leave our cells. We all breathed a sigh of relief. The downside to it was that Mano no longer had the ease of access around the Block that he had when Long was in charge and so that source of tobacco vanished.

We had thought that the new policy of refusing to allow us to wear a towel outside the cell was just the start of a much more intensive and brutal policy to follow; a policy to attempt to break us in H6. We thought that our wing would be made an example of and that if the prison authorities were successful in breaking us then they would extend their campaign throughout the other Blocks. In fact, it happened in reverse, some months later. In H4, for a brutal period of two weeks, the guards there introduced the policy prohibiting the wearing of towels outside of cells. Maybe they had heard from the guards in H6 about what had taken place with us and thought it a good idea to adopt it in H4. Maybe they even heard it from Davy Long himself who possibly boasted about what he had done. Either way, they started conducting cell searches as an excuse to implement their new policy. As a cell was being searched, one of its occupants (there were usually two people to a cell by that time) would be told to stand outside. When he attempted to walk out with the towel on, the guards would pull it off him whereupon he'd sit down on the floor of his cell and refuse to walk out naked. This provided them with the opportunity to then beat and drag him out of the cell, take him to Cell 26 and force him over the mirror. They would then do similar to his cellmate. The search had no rationale to it at all. It merely provided an opportunity to inflict brutality.

Likewise, the policy they introduced in forcing men to face the wall during wing shifts. During the shift you'd walk to the top of the wing and then have to wait in line as others ahead of you were forcibly searched by four or five guards over a mirror set on the floor. The guards now demanded that men face the wall when standing waiting. When prisoners refused to comply, the guards grabbed them by the hair and arms and shoved their faces against the wall, often with some force.

As 1979 progressed, brutality in H3 and H4 intensified. Leo Green (who was later on the 1980 hunger strike) was OC of H4 at the time and he vividly captures the horror of that experience in *Nor Meekly Serve My Time*.[51]

> "My own experience of brutality at its most intense occurred in the last two weeks of April 1979, one of which is indelibly etched in the minds of POWs who were in H4 at the time as the '*Seachtain dona*'(bad week). By then, incidents of ill-treatment and attacks on prisoners in H4 were almost a daily occurrence. During these particular weeks the situation boiled over and seemed for a few days to have gone irretrievably out of control, and likely to result in the serious injury of many prisoners."

Leo wrote those words many years later when we were compiling the book but at the time, when it was happening, he didn't know how long it would last for, or how much worse it would get. As I said in the Preface, that lack of knowledge, that uncertainty, intensifies the impact of the change to what has previously been the norm – even if that norm had been one of brutality. The other factor, besides not knowing how long it may last for or what might follow, is the fear of how bad it might become. Was the last beating during the cell search the worst I'll get? Or is that just the start of it? The uncertainty on all those levels vastly intensifies the impact of any such new development, and the fear that it generates. Believing that it must be happening with official sanction at the highest level, adds to a sense that it is inescapable.

And as for the guards, once they'd taken part in, or closely observed at first-hand, such brutality, then it became easier to engage in an even more extreme level of brutality. Any psychological barriers to inflicting brutality upon others that may have been in place before then were eroded. A new 'norm' was created – and repeatedly recreated.

I can vividly recall, for instance, returning from a visit one day. It was the mid-day lock-up, the dinner had already been served and empty dishes collected. The guard with me punched me several times from behind – fairly hard punches – to get me bent over the mirror in Cell 26. When the search was complete and I had stood up straight again, he turned to me and in a fairly civil voice inquired, "Did you get your dinner yet?" The two sat side by side; the brutal attack and the conversational tone. It was the 'norm'.

---

[51] Brian Campbell, Laurence McKeown, and Felim O'Hagan (eds.) (1994), *Nor Meekly Serve My Time: The H-Block Struggle 1976-1981*, Belfast: Beyond the Pale, pp. 88-90.

* * *

The guards who worked in the protesting Blocks could be roughly divided into three broad categories. There were those who were physically brutal (some, I believe, could be categorised as sadists); those who were extremely petty but not necessarily brutal; and those who were just there for the high wages and didn't really care much one way or the other about what happened. And then there was the occasional individual who demonstrated random acts of kindness, or, the likes of Kevin Lappin, PO of H5, who clearly abhorred what was happening and tried to avoid, as best he could, situations that would lead to assaults. It's easy to 'run with the pack'; it takes much more courage, moral fibre, and fortitude, to resist that, and to walk your own path.

The brutal ones could be sub-divided further into those who were naturally brutal people, or who appeared to carry anger issues, and those for whom the protest provided an opportunity to become brutal – the opportunity to become hard men or 'alpha-males' – which they weren't in their real lives in the outside world. In the protesting Blocks, with their uniforms, boots and batons, and with the overt or covert 'nod of the head' from their superiors, they had the opportunity to become the type of men they had only ever dreamed of before then. They could walk into a cell and slap someone around, punch them, kick them, and no one was going to say a word.

I recall observing some new guards who came onto our wings at various stages of the protest. They were instantly recognisable. They appeared fearful as they went around the wing with more experienced guards who were acclimatised to the conditions and practices. As the cell doors opened and slammed closed I could catch sight of them, their eyes wide open as they stared at the scene that greeted them from behind those locked doors. Prisoners wrapped in a blanket, hair down past their shoulders, beards, ribs showing clearly on their chests. The expression on the faces of the new guards was a mixture of horror, fear, surprise, and, even in some instances, pity.

It was interesting to then observe them over subsequent weeks and to watch how their demeanour changed, often significantly. Firstly, the horror, fear, surprise (and especially, the pity) disappeared. It was replaced with variations of contempt, disgust, hatred – or all three.

Attire also changed, as did the manner in which they 'carried themselves'. The peaks of their caps would often become slashed so that the tip of it, rather than jutting outwards, dropped and almost rested on their noses. This pushed their heads back in order for them to be able to see out from under the peak and thus gave a sort of militaristic impression – akin to the American marines in dress costume. Their shirt sleeves would then be rolled up to the elbow and metal studs fitted to the heels of their shoes to give that clicking sound as they walked. In just a matter of weeks they were transformed from the 'ordinary Joe-soap' to the Incredible Hulk. It was bizarre to observe the transformation. In the outside world they remained people who would jump out of their skins if you looked crossly at them. Even in other Blocks in the jail, with those not on protest, they would be less confident in their dealings with prisoners. But there, in the confines of the protesting Blocks, with naked, malnourished prisoners, they had the chance to live out their fantasies as hard men. And that's exactly what they did.

Then there was the other category; those who could claim, quite honestly, that they never assaulted a prisoner and only used the minimum of force required when, for example, we refused to squat for the mirror search. But for some of those, they had other means by which to inflict their sadistic inclinations. For instance, the Class Officer in our wing in H6 was a man called Al Parkinson, an Australian, though I don't imagine his ancestors arrived there from Ireland as he displayed no empathy towards us or our situation: quite the opposite. Or maybe he did have Irish roots and deeply resented that, as is the case of many who internalise the coloniser and go 'ag sodar i ndiaidh na n-uaisle' (aping the foreigner) and despise anything associated with their own culture, history, and heritage. He had a brother who was a Senior Officer (SO) and who was equally obnoxious.

Al Parkinson was not physically brutal but he had other ways to display his antagonism towards us; often much more insidious. Food was the primary means by which he did it. I had never seen before, and never saw afterwards, bowls that were as small as those in H6. Given that all prison items are standard-issue, I actually wondered if he had personally bought the bowls himself. They were not even really bowls. They were saucers. And small saucers at that.

One morning as we received breakfast, Sean Coleman, who was in a cell across from me, shouted next door to Bobby Sands: "Bobby, I just counted the number of cornflakes I got. Guess how many. Eleven!" Seán's experience wasn't much different from the rest of us. Although food wasn't great in most of the Blocks, with the exception of H5, we all visibly lost weight over the period of nine months that we spent in H6.

I'm not sure if it was Parkinson's idea or not, but one day the guards made an attempt to remove a ring from either Brendan Hughes or Bobby Sands. It may have been a wedding ring – which prisoners were allowed to retain. I think the guards tried the same with someone else in the wing. Bobby sent for Father Toner, the prison chaplain, and the issue was resolved but it highlighted just how petty and vindictive the regime could be. It reminded me of a quote from black American activist, George Jackson. Speaking about being imprisoned he says that everything can be taken from you and that you must be prepared to give up all possessions. "Even your hair is not your own." The blanketmen of H3 and H4 certainly experienced that with the forced washes and shavings.

* * *

In all the Blocks we were able to pass comms and tobacco around the wing by 'shooting a line' across the wing, or by passing them from one cell to another through the narrow space between the metal sleeve that encased the heating pipes that ran through the cells. The metal sleeve was there to allow for expansion of the pipes and, apart from only a few particular cells in all the wings I was ever in, it was possible to pass small items through the narrow space. Shooting a line entailed attaching a thread from the hem of a blanket to an object, and then 'shooting' the object under your cell door across the wing to a cell on the other side of the corridor. If it didn't make it cleanly into the opposite cell, it would hopefully get close enough to allow the occupants of the other cell to 'fish' it in using prayer leaflets acquired at Mass on a Sunday. The prayer leaflets came in handy for a number of purposes, especially around communication from cell to cell, and we were permitted to have them as they were of a 'religious' nature and therefore would have raised issues with the prison chaplain if we had not been permitted to take them back to our cells after attending

Mass. The religious magazines, had, however been stopped once we started the no-wash protest.

There were always cells that facilitated the process of shooting a line better than others; the space between the bottom of the door and the floor could be greater than other cells, or the floor from cell to corridor might be particularly flat. A lot also depended on what object was being used to 'shoot'. Generally, it was a religious medal as,

again, we were permitted to have them. We were also permitted to have rosary beads. Most medals were, however, very light and didn't shoot out a great distance whenever the 'sender' flicked it with his finger. A heavier weight was much better.

In H6, Jackie McMullan and I had ideal conditions for shooting a line, though only from Jackie to me and not the other way round. Of course, this had nothing at all to do with Jackie's expertise in shooting a line compared with my ability! Jackie's cell was directly across from mine and there was a large space at the bottom of Jackie's door. The floor from his cell to the corridor was smooth whereas that wasn't the case with my cell, and he had discovered a heavy washer in the canteen when attending mass. It wasn't the usual round metal washer with a hole in the middle of it but more a rectangular shape with protruding sections at the corners, not unlike the letter 'H'. I think it may have come off a radiator. It was weighty and Jackie could, on most occasions, get the line across to me on the first go. There were many instances where other people could take anything up to an hour to shoot a line across, with multiple attempts being made before one was successful. Usually the practical factors were the reason for that but in some instances it was probably that the person trying to shoot the line wasn't the most adept at it. However, Jackie could get it to me easily and often the washer would come straight under my door and several feet into my cell. Before shooting the line, Jackie would often shout, "Watch your eye, Laurny. This is coming to you now." He'd say this as often those receiving the line would have their head down on the floor trying to look under their door to see if the line was close enough to 'fish' in. From memory, the maximum number of attempts it ever took Jackie to get the line successfully across to me was three.

I would then pull the line towards me and take off it whatever Jackie was sending over – cigarettes or comms, usually. These would be held in an envelope tied to the line. Or, he would send over an empty envelope for me to put items into, which he would then pull back. Jackie kept the washer in his cell and it was only in that particular wing, C wing, that it worked, so when we were moved across to D wing for C wing to be steam-hosed, Jackie would hide the washer in his cell in C wing. Moving it across to the other wing would have risked having it detected by a metal detector.

Occasionally a guard would disrupt our procedure of shooting lines by pouring disinfectant along the corridor early on in the evening. The wet floor would stop the line sliding across to the other side. I don't know if the disinfectant was poured to deliberately prevent us shooting the line, or if it was done to pre-emptively improve the smell in the wing before we poured the urine out onto it. Either way, we always tried to get the lines across as early and as quickly as possible once the guards left the wings at 8.30 p.m.

Apart from the initial disruption in H6 when the guards changed who was in what cells and with whom, things pretty much settled down until our wing was eventually broken up in September of that year and all of us scattered back into the other three Blocks. Although I had initially been sharing a cell with Blute, I eventually ended up in a cell on my own. Jackie was across from me and, moving towards the top of the wing, Seán Coleman was next door to Jackie and next to Seán was Bobby Sands. Blute was on the other side of Bobby and Ian Milne from South Derry was in cell 25, next to the 'big cell'. On one side of me, moving towards the top of the wing, was Rab McCallum, from Ardoyne, and on the other side of Rab was Brendan Hughes. Willie 'Deek' Johnston was in the cell to the other side of me.

As there was a blockage at the pipes between my cell and Rab's, Bobby would shoot a line over to Rab, or vice-versa, to pass the cigarettes or comms. One night Rab had shot a line across to Bobby but as Bobby pulled it in, the line snapped on the bottom of his door. The worst thing was that the line had already left Rab's cell so Rab couldn't pull it back in. He had been sending cigarettes across to Bobby and now they lay in the middle of the wing. Both Rab and Bobby were working to see if either one could retrieve the ends of the line to pull it into one of their cells but they knew that the 'night guard' would soon be doing his rounds. The night guard would walk down each wing every hour to push an alarm at the end of the wing and thus confirm that the wing was being regularly checked. I could see out the side of my door fairly well so Bobby shouted over to me to keep watch for the night guard and if I recognised him, to let Bobby know. Shortly afterwards the guard arrived and it was 'Hack' Ramsay, a guard who was familiar to us but who never seemed to be posted to any particular Block. I think he was from South Derry. He was a bit of a raker/comedian. I shouted over to Bobby and as Hack passed Bobby's cell, Bobby called out his name. Hack stopped walking and looked around him, baffled that someone was calling his name. Bobby shouted out to him again and this time Hack identified where the call was coming from. He walked over to Bobby's cell, looked at the card outside the cell which recorded the name of the prisoner inside, then spoke in the side of the door to Bobby. I could see that he wobbled a bit on his feet; probably a bit drunk. Often the night guard arrived on duty straight from the guards' clubhouse. Bobby was familiar to Hack from regularly being out on 'appeal visits' – fifteen minute visits you could have every day if you had an appeal of your sentence lodged.[52]

"What's up Sands?' Hack asked. "Will you pass those cigarettes into me?", Bobby asked. "What?" Hack asked. "Those cigarettes on the ground," Bobby said. Hack looked at the ground and it took him a moment to see what Bobby was referring to. At night the wing corridor was only dimly lit. He then bent down, picked up the thread with the cigarettes attached, looked at them a moment, then pushed them in the side of the door to Bobby. He had difficulty doing it at one stage, either due to the drink or the narrowness of the door, and he called out to Bobby, "For fuck's sake, Sands, grab hold of that." Eventually Bobby got all the cigarettes in and Hack went on his way. A small moment of humanity.

'*Bia beatha*' (the food of life) – *tobac* (tobacco), *toitíní* (cigarettes). Morale in the wing soared or dipped, depending on whether or not there was bia beatha available. After we lost Mano's supply we had to rely on our visits, or maybe a priest at mass, or the Chaplain, Fr Toner, who occasionally brought us packages of tobacco that were given to him by our comrades in the Cages. I've often thought that Fr Toner was, to some extent, harshly and unfairly treated in historical accounts. When he is mentioned in Bobby's writings it's usually in a critical or disparaging manner and yet I think the moments Bobby describes were just that; moments in a period of five years during which Toner was daily in the Blocks carrying out a range of duties. I think we wanted him to be a republican and he clearly wasn't, and was never going to be. At the same time this didn't stop him from assisting prisoners on welfare/family matters. And I know he was truly devastated when Bobby died.

We shared whatever *bia beatha* we got. Often it meant that the cigarettes were very thin. Tom McElwee boasted one night that he had been able to make 45 cigarettes from one half ounce of tobacco! 'Very thin' was an understatement on that occasion!

---

[52] Some prisoners would lodge an appeal just to access the visits and then drop the appeal once it was due to go to trial. On such visits you were supposed to speak only about your appeal and if the guards overheard you mention any other topic they immediately stopped the visit. Such visits were good for communications, however, even if the conversation during them was totally contrived.

When there was little tobacco it was better to have the cigarettes made with something other than cigarette papers as the papers were very flimsy and burned too quickly. The Bible came in handy in that regard. The pages of it were thin, but not as thin as cigarette papers. They gave a bit of bulk to the smoke. They also gave an edge to it when you inhaled. One Sunday morning, as we left mass, an SO, who previously knew Larry Marley from the time he was in the Cages, said to Larry, jokingly, "Marley, we're told to read the Bible and digest its contents but you decided to smoke it." Most of us did at one time or another.

Larry was nicknamed, '*An Diabhal*' ('The Devil') – based on his sense of devilment. And he 'caught' me brilliantly with one of his pranks. We were at Mass one Sunday and we were expecting a wing-shift to occur at any time. I was talking to Jackie McMullan and a few others when Larry came over to us and said he had too much to bangle and could I take a *beart* (Irish for parcel/package) of tobacco. He took this *beart* out of his pocket and showed it to us. It was fairly big. Larry could put on the 'hush-puppy' eyes and he virtually pleaded with me to take it. I agreed in the end, even though I had a few things to bangle myself. That night Larry shouted up to me to make the cigarettes for our side of the wing. I took the *beart* out and opened it. And opened it. And opened it. There was layer after layer of toilet paper on it. When I got to the tobacco there was only a small amount of it and it was totally dried up. I had been caught! I shouted up to him out the window, "Nice one, Larry". He replied, "What's that, Laurny?" I said, "Thanks for the bit of dust. There's about enough tobacco here for ten cigarettes." At that, Larry raced to his door and called for Jackie and when Jackie got up to his door Larry said, "Jackie, you seen the size of the beart I gave to Laurny this morning? There was well over an ounce of tobacco in it and now Laurny says there's only enough for ten cigarettes. What do you reckon? Fly man, Laurny!" And then he laughed that famous impish laugh of his.

Jackie returned one day from a visit. There was no tobacco in the wing at the time and as Jackie came back onto the wing, he conveyed to us in Irish that he had secured some. I was delighted to hear it. I'd be smoking that night. Jackie was taken into Cell 26 to remove the prison uniform and return to his cell but the guards ran the metal detector over him and it started to 'beep'. Some Blocks used a metal detector and others didn't. It seemed to be left to the discretion of the individual guard. Jackie was then told he was being taken to the Boards where an internal examination would be carried out on him. Again, he shouted this to us before he was removed from the wing. When he arrived at the Boards he was told to voluntarily remove whatever it was that he had up his backside. Jackie told them he had nothing and said the detector was faulty as it had 'gone off' when someone else had been screened earlier in the week. The guard at the Boards then requested a metal detector from another Block to be sent to him and then he left Jackie in a cell. As soon as the guard had gone Jackie took the beart out of his body, unwrapped the cling film and began to search frantically for whatever was in it that set off the detector. All the time he could hear the guards pacing around not far from his cell. He could see nothing. He searched again and again. Eventually he discovered a small metal wheel from a petrol lighter inside the tobacco. He took it out, rewrapped the tobacco, and bangled it just moments before the guards returned to his cell with the new detector. They scanned Jackie's body with it and nothing; not a sound from it. The guard shook his head in disgust and said, "Take him back to his Block". Jackie arrived back in our Block with his tobacco – and he might have even still had the offending metal wheel hidden in his mouth. It was a wonderful day. We got a smoke, and Jackie had got one over on the guards. Sometimes there were days like that; good days that left you with a smile on your face even if you were going to bed on a piece of filthy sponge, cell walls covered in shit, and wind blowing through the bars of the concrete, glass-less windows.

In A wing of H6, a group of loyalists were on a blanket protest but not a no-wash protest. There was up to a dozen of them, belonging to both the UDA and UVF.[53] They had been on protest for several months before we arrived and in total, I think they remained on the protest for about 18 months. Following the introduction of criminalisation, some UVF prisoners, especially the younger ones, had gone on the blanket protest but were later ordered off by their OC, Lenny Murphy. From that time on, loyalists had not taken part in any protests, being instructed by their organisations on the outside that to do so would be to 'assist republicans'. The irony, as always, was that any concessions we would win would also apply to loyalist prisoners – which is exactly

[53] Ulster Defence Association and Ulster Volunteer Force.

what happened at the end of the hunger strike.[54] Not only did loyalists refuse to engage in the prison protest but on the outside they carried out a concerted assassination campaign against leading members of the National Anti-H-Block/Armagh Committee. In 1980 they killed four of them. The first to be killed was John Turnley, a Protestant and former member of the British Army. He was gunned down in Carnlough, County Antrim. One of those later convicted for his killing (in 1982), claimed during his trial that he had been working for the SAS and that they had supplied him with weapons, uniforms, and listening devices.[55] Miriam Daly, a lecturer at Queen's University, Belfast was shot dead weeks later at her home in Andersonstown, West Belfast. They had tied her to a chair and waited several hours on her husband to return home, no doubt with the intention of killing both of them. When he didn't arrive, they killed her. In October, Ronnie Bunting and Noel Little, both members of the IRSP, as was Miriam Daly, were shot dead at a house in West Belfast. Like John Turnley, Ronnie Bunting came from a Protestant background and was, ironically, the son of Major Ronald Bunting, a former close associate of the Rev Ian Paisley. In January the following year, the UDA also tried to kill Bernadette McAliskey in her home in County Tyrone. Although she was shot nine times she survived the attack. It was later revealed that British soldiers had been lying undercover in the driveway of her house but they had orders not to intervene or apprehend the loyalists prior to the attack. They arrested the loyalists as they attempted to make their getaway.

We had limited contact with the loyalists in H6. At this time we were moved regularly between D and C wings to allow for a rotation of cleaning. When we were in D wing, opposite them, they would shout over any news to us that they had got from the orderlies on their wing. It was strange, listening to them shout over reports about IRA bombings and killings. Other than that, we'd no real engagement with them. There wasn't really anything to discuss and they probably didn't want the prison authorities to form an impression that there was any level of fraternisation. I often wondered why they decided to go on the protest. Some of them were people who had rank or status in their own

---

[54] The excellent film, *81*, written and directed by Stephen Burke, very cleverly highlights this contradiction.

[55] Secret Air Service – a special forces unit of the British Army's.

organisations and by going on the protest they were going against those organisations. I tried some years ago to make contact with them through Billy 'Twister' McQuiston, a former UDA prisoner.[56] I'd met Billy a number of times after my release and he'd spoken publicly in the media about the respect he had for the hunger strikers. None of them were willing, however, to contribute anything more than what they had already said in a radio programme presented by Laura Haydon.[57]

At one stage, a non-political Protestant prisoner, Billy Maxwell, was put onto the loyalist wing. Billy was carrying out his own individual form of protest. He had made some sort of gift for his daughter and wanted to give it to her on a visit. The prison authorities would not allow him to do that and Billy challenged them. The outcome was that he was charged with an offence against prison discipline and sent to the Boards. Billy then refused to do prison work until the issue was resolved. When his time on the Boards was finished, Billy was placed in the wing with the loyalists and had his clothes and prison uniform removed. However, the loyalists decided that Billy's presence on their wing took away from the political nature of their protest and they demanded that the authorities remove him, which they did. They transferred him onto our wing. The first we knew about all this was when we heard some commotion in the wing. The empty cell next to Brendan Hughes was opened and a prisoner was put into it. We thought it must be a new blanketman but then we heard a Governor's voice saying, "Let's see how you get on with the Provies". Brendan got down to the pipes to talk through the wall to this new arrival and then got up to the door to tell Bobby what the situation was. He stated that Billy was welcome on our wing and could stay as long as he wanted to. No doubt the prison authorities imagined that we would not want Billy to remain on our wing, hence the comment from the Governor, but we had no desire to harm him in any way. Why would we? He was challenging the system and had never done anything against us.

'Maxi', as he became known to us, was on our wing for several weeks. During that time Brendan got him some legal advice and also told him that he should demand to get out for exercise as he was

---

[56] http://archive.northernvisions.org/related/thetroubles/1981-loyalist-recollections/

[57] *The Other Side of the Blanket*, broadcast on Newstalk 106-108FM, 16 December 2007.

entitled to one hour per day. Maxi started to do that though had to initially argue with the authorities to get the 'privilege'. Maxi's presence had its benefits. He could 'retrieve' any *bearts* someone had got on the visits but did not have the opportunity to bangle. They would leave it in the pocket of the jacket of the prison uniform. The guards never thought of searching the actual clothing; they were just interested in stripping the prisoner and carrying out the mirror search. Whenever it happened that someone returned to H6 with a *beart* still in their uniform pocket, they took note of which locker they left the uniform in and that information was passed to Maxi. The next time he went for exercise he'd wear the uniform in that locker and get the *beart*. Maxi was a bit of an 'old hand' in the prison system – this wasn't his first time in it – and he had no difficulty returning to his cell with the *beart* and passing the contents on to Brendan.

Eventually the prison authorities resolved the issue with Maxi and he was able to return to the conforming Blocks. He said goodbye to all of us and wished us well. Some years later, shortly after the end of the hunger strike, I met him down on the visits. He had been released from prison on the earlier charge but was now back in again on a new charge – for breaking into a Governor's house!

One day while we were still in H6, a guard was on our wing over the lunchtime lock-up who had known Bobby Sands from the time he was in the Cages of Long Kesh. He knocked on Bobby's door and started having a friendly chat with him. After a while Bobby asked him if he'd check the Class Office to see if there were any letters for us. I think all of us felt we were missing out on letters and were suspicious that the guards – particularly Parkinson – may not have been passing on incoming mail to us. The guard found a pile of mail and went around the wing and distributed it. He would have known it wasn't through oversight that the mail had been withheld. He must have known it was deliberate. I got one of the letters. It was from a girl who I had dated a few times before being arrested. The date on the letter was several months previous. It was a brief letter. In it she asked why I hadn't replied to her previous letters. I'd never received them. I felt anger at the letters having been withheld, mixed with a sense of joy that she had written. But I never did reply. I think, by then, I thought it best to leave the past in the past. Part of that process of shutting off from the outside world and a previous form of life so as to become fully focused on the

Laurence with daughters Caoilfhionn and Órlaith
in the yard of H-Block 4, 2005.

Caoilfhionn and Órlaith in the yard of the prison hospital 2005.

Laurence in H-Block 4, 2005.

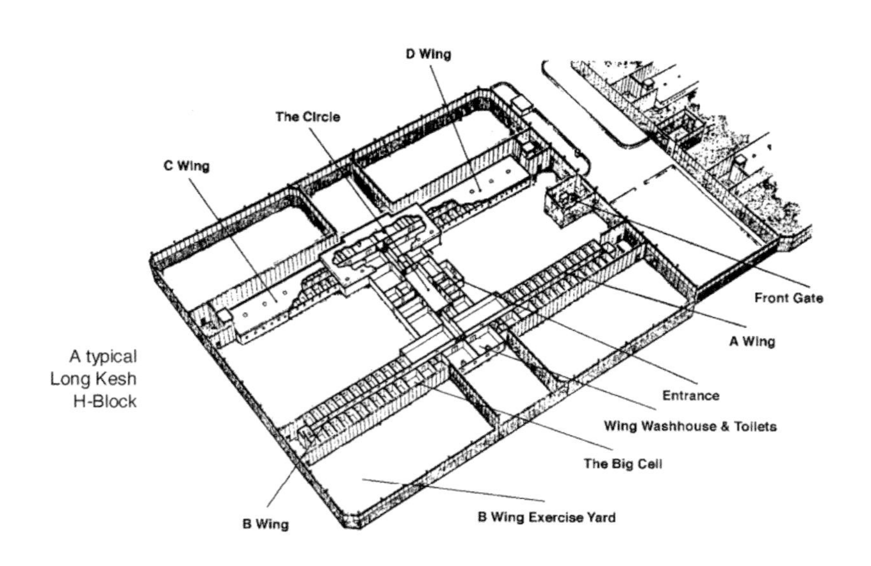


A typical
Long Kesh
H-Block

D081618.30m.10/78.D.gp.191

Form 21 AD

In replying to this letter, please address the envelope as follows:

Number 454 Name McKEOWN L.P.

C Wing H Block 2 H.M.P. MAZE LISBURN Prison

1-5-77

Well Mum,

I didn't expect to get writing a letter so soon but I've been lucky enough. Well I have been down here since Wednesday evening so I have become well settled in by now. The first few days were difficult as with every change in life but knowing me I soon became adapted to it. I didn't see Geraldine on Wednesday so I don't know if she was up or not or if she wasn't allowed in. You can tell her that I have wrote out and that if she still want's me to send her the next letter I will do so. Anyhow you can let me know when you answer this. As I think I said before I am allowed one letter in and one out each month so it is not so bad. I was talking to Geraldine's brother for a moment or two but he is not in the same wing as me now. I also hear that someone else has come in since I saw you last.

Well I hope dad didn't take it too bad when he heard the sentence. I know like yourself he worries a lot but you know that I am keeping healthy and I am not alone and some day soon it will be all over. I'm sure John and the rest of them got a bit of a shock when they heard but it wasn't really unexpected. Tell him it will not be long until I will be christening this new flat of his, or maybe I will be christening a "wee addition". Anyhow he is near enough to the bar if I ever drop in on him unexpected. I hope Gerry's father is no worse although from what Mary said a few weeks ago [illegible] it does not seem as if he will pull through this time. I was sorry I didn't say Good-bye to Mary on Monday but it will not be long until we meet. I forgot to tell you on Tuesday to collect my clothes from the 'Crum' but if you have got them you will get the hanky that I didn't get sending out. I would like you to keep it for me and get it framed if possible. It will always be something to look back on in years to come. Well there is no other news to tell you except as I have said I am in good health and spirits and am hoping for a brighter future. Tell the rest of the family that I am thinking of you all and that I include you all in my prayers as I know you do the same for me. Remember that there are those worse off than us and those who would be glad to be in the position we find ourselves in. Tell Geraldine I was asking about her and you can let me know if she wants the letter. Write soon.

Your Loving Son
Laurence

P.S. Mum I know that you and dad are suffering because of me now and have done so in the past but you know that any hurt I caused you both was not intentional and that I love you both. I wanted to say this on Tuesday but never got the chance.

Tell Mary I hope there is another 'wee Small' on the way by the next time I see her. Or maybe there already is. BYE FOR NOW. WRITE SOON.

Laurence's first letter to his mother after being sentenced and commencing the blanket protest in H-Block 2.

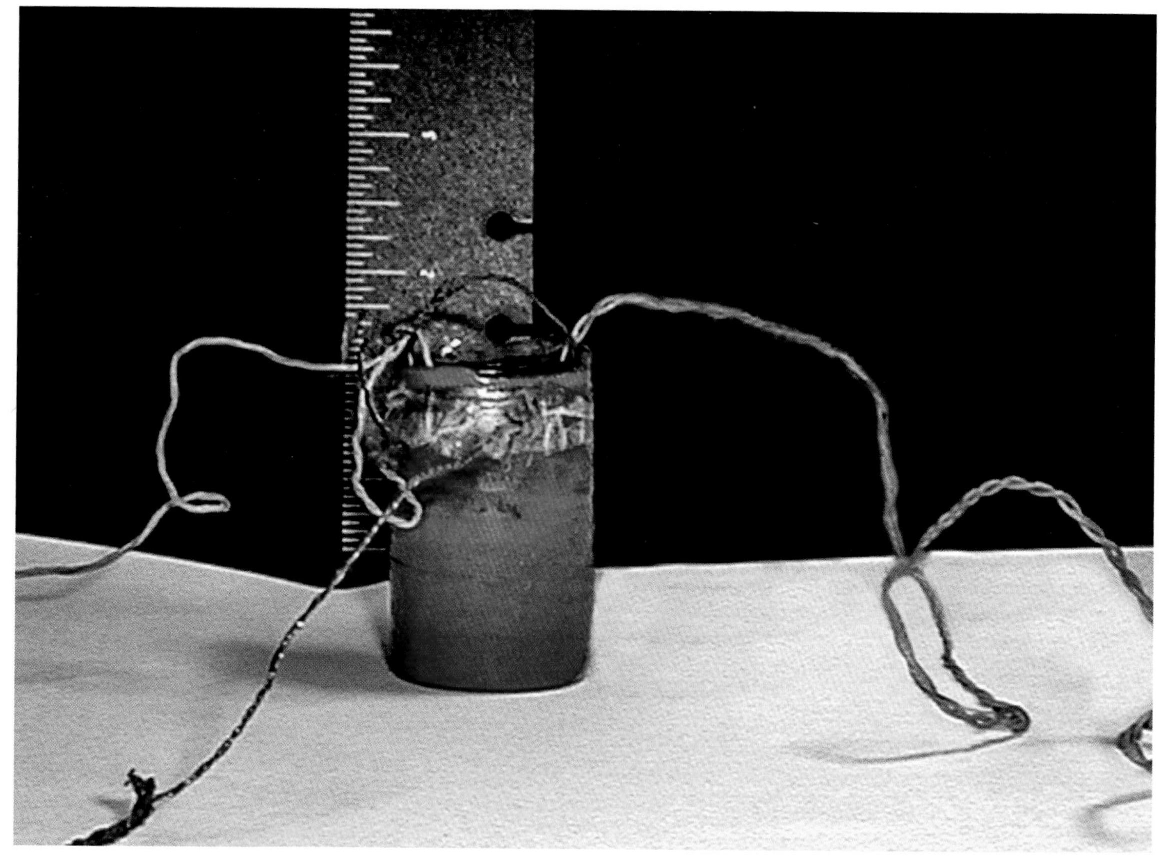

One of the radios manufactured by the IRA and smuggled into the H-Blocks during the blanket protest.

CONFIDENTIAL

A.

NORTHERN IRELAND OFFICE
DUNDONALD HOUSE
UPPER NEWTOWNARDS ROAD
BELFAST BT4 3SU

28 September 1978

S H Hilditch Esq
Governor
HM Prison
MAZE

PRISONERS WHO ARE PERSISTENTLY REFUSING TO CONFORM
WITH PRISON RULES IN H BLOCKS 3, 4 AND 5

MEASURES TO PROMOTE HEALTH AND HYGIENE

Following the recent exchange of views between the Chief Medical Officer, the Prison Medical Officers at the Maze, the Governing staff at the Maze and this office it has been agreed that the following arrangements should be introduced at the Maze Prison to assist in the control of health dangers given the difficulties caused by the refusal of some prisoners in H Blocks 3, 4 and 5 to be medically examined or to bathe.

2. It is agreed that -

(a) Prison Medical Officers will visit every prisoner in his cell at least once a week. This arrangement will provide adequate medical supervision for those cases where, upon adjudication, cellular confinement is not part of the punishment awarded.

(b) Where, however, a prisoner has been charged with an offence for which cellular confinement is a possible punishment, the Medical Officer will require the Governing staff to secure that the prisoner is bathed to enable the Medical Officer to assess the prisoner's fitness for punishment of cellular confinement.

(c) If a prisoner refuses to comply where the Medical Officer considers that the prisoner's state of personal hygiene constitutes a risk to the health of other prisoners or to the health of prison staff the Medical Officer will advise the Governing staff that they should bathe the prisoner.

CONFIDENTIAL

CONFIDENTIAL

A.

2

(d) If the prisoner refuses to comply where the Medical Officer advises that the prisoner should take some personal hygiene measures, including bathing, as a pre-requisite to examination or as part of treatment then the Medical Officer will explain to the prisoner that any consequences of not following the advice are solely the responsibility of the prisoner.

3. These arrangements are in accordance with the proposals made by yourself, as Governor, and the Prison Medical Officers to the Chief Medical Officer and to ourselves. The purpose of this memorandum is merely to record, for the avoidance of doubt, the details of the arrangements arrived at.

4. We are agreed that the Chief Medical Officer, the Prison Medical Officers, yourself and this office will continue to keep under review the measures necessary to deal with the problems for health and hygiene which the actions of these prisoners are causing.

E N BARRY

CONFIDENTIAL

Confidential document from the Northern Ireland Office, addressed to the H-Blocks' prison governor, Stanley Hilditch, outlining their plans to forcibly wash the blanketmen but placing full responsibility for the forced washings on the prison's Chief Medical Officer.

To B.B.C. Radio Derby, 56 St Helens St, Derby.

The recent election of Blanket Man, Hunger-Striker Bobby Sands as M.P. for Fermanagh / South Tyrone can hardly have gone unnoticed by many. Indeed had it not been for that election victory the present news coverage of the H Block hunger-strike would be absent from our T.V. screens, radios and newspapers. The election may well now be a thing of the past, but it would be very foolish for anyone to believe that the motives behind 30,000 people voting as they did are also a thing of the past. But it would be very foolish for anyone to believe that the motives behind 30,000 people voting as they did are also a thing of the past; on the contrary these motives still exist and are daily growing more intense as the hunger-strike progresses.

When Bobby Sands stood as a candidate in the Fermanagh/South Tyrone By-Election he asked the people of that constituency — who are like the people of most constituencies in Ireland — to vote against repression in the prisons. Those who were in favour of ending what they considered to be an inhumane prison policy voted accordingly, and by doing so have caused a major political embarrassment to British politicians who now seem to be finding it difficult to persuade many to believe that 30,000 people in one constituency alone support what is supposed to be a "criminal conspiracy". Their argument begins to appear even more ridiculous when the "respectable" policies of the British Premier Margaret Thatcher gain her 10,000 votes less than the "criminal" policies of Bobby Sands gain him.

Has the whole world suddenly gone mad and lost all sense of morals? Or would it be more reasonable to believe that the H Blocks and Armagh Jail are a festering sore in Irish society which the Irish people want properly cured by the implementation of a more humane and honest prison policy indicative of the true nature of the prisoners' offences rather than the continuous irritation of that sore by a stubborn Government approach.

The British presence in Ireland is for many people undemocratic and this view will surely be strengthened if the wishes of the electorate are now ignored.

It is the duty of the media to present the facts of each situation in a fair impartial manner and indeed the media by doing so have exposed many injustices in society. You the British media have in your power the means to persuade your Government to prevent a massive public explosion in both Britain and Ireland by defusing the hunger-strike time bomb. It is important for the media to act immediately if they wish to see some semblance of democracy remain in Ireland by working to ensure that the wishes of the Irish people are met.

Speak out now

Seamus McElhone, Political Prisoner,
H Block 3, Long Kesh

24/4/81

A smuggled letter Laurence wrote to BBC Radio Derby during the 1981 hunger strike, under the name of fellow-prisoner, Seamus McElhone, calling for public support for the protest.

Send to "Mid-Ulster Observer" to be printed

A Chara,

I don't know how anyone could say in a few words just what I want to say to you but then most of it has been said by someone countless times already, to some it has meant something, to others perhaps nothing at all, but at least ponder on what I have to say if only for a few moments.

As Christmas and the end of yet another year approaches fast and your thoughts turn to presents, parties and a time of goodwill and cheer for all, think of what this Christmas may mean to 7 men and their wives, children, parents and family. For them Christmas is something which might never come at all as they lie dying at this minute on hunger strike. A hunger strike which comes only after everything else has failed to gain us our right for recognition as political prisoners. For over 4 years we waited, asked, begged, beseeched for help without success until finally this year with the end of the Cardinal Ó Fiaich/Atkins talks and the blunt refusal by the British Government to even consider his suggestions for a reasonable solution, we were forced to take this drastic action. For anyone to make such a decision shows in itself the urgency and desperation of our situation as there are only two ways it can end — with death, or the granting of our demands.

You, as much as anyone can be the deciding factor in that final resort. You and your colleagues and friends actively participating in the protest marches and passive disruption campaign being carried out by the R.A.C.'s and H Block Committees could mean the difference between life and death to those men, some of whom are known to you. So if you care don't wait until some of them die before you decide to act as it will be then too late for them. Act now, then maybe they, us, and all our families could wish you too a happy Christmas.

Is mise le meas,

Laurence McKeown H4 Long Kesh

A smuggled letter Laurence wrote during the 1980 hunger strike, to be published in the local *Mid-Ulster Observer* newspaper, calling for public support for the protest.

# FACT FILE

LAURENCE PATRICK
PAUL McKEOWN
On hunger strike since
29 June 1981.

McKEOWN received four life sentences at Belfast City Commission for causing a series of bomb explosions at Randalstown and Antrim and a fifth life term for the attempted murder of a police constable.

Altogether he was convicted on 26 counts. In addition to the life terms, he was sentenced to a further 230 years, all to run concurrently.

McKeown refused to recognise the Court.

McKeown has refused to work or to wear prison clothes since going to prison. He is one of around 400 "protesting" prisoners in the Maze prison. They include 74 who have been convicted of murder; 45 for attempted murder; 118 for explosives offences; 92 for firearms offences and 15 for robbery.

McKeown's sentences also included five years for forcing a motorist to unlawfully relinquish possession of his car; 10 years for possessing firearms with intent to commit hi-jacking; 12 years for theft of the two pistols used to commit the offence; two years for maliciously damaging the car; and five years for membership of the IRA.

Daily Mail 30 JUN 1981

## THE CRIMES AND THE CONVICTIONS

*At Belfast City Commission on 26 April, 1977:*

McKeown was found guilty and sentenced to life imprisonment for causing a bomb explosion at Randalstown on 9 March, 1974. He was also sentenced for:– possession of a bomb (20 years); forcing a motorist to relinquish possession of his car (five years); possession of an Armalite rifle (10 years); maliciously damaging a motor vehicle (two years).

Belfast Telegraph

**Bombers fire shot at cafe owner**

By Telegraph reporters 9 MAR 1974

A RANDALSTOWN businessman had a lucky escape today when terrorists planting a bomb at his cafe opened fire on him. And in the Oldpark area of Belfast a car-bomb exploded without warning outside a bar, but although several people had to be treated for shock there were no injuries.

*At Belfast City Commission on 26 April, 1977:*

McKeown was sentenced to life imprisonment for causing a bomb explosion at Antrim on 2 April, 1974; possession of the bomb (20 years); forcing a motorist to transport the bomb to Antrim (five years); possession of an Armalite rifle and a .45 hand gun with intent to endanger life (14 years); possession of the weapons under such circumstances as to give rise to a reasonable suspicion that they were not for a lawful object (10 years).

The Irish News 3 APR 1974

**Car bomb shatters centre of Antrim**

A MASSIVE car bomb blasted the centre of Antrim Town last night leaving a trail of damage to business property.

## THE CRIMES AND THE CONVICTIONS – CONTINUED

Belfast Telegraph

**Proxy car bomb attack foiled by civilian**

10 JUN 1974

AN ALERT passer-by helped police foil an attempt to plant a large "proxy" car-bomb in the centre of Randalstown at the weekend.

*At Belfast City Commission on 26 April, 1977:*

McKeown was sentenced to life imprisonment for causing a bomb explosion at Randalstown on 8 June, 1974; possession of the bomb (20 years); possession of an Armalite rifle and a .45 hand gun with intent to intimidate (10 years).

*At Belfast City Commission on 26 April, 1977:*

McKeown was sentenced to life imprisonment for causing a bomb explosion at Randalstown on 27 February, 1976; possession of the bomb (20 years); hi-jacking a motor vehicle (five years); possession of a rifle with intent to commit a hi-jacking (10 years); forcing a motorist to transport a bomb to Randalstown (five years).

**Gunmen leave one dead and two injured**

28 FEB 1976

Belfast Telegraph

*At Belfast City Commission on 26 April, 1977:*

McKeown was sentenced to life imprisonment on a charge of attempting to murder members of the Security Forces travelling in a Land Rover along the Barnish Road, Antrim, on 11 July, 1976; wounding a police constable on the same occasion (20 years); possession of a rifle and ammunition with intent to endanger life (20 years).

**Policeman—youth shot in 2 incidents**

12 JUL 1976

Belfast Telegraph

*At Belfast City Commission on 26 April, 1977:*

McKeown's sentences also included five years for forcing a motorist to relinquish possession of his car on 4 March, 1974; 10 years for possession of firearms with intent to commit hijacking; 12 years for theft of the two pistols used to commit the offence; two years for maliciously damaging the car; and five years for membership of the IRA.

*Published by the Northern Ireland Office, August 1981.*

'Fact file' published by the Northern Ireland Office in 1981 as part of their propaganda campaign against the hunger strike and those participating in it.

Ledger from the prison hospital which shows Laurence's father visiting him during the hunger strike.

12. DOES HE/~~SHE~~ TALK ABOUT HIS/~~HER~~ PLANS FOR RELEASE? WHAT ARE THEY?

DOES NOT RELATE THIS TO STAFF

13. DO YOU THINK HE/~~SHE~~ WOULD RETURN TO VIOLENCE IF RELEASED? IF SO - WHY?

LIFE
HAVING SERVED SO LONG IN PRISON I DOUBT IF HIS ATTITUDE TO THE TROUBLES HAVE CHANGED. I THINK HE WOULD STILL BE INVOLVED IN THE PARAMILITARY STRUGGLE.

14. ANY OTHER ADDITIONAL INFORMATION/COMMENTS.

COULD CAUSE PROBLEMS IF IT SUITED THE ORGANIZATIONS ENDS.

Part of a confidential document containing comments written by a prison guard about Laurence on 28/06/1991. The document formed part of the lifer review process which determined a prisoner's 'suitability' for release, or otherwise.

LICENCE

PRISON ACT (NORTHERN IRELAND) 1953 SECTION 23

WHEREAS LAURENCE PATRICK PAUL McKEOWN was convicted at Belfast City Commission held on the 26th day of April 1977 of causing explosions and attempted murder and was sentenced to life imprisonment.

NOW I, THE RIGHT HONOURABLE SIR PATRICK MAYHEW, QC, MP, one of Her Majesty's Principal Secretaries of State, in exercise of the powers conferred by Section 23 of the Prison Act (Northern Ireland) 1953, hereby direct that the said LAURENCE PATRICK PAUL McKEOWN be released on licence within 15 days from the date below.

Dated this 29th day of March 1993

P. B. B. Mayhew

ONE OF HER MAJESTY'S PRINCIPAL SECRETARIES OF STATE

Note: A person serving a sentence of life imprisonment who is released on licence is liable under the provisions of Section 23 of the Prison Act (Northern Ireland) 1953 to be recalled to prison at any time by order of the Secretary of State.

LSU 40

Laurence's release on licence signed by British Secretary of State, Patrick Mayhew, 29 March 1993.

Laurence at his grandmother's house in Randalstown circa 1968.

Laurence with his sister, Mary, and brother, Eugene, at their home in Carngranny, Antrim, circa 1964.

Laurence's parents, Margaret and George, and sister Mary, pictured at their home shortly after Laurence went on hunger strike on 29 June, 1981.

Laurence's parents in Washington in 1982 when they went there to visit her father's grave.

Laurence while released on 12-hours 'compassionate parole' on 10 June, 1983, to attend his mother's funeral.

Laurence with his maternal grandmother whilst released on compassionate parole to attend his mother's funeral.

Laurence with his sister and brother, Mary and Eugene, at his home in Randalstown when released on his first summer parole, 1989.

Laurence graduating with his doctoral degree from Queen's University Belfast, in 1998.

immediate – and better able to psychologically and emotionally deal with the immediate.

* * *

The H-Block camp was split up into 'phases' with high concrete walls separating the different phases. H3, 4, and 5 were in one phase; H6, 7, and 8 in another; and H1 and 2 in the remaining phase. Heavy metal gates provided access from one phase to another. The Visiting Block was closest to H5, just to the rear of it, on the other side of another high concrete wall. We walked to visits. Apparently the authorities thought we would stink up the mini-buses that took conforming prisoners to and from the visits. It may have been, though, that they didn't want us to associate in any way with conforming prisoners. I enjoyed the walk to the visits. H6 was much further away from the visiting area than the other Blocks; about a 15-minute walk. That was sheer bliss. I didn't care what the weather was like – rain, hail, or shine – it was just great to be out in the air, and actually walking. Pacing up and down the cell with a blanket wrapped around your legs wasn't really walking; not real walking, not stretching your legs. Going to and from the visits, one day per month, twelve times per year, was the one time I got out into the fresh air and I loved it.

Walking to the visits from H6, I passed the newly-constructed gymnasium and playing fields. The gym was quite large and there were two full-sized, all-weather soccer pitches. Sometimes when I'd walk past I'd see conforming prisoners out playing on the pitches and hear the sounds of play – shouts of encouragement to teammates, or calls of abuse to those on the competing side. It was just a few feet away from me and yet it was a different world entirely. By that stage, 1979, I had been on the blanket protest for two years and on the no-wash protest for a year, hair grown down below my shoulders, straggly beard, wearing (for the visit) an ill-fitting prison uniform with sock-less feet stuck into lace-less boots. Those I saw on the pitches would return to the Block after the game to get showered; I'd return from my visit to a mirror-search.

It was during 1979 that the authorities introduced yet another new search procedure. At the rear of H5 they constructed a small wooden hut, like a large shed you'd get today for your garden or back yard. We called it the 'Romper Room'. It was where blanketmen – and only blanketmen – were searched immediately after we left our visits. We exited the Visiting Block into a fenced corridor and then through a heavy metal pedestrian door in the concrete wall that separated the Visiting Block from the phase where H5 sat, and then into another fenced-off waiting area. The new search box sat outside this fenced-off section in a sort of 'no-man's-land'. Depending on how many blanketmen were out on visits at the time there could be two to three waiting to be searched. It was an opportunity to pass *scéal* or comms but there was always an anxious energy, knowing that the search was ahead of you. Like wing shifts, the waiting was the worst. As you stood there, you'd hear muffled sounds from inside the box as someone was being searched – and thrown around. I thought the box shook at times. It may have, as it was made of wood, though I don't know if it actually did shake or if it was just my imagination. Occasionally, when the person ahead of you left the search box, they'd shout over, "*Níl sé ró-dona*". ("It's not too bad.") When they were silent, you didn't know if they didn't have Irish, didn't think of commenting, or didn't want to comment on how rough it was.

It's always interesting how people can adjust to varying degrees of abuse – whether that's in prison on the blanket protest or on the outside in a domestic or work situation. Today's abuse or brutality is compared to some previous instance of it which may have been worse, so today, *níl sé ró-dona*. We can live with it. It's our way of coping with life. But it's not how life should be. It's not living. It's existing.

* * *

The routine at night in all Blocks was that after any lines across the wing had been completed the OC would ask if there were any issues or any *scéal* from the visits to be shared. Once that was completed, he would give the order to slop out, the guard would later 'squeegee' the corridor, and then it was the quiet time of night, usually around ten o'clock. It was in H6 where I was introduced to 'story-telling' which involved someone telling the story of a novel they'd read. I don't know if this practice had taken place in any other Block before then but it was a first for me and the first person to tell a story – *Trinity* by Leon Uris – was Bobby Sands. This was a huge novel (896 pages) published in 1976, which Bobby had read while on remand, and although it is a fictional text, it is based on fact. The story is set in Ireland, in Co Donegal, in the late 19th century and links the great hunger (Famine) with rebellion. I read many books while on remand but would have been hard-pressed to recall their full story. Bobby remembered *Trinity* in detail. Any facts he was unsure of, he checked with others who had read the book. He even wrote comms to outside to check on some details. Bobby would give us advance warning of when the story was about to start – maybe ten minutes – so that we could finish off whatever we may be doing. Maybe, if we had tobacco, to get some cigarettes ready for when he would start the story. It would be similar to sitting down today to watch a film on TV but first getting the glass of wine poured and the chocolate bar opened and left sitting on the table beside you, ready for the viewing.

It took Bobby several weeks to tell the full story – such was the level of detail he engaged with and his ability to recall the most minor elements of the story – and he told it most nights. If he was too busy, or too tired (a rare event for Bobby) to tell it on a particular night, depression settled into the wing; we had become so used to ending our days hearing of the exploits of Conor Larkin, his father Tomás, and mother Finola.

The sing-songs also continued in H6 – and with them the dread I always felt at being called up to sing. I don't think I ever did sing while I was in H6; the experience in H5 had been enough for me. There were some good singers in the wing though; Bik McFarlane, for instance, and especially Bobby Sands. I often wonder, now that Bobby has become an international icon, if it appears sycophantic when those who shared a wing or cell with him refer to his talents. But he had an amazing voice, just as he had an amazing talent as song-writer, poet, and writer. When the sing-songs were organised, Bobby was kept until the end, in the hope that he would sing several songs, or even treat us to a one-man mini-concert lasting for 30-40 minutes.

The Blocks were very quiet at night. There was no traffic to be heard or no late-night revellers making their way home. And when Bobby sang, his voice reverberated the length and breadth of the wing – and beyond. It wasn't because he had a loud, deep voice – he had a 'folksy' sound; a light touch – but his voice carried emotion and depth. Paul Simon, from Simon and Garfunkel, reminds me of the type of voice Bobby had. He would regularly include in his repertoire, *Me and Bobby McGee*, the song written by Kris Kristofferson, which was one of his favourites. I often wonder whether it appealed to him because he wished for the carefree life that the song depicts.

Busted flat in Baton Rouge, headin' for the trains
Feelin' nearly faded as my jeans
Bobby thumbed a diesel down just before it rained
Took us all the way to New Orleans

I took my harpoon out of my dirty red bandanna
And was blowin' sad while Bobby sang the blues
With them windshield wipers slappin' time and
Bobby clappin' hands we finally sang up every song
That driver knew

Freedom's just another word for nothin' left to lose
Nothin' ain't worth nothin' but it's free
Feelin' good was easy, Lord, when Bobby sang the blues
And buddy, that was good enough for me
Good enough for me and my Bobby McGee.

But the one I still most vividly recall him singing was one he composed himself, *Sad Song For Susan*:

I'm sitting at the window, I'm looking down the street
I'm watching for your face, I'm listening for your feet.
Outside the wind is blowing and it's just begun to rain,
And it's being here without you that's causing me such pain.
My mind's wandering back again, to when you were here
And I wish I had you now, I wish that you were near.
I remember the winter nights when you warmed me from the cold
And in the spring when we walked through green fields and skies of gold.
You're gone, you're gone, but you'll live on in my memory.
In summer we played with the kids and you brought us young Jane,
But now – now it's lonely and cold and it's winter once again.
It's dark now, I see the stars are all out way up in the sky,
And oh! how they remind me of the sparkle in your eye.
I'm lonely, yes, I'm lonelier than the cold wind that blows,
Are you happy? Are you all right? I suppose God only knows.
And darling all the people are going to bed and the kids are crying for you,
How can I tell them that you're dead?
You're gone, you're gone but you'll live on in my memory,
You're gone, you're gone but you'll live on in my memory.

The words of the chorus now take on a whole new meaning. They remind me so much of the author. And yes, Bobby, you do live on in my memory.

We stayed in H6 for nine months. Our time spent there was mundane in many ways with just the one wing, but it was an important time for me. I was exposed to the ideas of people (Bobby Sands, Larry Marley, Brendan Hughes, Pat McGeown, Joe Barnes, Brendan McFarlane, and others) who had been in the Cages for several years; people just slightly older than me but a few years made a big difference back then. Learning about the development of republicanism in the late 1960s/early 1970s was particularly interesting because they were able to speak of their own personal experiences and involvement in the Republican Movement at the time. It was the first time that I had ever heard such a detailed account of how events had evolved to where we were at that time. Although I had experienced a gut reaction to the removal of political status, believed that I was a political prisoner and demanded the right to be treated as such, the rationale behind the policy of criminalisation, and the role it played in a much more comprehensive counter-insurgency strategy, had never been explained to me. No doubt this was because those who had entered prison at the same time as myself had no clear notion themselves about what was happening other than that we were refusing to be classed as criminals.

In the lectures and discussions held in H6, the policy of the British government in relation to the entire conflict became much clearer. This deeper insight into our struggle, and how we had reached that particular point in our history, made me shake off many of the naïve notions which I had still harboured until then about how the 'Brits' would eventually 'wise up and have a bit of sense' and restore special category status. I began to realise that our struggle in the prison was going to be more difficult and protracted than I had imagined. I wasn't aware at the time, though, that Brendan Hughes and Bobby (and a few others) were discussing the option of a hunger strike to occur during the Pope's visit which was planned for September of that year. The proposal was sent to the Movement on the outside but they asked to hold off on it as Tomás Ó Fiaich (by then, Catholic Cardinal of Ireland) was in ongoing talks with the British Secretary of State, Humphrey Atkins. Those talks dragged on for six months and ended inconclusively. The Pope came and left and in October the Movement established the National Anti-H-Block/Armagh Committee to coordinate the campaign of street protests so as to maximise their impact and also to utilise resources to the best effect.

# 7
# A New World Record

In September 1979, H6 was split up and we were scattered back around the other three Blocks. I was sent to H4 with about eight or nine others where a 'reception committee' of guards awaited us. Larry Marley, Paddy Quinn, and I were sent to C wing. The three of us were first held between the grilles leading into the wing and then Larry was called. We watched him walk to Cell 26 and soon afterwards could hear scuffling and muffled sounds. Larry reappeared onto the wing, dishevelled, and was taken to his cell. It was then the turn of Paddy Quinn. The same sequence of events and noises ensued. And then it was my turn. When I walked into Cell 26, Brian Armour, a guard, was sitting on a table with his legs swinging. I knew Armour from C wing in H5 before the no-wash protest began. He was a small man from East Belfast with red hair and beady eyes. His nickname was the 'Red Rat' and he was Deputy Head of the POA – the Prison Officers Association. He was bigoted to the core. The PO of H5, Kevin Lappin, had previously had Armour removed from his Block because of his attitude towards us.

Armour sat there on his table like a king on his throne and in front of him, on the floor, was the mirror. He motioned to the other four or five guards to bring me closer. Two of them took me by the arms and pulled me towards Armour so he could look at me. Even though he was sitting on the table I was still much taller than him. The guards either side of me then thumped me and kicked behind my knees to force me to squat over the mirror. They held me in that position and Armour, now looking down on me, said, "Welcome to H4, McKeown".

It was the first time since going on the protest that I had personally been on the receiving end of such casual, yet organised, brutality. Any assaults I had previously suffered had been when particular events occurred, such as the smashing of the furniture when the protest first began, or during the wing shifts. This encounter was more frightening as it was evident that this would be the norm for the Block. Not long afterwards, I came to realise that what I had experienced on that day was quite minor in comparison to what had already taken place in H4. I discovered that Armour determined the daily practice and culture of the Block. In other words, he set the level of brutality. Armour was the one in charge of the Block, not the Principal Officer, Dessie Stewart, or the Assistant Governor. Armour was a very powerful man. His sidekick, Tommy Keenan (nicknamed '*An Fear Ramhar*' – 'The Fat Man' – by the blanketmen), grew in power with him. An equally insignificant guy at the start of the protest, several stone over-weight and awkward in his gait, Keenan, like Armour, in the artificial world of the H-Blocks, adopted a new 'alpha male' persona.

Neither Keenan nor Armour seemed to have a life beyond the Blocks. They were always there. Maybe it was the money, or maybe they had become addicted to the adrenalin and the status that was afforded to them in that environment. They could open the door of a cell at any time of the day, walk into it and slap prisoners about. They could take a tray of food and just dump it into the dustbin. They could put disinfectant into the tea boiler or piss in it – all of which happened at one time or another – because they were in charge, without meaningful oversight or scrutiny. Either a blind eye was turned, or, their behaviour was actively encouraged. Irrespective, they got to become their own version of 'Rambo'; little men transformed into big men in the confines of Long Kesh. Post-hunger strike, the bubble burst. The H-Blocks became a different place. Armour didn't appear in the Blocks again, though that didn't stop him from carrying on his personal war with republican prisoners. Using his very influential position within the POA he consistently tried to stop the implementation of reforms and concessions for which we continued to struggle. His agitation didn't go unnoticed, and on 4 October 1988 Brian Armour was executed by the IRA. A booby-trap bomb exploded under his car in East Belfast.

Armour wasn't killed in an act of revenge for what he had done during the period of the protest, but rather because of his ongoing attempts to frustrate, in any way he could, our struggle to achieve our outstanding demands. Of particular interest is the internal politics of the prison authorities vis-à-vis the POA. At the time of Armour's death, the prison authorities were trying to wrestle back authority from the POA. They had lost that authority during the period of the protest and this was made more evident in the aftermath of the mass-escape of 1983 when once again the POA, rather than the Governor, assumed control of the prison for several days and thereafter attempted to ensure that their writ ran. In the aftermath of Armour's killing, IRA prisoner Martin Meehan made a comment about his death to a very senior official in the prison authorities. The response from the official was unexpected, if very true; "Well, if you play with fire you're going to get your fingers burned".

Despite that initial 'welcome' to H4 I settled in quickly. I never really had a problem settling into any wing or Block, either during the protest or in the years that followed. Moving onto H4 though, it was surprising to be regarded as a member of some form of elite group – those who had been in H6. We were referred to as the 'elders' by some in the wing but it was all light banter and although I knew I was now in a situation that was more brutal than H6, or H5 where I'd been previously held, I sensed a good atmosphere about the wing and was glad to be back in one of the original blanket Blocks.

Looking back, it is clear to me that my time in H6 *had* been, for me, a time of personal growth and intellectual development. By the time I arrived onto H4 I had already been on the protest for two and a half years and had experienced a lot during that time. I had discovered much about myself and had begun to formulate a clearer politic. And while in H6 I had continued Irish classes with Séanna and by the time we left there I had more or less exhausted all that he had to teach, certainly in terms of grammatical rules, if not vocabulary. In H4 I began to teach Irish to others; *an árd-rang* (high class). Some of those who were students in that class then taught *meán* and *bun ranganna* (middle and basic classes) to others in the wing, as was the case throughout the Blocks. Talking to participants of a class out the side of a door is not always the easiest, especially when you're at one end of the wing and they're at the other and you're trying to explain the rules governing the habitual past participle! But I enjoyed giving the classes and preparing for them challenged my own understanding and grasp of the language.

I was always on the lookout for new articles in Irish or new words to add to my vocabulary.

One day, whilst pacing up and down the cell, reciting new words and phrases in Irish that I'd just got from an article in the *Irish Press*, I made a sudden, and wonderful, discovery. When I was growing up in Carngranny I had attended Farinflough primary school. It was a very small school consisting of just two classrooms. Years 1-4 were in one classroom and years 5-7 in another. The school sat out in the countryside, a stream ran beside it and behind that there was what had once been an old flax dam. We were warned not to venture near it as we could easily slip into it and drown. My intention was to move on to Antrim Technical College once I left primary school. I liked to work with my hands and wanted to be an engineer. However, the year that I ended my primary education (1968), the Tech stopped taking new pupils aged 11/12 and would only thereafter take them aged 15/16, after they had completed several years at a secondary school. Ordinarily, I would have moved onto St Olcan's Secondary School[58] in Randalstown, but I passed the 11+ exam and my teacher, Rose McKeown,[59] decided that my parents should apply to have me accepted into St Malachy's Grammar School in Belfast. It was the summer, I had just finished primary education, and the thought of what happened next didn't really concern me one way or the other. Come that September I was enrolled in St Malachy's – and the moment I arrived there I hated it with a passion. I got up at about 6.30 in the morning, cycled three miles to the main road, and took a bus for the twenty miles to Belfast to start school before 9.00 a.m. I didn't get home until after 5.00 p.m. To crown it off I suffered from travel sickness too.

It was a different world entirely from what I had experienced at Farinflough and one abiding memory is of the day when a particular teacher inquired as to what schools we had previously attended. I was one of the last to be asked and all the others before me had quoted a variation of 'Saints'. They'd attended Saint Patrick's, Saint Joseph's, etc.. When I said I had attended Farinflough the entire class burst out laughing. I think the teacher also laughed. I was so embarrassed. I felt that it was a really fucking stupid name for a school and I'd have laughed too if it had been someone else who had said it. But all those

[58] Renamed St Benedict's College in 2006.

[59] No relative of mine but mother of current Catholic bishop, Donal McKeown.

years later, as I paced up and down my cell in the H-Blocks, wrapped only in a blanket, reciting new words and phrases in Irish that I'd just got from the article in the *Irish Press*, I stopped dead in my tracks. One of the words was '*fearainn*', or '*baile fearainn*'. It meant townland. *Fearainn fliuch* (pronounced 'farin flough') would mean wet townland. My primary school had the old flax dam out the back of it, the one we were told to stay away from in case we drowned. It was a 'wet townland'. It was a '*fearainn fliuch*'. The embarrassment I had felt on that day in St Malachy's instantly disappeared and in its place came an immense pride. I had actually grown up in an area that still retained the old Gaelic names, even if since Anglicised. My own house sat in the townland of Carngranny (*Carn Greanaí*) and that was next to Drumsough (*Droim Subhach*). What I was learning now, wasn't the formal education of St Malachy's or education in a formal setting. This was education as it should be. This was about discovery and self-learning. Discovering who I was and where my people came from and what we were about. I felt immensely proud of my roots.

The teaching of the Irish language was one of the earliest examples of how we developed an informal system of education during the years of the blanket protest in which the 'pupil' became the 'teacher' once he had arrived at a particular level of competence. No one had to be fully qualified according to some official criterion. All that was required was that those more advanced than others passed on what they knew and attempted to raise others up to their standard whilst simultaneously trying to acquire a higher standard themselves. The same applied to other knowledge that people acquired, be it about economics, socialism, or history, but it was in the teaching of the Irish language that the principle was most apparent.

In the Cages, republican prisoners had at one time used flags through which to communicate with one another (flag semaphore).[60] Codes were changed daily so that the prison authorities could not break them. In the Blocks the Irish language became our 'coded system' for secretive communication. Verbal messages could be passed from wing to wing and Block to Block without the authorities knowing what was being said. We heard of attempts by the guards to learn Irish but they never came to anything. Occasionally, they discovered bits of Irish written out

---

[60] Ronan Bennett (1994), *Fire and Rain*, Broadcast on BBC Radio 4 in October 1994, Unpublished.

on toilet roll when they searched the cells and took them away with them. Some tried to read what was written but never with any success as they could never match sounds to the words and there was no real commitment on their part to learning the language.

One day, however, when I was in C wing H5, not long after the start of the no-wash protest, the Class Officer of the wing and a couple of other guards walked down to Séanna's cell and opened the door. They knew Séanna was the main teacher of Irish in the wing. They had a new guard with them; a small man with a red face who we later learned was from the south of Ireland. The regular guards smiled and said something to Séanna along the lines of, "We have youse now". They then motioned to the monkey on the organ grinder to perform. The new guard started to recite the 'Hail Mary' in Irish. Whilst he was doing so, Séanna started to address him in Irish. "*Tá tú go h-uafasach. Tá cuma an moncaí ort a mhic oh!*" ("You are horrible looking. You look like a monkey, son.") Séanna continued in a similar vein as the new guard continued his recitation of the 'Hail Mary', clearly not understanding Séanna's insults. When the latter had finished, the other guards smiled with glee at Séanna, closed his cell door and walked off laughing. They thought they'd achieved some major victory but instead the new guard had been exposed as knowing absolutely no Irish at all – other than something he'd learned by rote when attending school. Séanna could be a cocky bastard that way.

It often surprised us that they *didn't* make a serious attempt to learn Irish but looking back on it, it was an indication of how they viewed us and the protest and maybe an indication of how they viewed Irish culture and identity – with utter disregard and contempt. We did catch on, however, that certain phrases would alert them, or they could get a sense of what they meant which might get their attention. A prime example of this was someone returning from a visit and walking up the yard at the front of the Block. Prisoners in A and D wing (the wings at the front of the yard) would shout out to them, sometimes abuse about how they looked in the prison uniform with unkempt hair and walking in boots too big and with no laces. All good-natured banter. But if the prisoner was from one of those wings and his comrades were eager to find out if he had got tobacco on the visit they would shout out to him, "*An bhfuair tú?* (Did you get?) And if he replied, "*Fuair*," a cry of joy would go up in the wing. There was nothing in the words exchanged to indicate precisely that they related to tobacco and smuggling but we became aware that the guards got some sense that something was up and often did a more rigorous search on the prisoner once he got back into the wing. When I was in H6 we were told not to shout out "*An bhfuair tú*" to prisoners returning from visits but due to our eagerness (and craving for tobacco) we'd use various other words such as, "*An bhfuil athas ort?*" (Are you happy) and if someone said "*Tá*" or "*Tá athas orm,*" we'd know we were in luck but were still careful not to shout out or cheer.

Toilet paper was especially important to us during the blanket period – for writing on, rather than the use for which it was originally intended. We were only allowed four squares of toilet paper per day, which the guards put through the top of the door each evening. However, with the commencement of the no-wash protest the guards refused to give us the toilet paper as they said we were not using it for the correct purpose, alluding to the fact that we had repurposed it into writing material. The OC in one of the wings I was in, however, instructed us to ask for toilet paper in the evening when the guards came round with the supper. Generally they ignored our request. The response from one guard was always, "Show me your pen and I'll give you the paper". Charlie Talbot, an old guard in H4 who wore a wig and was the butt of jokes amongst his colleagues, never mind us, would hold a roll of toilet paper behind his back as they came round the wing with supper. Charlie thought he was hiding it from us. He seemed to be unaware that our comrades on the other side of the wing could observe him through the side of their cell doors and were able to inform us, in Irish, that Charlie had the bog roll. So we asked him for it. And he provided it. A fucken pantomime!

With the general loss of toilet paper after the start of the no-wash protest we started to write Irish on the cell walls. To write on the wall we'd use anything with a lead content. Some people got the lead innards from pencils smuggled in on their visits but religious medals or crucifixes would usually suffice. I had a Celtic cross for most of the time on the blanket. It hung around my neck on a thin chain and was very handy for writing with. I didn't have to take the chain and cross off to write but just lean closely to the wall. The chain broke several times – maybe five or six times – over the course of the protest but I was able to repair it with thread from our small white towels by forming a link out of the thread and tying it in a knot.

It was easy to rub out writing on the wall by spitting on it and rubbing it with your finger or a bit of your blanket if you made a mistake. Although during the no-wash protest we covered the cell walls in our own excreta, we'd leave a piece of wall clean, close to the door where we stood to take part in the classes, and usually on another part of wall, either over at the window where we would stand and look out, or low down on the wall close to our mattresses so that we could read the words and phrases as we lay in bed.

I remember meeting Cardinal Tomás Ó Fiaich, a fluent Irish speaker, when he came into the Blocks to visit us in late 1979 or early 1980. He had previously visited in 1978 and made his famous 'Streets of Calcutta' reference in a media interview upon leaving the prison. I shared a cell with Paddy Quinn from South Armagh and as that was in the Cardinal's diocese he came to our cell to visit Paddy. I had an article *as Gaeilge* which I'd got from the *Irish Press* written on my wall in a corner of the cell close to the window. There were a few words and short phrases that I couldn't understand and I asked the Cardinal if he'd take a look at them. He agreed and stepped over into the corner with me. When the Cardinal visited, the guards kept the cell door open and they stood outside looking in. They said it was for the Cardinal's safety; really it was to keep an eye on him and his interactions with us given his previous statement about conditions in the prison. That day he very quickly identified the words and phrases and was interpreting them for me and giving me examples of how they could be used. The Cardinal stood directly facing me, looking at the wall with his back to the guard at the door. The guard could therefore only see my shoulders and head above the Cardinal's body. As the Cardinal spoke to me, whilst looking at the words written on the wall, he put his hand into his inside pockets and pulled out packets of cigarettes which he handed to me and which I immediately hid in the folds of my blanket at waist level. It was a perfectly smooth operation. I thought he'd be a great asset on the wing as a blanketman! The guard saw absolutely nothing.

I always thought that it was somehow poetic that it was through the medium of the Irish language that we conversed that day whilst carrying out this minor covert operation. I had major criticisms of the Catholic Church – and he of the IRA – but we shared an understanding of Irish history, of colonialism, of how the Catholic Church was once suppressed under British rule. And I believe he genuinely identified with our plight.

As all this demonstrates, learning and speaking the Irish language in the H-Blocks, especially during the time of the blanket protest, had significance for a number of reasons, some practical, some political, others to do with culture, and a sense of identity that went beyond mere nationalistic opinions and beliefs. There was a growing emotional attachment to the language and a deepening awareness that, as humans, we think in a specific language. Our values are reflected in our language. Words and phrases in Irish convey different concepts than they would in English. On a more practical level, the language was a means through which to communicate to comrades, to exclude enemies, to relieve boredom and stimulate the mind, but ultimately it was a means through which to express our identity as Irish republicans. Learning the language was, therefore, a very political and subversive pursuit.

I often refer to the four and a half years I spent on the blanket protest as the most educationally valuable time of my life even though I had no access to books, papers, magazines, radio or TV. Even though in later years I went on to complete a university degree while still in prison and, following my release, a doctorate, I regard those years on protest as the most important, educationally, because it was a time of 'unlearning'; unlearning all the crap that I had soaked up from state, church, and the media up until then. It was during the protest that I became aware that I held opinions that were often contradictory and I came to realise that I'd never actually sat down at any stage of my life and seriously thought through, in any coherent or organised manner, what I really thought about the world and various socio-political issues. I just had loosely-held opinions which I flippantly trotted out. But, on the blanket, you couldn't have your say and then just walk away from a conversation. You were going to be there the next day and the day after that, and you were going to be challenged by others and would need to justify your position. I began to realise that some views I held were incoherent or contrary to values and principles that I otherwise espoused. And what were those values and principles? This question had begun to occupy my thoughts.

The 'culture of education' that developed in such circumstances was impossible to escape. Our conditions created a new mode of discussion. Without written materials we shared what knowledge we had in our heads, such as Irish history, economics, and geography, but discussions often covered the broadest of topics including religion, atheism, abortion, divorce, communism and so forth. Some debates lasted for days on end. Some discussions never reached any firm conclusion and periodically re-emerged. In one sense, discussion and debate was a means by which to occupy our time, but it also played a critical part in developing a new awareness about the acquisition of knowledge. Most significantly, however, in the absence of books and the usual 'opinion formers', we began to look critically at the orthodox republican values, principles, and beliefs we had held up until then. We became more knowledgeable about the origins, history, and diversity of Irish republican ideology. We also began to re-interpret the content of academic studies we had pursued earlier in life, especially those relating to Irish history. These educational experiences during the period of the blanket protest greatly influenced the manner in which, post-hunger strike, we developed our camp-wide system of political education and organisation. The critical approach to education, adapted during the protest years, combined with a co-operative as opposed to a competitive pursuit of knowledge, shaped our approach to learning and our outlook on the world and the struggle we were engaged in.

A part of that change in outlook involved changes in regards to my religious belief. I was far from being a devout Catholic to begin with but was, nevertheless, reared with a Catholic belief in a Catholic household and attended Catholic schools. As such, I was immersed in a Catholic ethos. In general, the Catholic hierarchy condemned the IRA campaign, though several individuals, including Tomás Ó Fiaich, could at least understand where a republican belief arose from. The Church's condemnation sat heavily with some people who regarded themselves as observantly Catholic but who also believed in the legitimacy of the IRA's armed struggle. It was during the blanket protest that I became aware of 'Liberation theology' which had developed within the Catholic Church in Latin America in the 1960s as a moral response to poverty and social injustices. Liberation theology developed in the era immediately after the Second Vatican Council which saw a move away from the much more orthodox, conservative elements of Catholic Church teachings and practice.

That experience in Latin America resulted in many priests, nuns, and religious lay-people taking up arms or at least openly siding with various guerrilla movements. This gave us heart, as well as ammunition to use against those priests in Ireland who preached against the IRA. It was always heartening, too, when Catholic missionaries from Latin America, or the Philippines, or other conflict zones would come in to say Mass in the H-Blocks when in Ireland. Other religious allies closer to home were the monks of Portglenone Abbey and the likes of Fr Brian Brady whose integrity was very apparent and encouraging. Missionaries totally understood our protest. They understood it because their congregations lived in poverty and under oppressive regimes. They knew that many in their congregations were tortured or murdered by the military or just 'disappeared'. They understood completely. And their sermons weren't sermons as we generally were accustomed to; they didn't lecture us. They were more akin to conversations which made them so very different to the ones delivered by local priests who had always practised their ministry in Ireland. Even as my belief in religion withered and died, my respect for those priests, nuns, and religious lay-people who threw in their lot with their oppressed and downtrodden congregations, increased.

Some months after we arrived in H4, the guard from H6, 'Hack' Ramsay who put the cigarettes into Bobby's door, was again on our wing one night. I still shared a cell at the time with Paddy Quinn; cell 25 at the top of the wing. At around ten o'clock, Hack placed a chair almost immediately outside our door and then took the record player out of the canteen, set it on the chair, and played the Electric Light Orchestra album, *A New World Record* (1976). When the A side was finished, he turned it over and played the B side. And when the B side was finished he played the entire album over again. The wing was totally silent. Most of the songs were familiar to us but this was the first time we'd heard music since our time on remand years previous. I've no idea why Hack decided to do that. Maybe he just liked ELO's music. Maybe he was bored. More likely it was a simple gesture of humanity.

When guards worked night duty they were off the next day and then returned to the same Block at lunch time the following day. When Hack returned that lunchtime he again played the album, though this time in the canteen; it would have appeared too blatant to take the record player out into the wing in the middle of the day and play it. A few minutes after the album began to play, and we had all settled down to listen to it, we heard grilles opening and closing. The Block Senior Officer, a Catholic called Carey, came from the Circle and shouted down our wing, "Hack, turn that down. The Provies will hear it." Hack uttered some grumbled response but turned it down.

Once again, a Castle Catholic had carried out his duty on behalf of the Empire.

# 8
# Hatred

IN LATE 1979 (or early 1980) someone in the NIO decided that we should be given chairs for our cells. We had no beds, sheets, TV, radio, books, or magazines. We had no exercise, no showers, no access to toilet facilities, but someone in their wisdom decided that what we most needed was a plastic chair. In line with the directive, the guards came around one afternoon and put the chairs into our cells. The Block PO, Dessie Stewart, was with them. As they put the chairs into our cell Stewart said, "You can sit on them, shite on them, or whatever". I think I sat on the chair for a while just to try it out. It was strange to have these two new additions to the cell. They looked out of place, sparkling clean, sitting there amongst the squalor.

They didn't last long, however. That night we got orders from the Block OC to destroy them. Paddy Quinn and I went to it with a passion. They were easy to break. We just jammed the legs down the back of the heating pipes then leaned heavily on the chair causing the metal tube legs to bend. We then wiggled them to and fro a few times and the metal soon snapped. This provided us with weapons – a clear oversight by the guards. Now armed with the metal legs of the chairs we got stuck into the metal grilles covering the windows. We used the chair legs like a tin opener and soon had the grille ripped apart and rolled up to the ceiling, thus giving us access to the Perspex boxes on the outside of the windows, which we promptly smashed. We also dug holes into the concrete wall at the sides of our doors so that we could better see out.

Shortly afterwards, we heard a lot of commotion in the Circle and knew that the riot squad had arrived. Soon they came into our wing and our cell was the first one they entered. The guards didn't know what to expect when they opened the doors. They knew we now had potential weapons but didn't know if we had been instructed to attack them or not. You could see the fear on their faces as they came through the door. Thankfully, however, we had been directed by our OC not to engage in any fight with them. Paddy and I were standing at the back of the cell, against the wall with the window in it, and all the parts of the chair were lying in the middle of the floor. The guards rushed into our cell and while a couple of them stood immediately in front of Paddy and me, the others gathered up the remains of the chairs and threw them outside. They then left. As they moved around the wing, however, they became more confident. And more aggressive. Soon you could hear thumps and the sound of bodies thrown against walls. I remember talking across the wing to Dessie McCallion and Pius McNaught from Derry. They were in the last couple of cells to be searched and therefore had to wait and listen to the assaults taking place, knowing that their turn was soon to come. Waiting. Waiting. As was often the case, someone down the wing shouted out, '*Níl sé ró-dona*' (It's not too bad).

When the guards had completed the search and left the wing there was a great sense of euphoria – coupled with relief that no one had been seriously beaten. The act of smashing the chairs and destroying the grilles and boxes outside the windows gave us a great sense of achievement. We had once again smashed the system, and whoever it was who had decided to give us chairs had possibly now lost their job!

Pat Sheehan was at the very bottom of the wing on the same side as me. He had received a visit that day and had returned with tobacco but because there was a blockage in the pipes between several cells, the tobacco could not be passed up the entire length of the wing. Now, with the grilles smashed, it was possible to swing a 'line' (thread with a weight tied to the end) out the window and connect with the prisoners next door – just as we used to 'swing' the prison trousers when they had been in our cells. On this occasion, I think I used a dried chicken bone to weight the line. Slowly the tobacco began to make its way up the wing. Next door to me was Pat 'Beag' McGeown and Blute. As it got later and later in the night Pat teased me by saying they were off to sleep and, anyhow, sure I'd get the tobacco the following day. I told him in no uncertain terms that there was no way he'd get to sleep. I'd be battering the wall between us with my pisspot until I got the tobacco!

The tobacco did eventually arrive with me, around midnight. The cell lights were long out by that time. The guards controlled the lights switches from outside the door. We had no control over them. They usually switched them off at around ten o'clock, though some light still shone into my cell from the outside yard perimeter lights. I had a very small remnant of a flint in a bit of pen refill and knew there was a grave danger that the flint would pop out of the refill once I'd strike it with the metal wheel from the lighter to get a spark. If that happened it would be difficult to find it in the dark. Sure enough, that's exactly what happened. I had, however, crouched down close to the floor in the corner when striking the flint so that if it did come out of the pen refill it would be confined to a small area of the floor. The problem was, the corner was particularly dark. Very little light shone into that area. I groped around slowly with my fingers and found the small piece of flint and, standing at the window, with the aid of the yard perimeter lights, was able to get the flint back into the refill. Kneeling down in the corner again I tried for the second time. And it worked! I lit my cigarette, stood up at the window, inhaled on it deeply, then blew the smoke out into the frosty air.

I can state categorically that the cigarette I had that night was the most enjoyable smoke I've ever had. Ever. The place was totally quiet. Others, including my cellmate Paddy, were asleep. It was a very still, frosty night. I stood at the window and watched the smoke as I exhaled. I felt a great sense of achievement. I was smoking a cigarette made from tobacco that someone bought on the outside, then wrapped in cling film, carried into the prison, and then smuggled to Pat. There was a lot of love, care, and commitment involved in that process. The tobacco had reached me at the bottom of the wing through various convoluted processes and collective effort. The flint had almost let me down, but there I now was, enjoying the smoke. In this way it wasn't just a smoke. It was the overcoming of many obstacles. It was a huge victory.

* * *

New Year's Eve is generally a time for celebration. People reflect upon the year just passed and look forward to the start of a new one. For us, in H4, New Year's Eve 1979 summed up for us what the year had been like and gave a glimpse of what 1980 might hold in store for us. An SO, MacIntyre, came onto our wing that night. He wasn't a

regular in the protesting Blocks but had been seen in them from time to time – and not in a good way. A small, obnoxious man, it was soon apparent that he was drunk that night. He did a tour of the wing as if he was a Governor, the guards opening cell doors for him to stick his head in. He looked at prisoners and asked some of them how they were. I watched him through the side of my door as he made his way up the other side of the wing. I could see him sway on his feet and some of those in the cells he had already visited, shouted out in Irish, '*Bí cúramach. Tá sé ar meisce*' ('Be careful. He's drunk'). He looked into my cell, didn't say anything, then moved on. Two doors away from me were Ciaran McGillicuddy from Strabane and Liam Berkery from Belfast; two of the youngest blanketmen. Ciaran was aged 15 when arrested, aged just 16 when he joined the blanket protest, and was 17 at that time. Liam was 19.

The guard opened their cell door and shortly afterwards I heard the 'bolt shoot'. A cell door lock has a 'snib' on it like an ordinary front door of a house but when the door is being closed and the snib goes into place into the frame of the door it automatically prompts a bolt to shoot out to lock the door in place. If a guard was entering a cell he, or another one with him, would first kick the snib of the open door, thus shooting the bolt out and ensuring that the door could not be accidentally locked closed behind him, trapping him in a cell with the prisoners. It was usually an ominous sign when you heard a 'bolt shoot'. A guard was going into someone's cell and that didn't bode well.

Soon afterwards I heard a commotion in the cell. Ciaran McGillicuddy wrote about the incident years later in *Nor Meekly Serve My Time*:

> When he (MacIntyre) got to our door he asked my cellmate, Liam Berkery, how he was. He didn't get an answer so in he came and hit Liam on the face. He asked him again and again how he was but he still didn't get an answer. This went on for a few minutes and then he started talking to the wall like a madman. He turned to me and asked me how I was. By this time I was really afraid but there was no way I would have answered him after what he had done to Liam. So it was my turn for a few slaps around the head. By this time he was starting to get mad because he was getting nowhere. He turned to Liam and once more asked him how he was. With this he hit Liam a punch in the face. I remember Liam's head rocking back and the blood splashing over the back wall. It was like the slow motion action on TV. At this the SO started to worry about what he had just done so he told Liam that he had fallen and hit his head on the pipe and that was how he had bust his nose. He beat him again so he would agree. He turned to me. As soon as I saw him looking at me my arms were around my head. I didn't want my nose busted but he tried his best to get at me. He kept going from Liam to me shouting, "He hit his head on the pipe!" There were three screws around the door.
>
> He turned to me, grabbed me by the hair and pulled me into the wing. He ran me up the wing. I didn't know what lay ahead. He ran me into the canteen and pushed me forward, making me fall onto the floor. I jumped up. He just kept shouting, "He hit his head on the pipe, didn't he?" He pushed me over to a table and pulled my hair back so I was bending backwards. It was so hard it brought my feet up onto the table. I rolled into a ball and he kept hitting me, more on the back as I had covered up. I could see his face and it put the fear of God into me

> because I could see that he had lost control of himself. I could also see fear in the faces of the other screws as they didn't know what would happen next. I was pulled off the table onto the floor and kicked. After about a minute a screw, who was in another wing across from us, came running into the canteen to pull him off me. The SO was like a drunk man being held back from a fight in the pub. He was shouting at me that he'd kill me. I was sent back to the cell.
>
> The next day Fr Toner was in our cell and saw the blood on the wall. Liam had a black eye and was bruised all over. Fr Toner made a protest to a Governor. We put our named down to see a doctor so he could do a body sheet. It wasn't until ten days after the beating that we got to see a doctor, nine days after we had asked to see him.
>
> We took a case against the prison Governor. A man from the NIO came to ask questions about what had happened. We refused to go out because it was the NIO who ran the H-Blocks and paid the screws extra money for the job they were doing. There was no way he would have found against the screws. When we refused to see him we were dragged from our cell by the feet along the wing into the Circle and then asked if we had a complaint to make about a beating.

That was how we began 1980. However, things began to quieten down a bit after that. There was talk in the air about a possible hunger strike as we were aware that the talks between Cardinal O'Fiaich and the Northern Ireland Office hadn't gone anywhere. Conversely, there was a rumour about some concessions being made on the clothing issue. Speculation extended to the guards who, ironically, turned to us for information. I think they began to fear that things in the Blocks were going to change, and in our favour, so even the worst of them began to behave in a less aggressive manner.

In January, 1980 the National Anti H-Block/Armagh Committee, campaigning on our behalf on the outside, formulated the 'five demands'. It was thought that the term 'political status' was too vague and that it should be broken down into something more tangible. Hence, the five demands:

1. the right to wear our own clothes
2. the right not to do prison work
3. free association with other prisoners
4. a visit, parcel and letters per week
5. the return of remission lost during the protest

There was much debate in our wing when we learned of the articulation of the five demands. Not everyone was happy with them.

Up until then I think we had all pretty much held onto the belief that getting political status would mean we would be moved to the Cages where our comrades still enjoyed that status. Political status was somehow synonymous with the Cages. It didn't occur to us that we could be held in the Blocks and have status. The Blocks were associated with the criminalisation policy. Some pointed out, however, that when political status was first introduced it applied in the Crumlin Road Prison, which was a cellular system prison unlike the Cages. And prisoners in Portlaoise had political status but were not housed in Cages but in a normal prison building. Others added that it would probably be impractical to move about 400-500 republican prisoners alone (never mind loyalists on top of that) to the Cages. There just wouldn't be enough room. Slowly, the image we had held of one day moving en masse from the Blocks to the Cages faded. There was, however, the occasional person who still thought that the five demands was a weakening of our claim to political status and one in particular said to me one day, "What about the repatriation of our comrades from English prisons? That was also part of our demands for political status." He was correct; it had once been part of our overall demand, but for most of us, some degree of pragmatism had kicked in over the intervening years. We were now much more realistic about what could, or could not, be achieved. The campaign to repatriate IRA prisoners held in prison in England would continue but was not linked to our demand for political status.

Whether it was the publication of the five demands, the rumours about a possible hunger strike or imminent concessions, another factor in the apparent reduction of systematic, casual brutality in the protesting Blocks as we moved into 1980 was the removal of a number of the worst guards. Assaults still took place but not on the same level as in 1979, the worst year by far. We took this as a sign that the NIO was moving towards some form of concessions or at least beginning to develop a political climate wherein compromises might be reached and concessions made. Another factor, however, may well have been that the prison authorities were becoming concerned by the behaviour of some of the guards, not in regards to their treatment of prisoners, but their lack of discipline and the insubordination they were by then openly displaying towards senior members of their own prison staff. On at least one occasion in H4, a Governor, on an unexpected visit to the Block, caught a guard drunk on duty. The guard wasn't at all concerned about it. Whatever the reason for the redeployment of particular guards, the period from the beginning of 1980 onwards saw a relaxation in tension in both H4 and H3; H5 had always been relatively calm, in comparison to the other Blocks.

One practical expression of that change in H4 was when Freddie Spence, a regular guard in the Block, was made Class Officer of the wing adjacent to us in early 1980. Class Officers were rotated every year or so. Spence had been working in the Block for some time and was regarded as one of Armour's henchmen – a '*fear dona*' ('bad man'). He was a heavy-set man, with a big belly, giving him an intimidating physical presence. He was a bit of a joker amongst the guards and well-liked by them. In our wing, we knew we were going to get Stevie Binx as the new Class Officer. He was considered OK: a stocky, fair-haired man, usually fairly quiet. At least he didn't have a bad reputation. Micky Fitzsimons from Lenadoon, Belfast, was the OC of the other wing and when we heard that Spence was to be made Class Officer there, we joked with Micky about how we were relieved that they were to get Spence and not us. As it turned out, however, they got the better deal. No sooner had Spence appeared on their wing than the food portions dramatically increased. Not only were the men getting the usual basic portion of fish, or pie, or whatever was on the menu but some were getting an additional half portion, or extra potatoes or veg. On the Friday of the first week that Spence had taken over, one of his close colleagues, a guard called Hassan, shouted down the wing to Spence, "Freddie, throw me out a couple of fish". Spence walked up to the grille leading out of the wing and said, "Mr Hassan, from Friday (and he said whatever date it was) you buy your own food." Hassan replied, "For fuck sake, Freddie, stop fucking around and throw me out the fish." And Spence told him, "No". Initially, I don't think Hassan believed it – it was so far from the norm – but when it did eventually sink in he said, "Fuck you, Freddie," and left.

We always suspected there was more food arriving into the Blocks than was given out to us. We knew the orderlies more than likely had double helpings of whatever they wanted but hadn't been aware that the guards also ate a lot of it. We did know, however, that some of them occasionally threw trays of food into the rubbish bins as we had witnessed it.

A few weeks after Spence had become Class Officer he was escorting Micky Fitzsimons down to the visits and although there had been little dialogue between the two of them while in the wing, Spence knew that Micky was the OC. He asked Micky if everything was going OK and Mickey said that it was, and Mickey referred to the food. Spence then asked how things were when he wasn't on duty and Micky told him that the assistant Class Officer, Ronnie Lynas (known to the blanketmen as, 'Sammy Pastie Face'), messed around with the food. Spence said nothing but the next time Spence and Lynas were working together on the wing, Spence grabbed Lynas, put him against the wall of the canteen and told him that if he ever heard about him messing about on 'his wing' that he'd 'beat the livin' daylights' out of him.

I have no idea why Spence went through this 'transformation'. It could have been that he regarded an end to our protest as imminent and thought it likely we would soon win concessions. Or it may have been that with his new position of authority he felt a sense of responsibility. Only he can answer that.

As an aside, while writing this book I checked some of the details (above) with Seamus Kearney. Seamus was also from Lenadoon, had been sentenced along with Micky Fitzsimons, and was on the same wing with him in H4. On the afternoon of the 12th July 1979, Assistant Governor Chambers entered Seamus's cell. He asked Seamus how many brothers he had and what their names and ages were. Seamus told him he had two, named Michael and Sean, and that they were twins, aged 20. Chambers replied, "Do you see the one called Michael? Well, you don't call him Michael anymore. How do you feel about that?" Later that day Seamus was taken out on a visit to meet with a local priest who told him that his brother Michael had been found dead on the border. The following day, Seamus got a special family visit with his brother Sean. He was escorted to the visit by Stevie Binx, the Class Officer from our wing, who sat between Seamus and Sean. Sean told Seamus that Michael, who was an IRA volunteer, had been discovered on the border near Newtownbutler, Co Fermanagh. He had been executed by the IRA as an informer. According to Seamus, Stevie Binx looked visibly shaken, dropped his head and shook it from side to side. He never opened his mouth. Later, when he returned from his visit, the Governor told Seamus that he would make a request of the Secretary of State, Humphrey Atkins, that Seamus be granted compassionate parole to attend the funeral – on the condition that Seamus signed a document stating that he would come off the blanket protest and conform. Seamus refused to sign and Atkins refused his request for parole.

Seamus remained on the blanket until the very end and never conformed. Binx never ever mentioned what he had heard on that visit though other guards taunted Seamus about the IRA killing of his brother for weeks afterwards. In 2003, after a protracted investigation, the IRA cleared Michael of any suggestion that he was an informer and apologised for his killing.

* * *

Royal blue plastic plates. Light blue cutlery – plastic too, of course. Funny how quickly you get used to eating with plastic cutlery from plastic plates and bowls. How normal it becomes. Humans are adaptable – we have such a capacity to adjust to new conditions, routines, and practices.

The blanket protest is largely known about today because of the 1981 hunger strike; because of ten men fasting to death. But food was something that preoccupied our minds throughout the five years of protest. Usually a lack of food, or getting cold, inedible food and dreaming of hot, tasty meals. Mealtimes were significant to us. They gave structure to our days or at least broke them up; breakfast, lunch (or dinner as it was referred to), tea, and supper. The food was cooked in the prison kitchen and then distributed to the Blocks. Depending on what direction the wind was blowing we could smell the cooking from our cells. Often it was the smell of over-boiled cabbage, not the pleasant smell of home-cooked food that whets your appetite. The cooked food was put into aluminium trays which fitted into aluminium containers that then fitted into a small upright trolley with four wheels on the bottom, allowing for easy manoeuvring on to and off the lorry that transported the food around the camp to the various Blocks. The same lorry that years later – September 1983 – was used to transport 38 IRA prisoners to the front gate of the prison in what became the largest escape ever in British penal history.[61]

---

[61] See Gerry Kelly (2013), *The Escape*, Belfast: M&G Publications, and other books. Also the 2017 film, *Maze*.

When it arrived into the individual wings the prison orderlies ladled the food onto plates and bowls and then placed those onto a long aluminium trolley. The plates sat on top of one another as there was not enough space to set them side by side. Like any 'total institution', prison or hospital, where a lot of meals have to be cooked in one place and then distributed elsewhere, the food was often already soggy and lukewarm by the time it reached the Blocks. On top of that, it depended on what cell you were in whether or not you got the food either moderately hot, cooler, or cold. If you were in cell 25, for instance, it was usually (though not always) the last cell opened. The cell doors swung open to the left and on a practical level it was handier for the guards to start at cell 3 and work their way round the wing. You stood at your door and if it was dinner you took the dinner in one hand and the dessert in the other. If you had a cellmate you usually grabbed the two dinners and he collected the desserts or vice versa. When I mention to people on the outside that we got a dessert every day in prison, even during the blanket protest, it jars with their mental image of our conditions at the time and sounds more like we were enjoying some sort of all-inclusive holiday package.

Breakfast was distributed around 8.00 to 8.30. It consisted of either porridge or cornflakes plus two rounds of white pan bread and a blob of margarine. Usually the bread was lying in the 'milk' of the cornflakes. I put 'milk' in inverted commas as the prison established its own variety of skimmed milk long before it ever became a fad on the outside. We were entitled to at least half a pint of milk each day, maybe a pint, but we never received that. When the milk arrived from the kitchen each morning several pints of it were poured into a large cylindrical aluminium container. Water was then added to top it up. So the cornflakes had watery milk in them. Either the guards or orderlies, or both, drank the extra milk.

The porridge was thick and tasteless. There was neither sugar nor salt on it and no milk, watery or otherwise. But I ate it. It was food. Some threw it onto the walls of their cell. It stuck well to the walls. In fact, trying to remove porridge that had dried onto the wall was almost impossible. It probably gave the cleaners additional hassle. Others, who didn't eat the porridge, just dumped it in the corner of their cell with any other left-over food. In this instance 'left-over' did not have quite the same meaning as it would have on the outside where you might eat your fill until you felt sated, and then have left-overs the following day. During the no-wash protest, left-over food was anything which could not be eaten because it was so tasteless and revolting.

The flies loved the pile of rubbish in the corner of the cell. They laid their eggs in it, which then turned into maggots, which then became flies and then the whole cycle began all over again. Some men claimed they could see the pile of food move if they looked closely enough, carried on the backs of dozens of maggots underneath.

The cutlery lay on the plate. The plate sat on the floor beside the door. It rested on fragments from last night's dam – the dam, removed from the floor in front of the door and placed in the corner for use again tonight. Sometimes the dam needed to be bolstered with additional bread. That meant sacrificing a round of bread, or possibly two. We got eight rounds of bread daily, the two in the morning and six more in the evening – with a square of margarine each time. The one square did not suffice for six rounds of bread so I spread it on three of the rounds and placed a dry one on each of them. There was usually some margarine left from the two rounds in the morning but you couldn't keep it until the evening as there was nowhere to place it that wasn't filthy. I stuck it to the wall, to be used at a later stage for bangling. I'd dip my finger in the margarine until my finger was well-coated and then insert it into my arse and twist it around a few times to ensure the sphincter was well-lubricated. Any remaining margarine was then used to coat the *beart*. If I didn't have enough margarine I'd spit on the *beart* for lubrication.

Maybe it was just paranoia but I often wondered if the guards and/or orderlies deliberately tried to sow discord between cellmates when distributing the food as often one plate contained more food than another. It may well have been that it was simply due to their hurry to dish up the food, or, maybe initially they were more frugal in what they ladled onto the first plates but when they got near the end of the plates they discovered they had plenty of food left so gave out more generous amounts. Either way, innocently or otherwise, you could often end up with plates with very different portion sizes. This was especially so with the dinner meal as it had mashed potatoes, or maybe stew, which had been ladled out rather than, for instance, individual items such as bacon or sausages, where everyone got the same number of portions.

This is where it was important to have a good relationship with your cellmate, or for both to act with some integrity. For instance, if my side of the cell (the side where my bed was) was on the right-hand side of the cell as you walk into it, and I collected two plates of food at the door and turned round to walk back into the cell, I could choose which plate to give to myself and which to my cellmate. If, as I walked back into the cell, with me facing the window, I set the plates down immediately, it meant that the plate in my right hand was set at the right-hand side of the cell (my side) and the other plate went to my cellmate. If, however, I walked back into the cell, walked to the window and then turned around before setting the plates down then the one in my right hand went to my cellmate and the one in my left hand to me. It all depended on whether I was facing the window or door when I set the plates down. In most cases – and if the plates held equal amounts of food – it was irrelevant what hands they were held in. But if one of the plates in my hands contained much more food than the other then it was very significant what way I was facing when I set the plates down. I could easily decide to give myself the plate with more food on it, or my cellmate could equally make such a decision.

The easiest way to resolve the issue, like most issues, was, of course, to firstly name it. We had no say over what plates of food were handed to us. It was a lottery. It may well have been that the guards and/or orderlies were trying to put the mix in and sow discord but we could decide what to do once we got the food; that is, share it out evenly. If there was more on my plate than my cellmate's then I gave him some of mine, and vice versa. Thankfully, most cellmates were on good terms with one another, though there were the odd exceptions.

'Tea', around 4.00 in the afternoon, was a smaller meal, though it came with a cup of tea and the six rounds of white pan bread. One example of tea was the 'fry', which we got once weekly. The fry consisted of one rasher of thick bacon, one piece of potato bread, and a boiled egg. They definitely didn't do the full-Irish! Willie 'Deek' Johnson, for some reason, referred to the boiled egg as the 'dreaded lady'. Why he should refer to the egg as a 'lady' and to be dreaded, was beyond me.

Supper, served any time between 6.00 and 7.00 p.m. generally, consisted of a cup of tea and a piece of cake – often the dreaded 'yellow cake', which was basically just a piece of sponge cake though often not fully baked. I ate it; it was food. Depending on the culinary likes and dislikes of my cellmate, if I had one, I ate his too. Big Doc

(Kieran Docherty who died on hunger strike) also ate it and others in the wing would send their portions down to him[62] by swinging it out the windows (at a time when we had no grilles across the windows).

On Sundays we got a salad for tea and a piece of fruit for supper. The salad contained a few slices of beetroot, a slice of cheese, and either corned beef or spam. From the time I was a child I hated cheese. I also hated tomatoes. If we were visiting relatives or neighbours and were offered sandwiches they were most often made of cheese and tomatoes. I'd try to be polite and attempt to eat one but would gag on them. In H4 I'd give the cheese to my cellmate, Paddy Quinn. That left me with the slice of corned beef and the beetroot. At some stage, however, I began to imagine that I could eat the cheese if it was mixed with the beetroot. The beetroot would change the taste of it and make it more palatable, whereas, for instance, the cheese and corned beef or spam would not taste quite so good. When I announced to Paddy one Sunday that I was going to eat the cheese he tried his best not to show his disappointment. A substantial portion of his Sunday tea had just disappeared off his plate. And I found the cheese with beetroot quite tasty.

Even though days of the week should not have made any difference to us in our situation, Sundays always seemed particularly dismal and depressing and they certainly were not helped by the salad. If it was the middle of winter, cold or raining, the salad was really fucking depressing. And then to get an apple or orange later for supper rather than a piece of cake just added to the torment. The last meal Bobby Sands got, on the Sunday night before he began his hunger strike, was an orange. "I ate the statutory weekly bit of fruit last night. As fate had it, it was an orange, and the final irony, it was bitter."[63]

It was in relation to food in the prison that I learned how to hate. I don't think I'd ever really hated anyone or anything in life before then. Thoroughly dislike, maybe, but not really hate. I vividly recall the moment I began to hate; it was in H4. It was one guard, Peter Ward, who prompted this emotion in me. Ward was an average guy, mid-40s probably, red wavy hair combed back, not that tall, with a slim build.

---

[62] Brian Campbell , Laurence McKeown , and Felim O'Hagan (eds.) (1994), *Nor Meekly Serve My Time: The H-Block Struggle 1976-1981*, Belfast: Beyond the Pale, pp. 77-78.

[63] Bobby Sands (1981), *The Diary of Bobby Sands*, Dublin: Sinn Féin Publicity Department.

In other words, pretty insignificant, certainly in terms of physique. But my experience during the protest, was that it was never about physical size. The guards had the numbers on their side, and the opportunity, so even the most physically-challenged amongst them had the opportunity to be brutal. But there were also many others, as was the case with Parkinson in H6, who had a propensity toward pettiness, rather than brutality. Peter Ward was one of them. I don't recall him ever thumping me, even over the mirror search. In fact, I don't think he ever laid a finger on me throughout the entire period that we interacted during the protest years.

The day, or precise moment, that he prompted me to hate was when the wing orderlies set out the dinner onto the trolley. Paddy and I were at the top of the wing in cell 25, closest to the canteen. We could smell the food and knew it was stew. We liked to get stew as it was usually warm and tasty and you could mix it in with the two mashed potatoes that came with it. It was baked with a crust on top which was also nice. But when the orderlies wheeled the trolley out of the canteen, ready to go around the cells, Ward told them to stop and ordered them to leave it sitting. He said out loud to them, (probably deliberately for us to overhear), "It's too hot yet. Don't want the Provies burning their mouths." The orderlies did as they were told and parked the trolley outside our cell. The food sat there, on the trolley, outside our cell door for about 15-20 minutes and it was during that relatively short period of time that I learned how to hate. I could smell the food. I could see the food out the side of my door, sitting there on the trolley. Sitting getting cold. And I hated Ward for it.

It was the pettiness of it that got me. The deliberate pettiness. But like the withholding of letters from family and loved ones, it was also sadistic. It was done simply because Ward had the power to do it.

It was a good lesson for me, in one way. To identify pettiness. To identify power and the abuse of power and never in later life to use power in such a manner.

Years later, after the hunger strike, when we were attempting to build amicable relations with the guards[64] and thus make our lives as relaxed as possible in the Blocks, Peter Ward ended up as a regular guard in my wing. I think I was OC of the Block at the time but even

---

[64] This had worked especially well in the lead up to the escape in 1983.

if I wasn't, our policy (which I totally agreed with) was very clear; we were not to allow past antagonisms, especially from the period of the protest, to influence our behaviour and attitudes to the guards now. In general, I didn't have a problem engaging with those guards who I occasionally came across from the protest years. Not so in regards to Peter Ward. I had a huge mental and emotional blockage regarding him. I just had to look at him, or hear him speak, and the past flooded back to me in a very visceral manner. I knew I shouldn't and couldn't act on those feelings and also knew that I had to deal with the emotions I felt, rather than just bury them. I realised too that there was an evident tension when the two of us were in the same close physical space and that others had become aware of that. I knew he was certainly very much aware of the tension and was no doubt anxious about the situation. We were no longer on protest and behind closed doors. There was up to 40 men housed on the wing and at times practically all 40 of us were on the wing at the one time. There were only 3 or 4 guards. The power dynamic had shifted, dramatically.

I thought about the situation. I went over in my head, time and time again, that specific moment those years previous when the trolley of food had sat outside my door. I could smell the food, until I could no longer smell it as it had grown cold. And I could recall eating it, cold.

I relived that image several times in my head and allowed myself to experience all the emotions that came with it. And then I planned how I would orchestrate a situation that would allow me and Peter Ward to speak to one another.

As it turned out, I didn't need to orchestrate a situation. A few days later I was due to get a visit. The practice was that your name would be shouted from the Circle of the Block. The guard between the wings would then shout down to the guard in the specific wing where the prisoner was, and finally a guard on the wing would shout down the wing to the prisoner. I could hear my name called from the Circle and, shortly afterwards, Peter Ward shouted down the wing, "McKeown for a visit". I psyched myself, stepped out of my cell, and shouted down the wing, "Peter, was that me called for a visit?" (I deliberately addressed him by his first name.) He walked towards me and said, "Yes, Laurence. That's you, Laurence," (repeating my first name). I said, "No problem. Be there in a moment." I walked down the wing a few moments later, he unlocked the grille for me, smiled and nodded at me and I responded likewise. That was the ice broken; and the past put where it belonged – in the past. I've always found it amazing the difference it makes if you address someone by their first name – or they address you in that manner. If you smile, stretch out your hand to shake hands, offer them a seat, a coffee, a cup of tea. Just very basic, simple human gestures of civility that can have such a profound effect.

I'm sure it was difficult for Peter too. It's been difficult for all of us to forever live with tragic and horrific events that are still very fresh in our minds but not allow those events to shape our thinking and behaviour today. Going through that process of engaging with him was liberating for me. I had acknowledged how I felt but understood that the emotion belonged to the past. It wasn't happening to me now. The food wasn't sitting cold outside my cell. I now ate my food in a canteen surrounded by the laughter and chat of comrades and friends. And the food was hot.

# 9
# Promises Promises

AFTER FOUR YEARS of the blanket protest it was very obvious that it was taking its toll on people. Some had left it as a result of physical or mental ill-health, family pressures, or simply through losing hope and thus their commitment. Hope was what we clung to. Even if it was irrational and offered nothing concrete, it was something to help us through each day. I often thought that if you were to wake up one morning and find that hope had vanished then it would truly feel that you were living in a hellhole: walls covered in shit, rotten food in the corner, barefoot, bearded and unwashed. And having been in that state day after day, week after week, month after month, year after year.

I had hoped that something would have come from the contact between Cardinal Ó'Fiaich and the NIO. That hope, again. Not the sort of wild hopes I once had – my experience during the intervening years had knocked a lot of naïve notions out of me – but, nevertheless, I still held on to a hope that something might yet materialise. I also hoped that the actions of the National Anti-H-Block/Armagh Committee on the outside would bring enough international pressure to bear on the Brits to move them.

In the latter part of 1980 we received word from Cardinal Ó'Fiaich's office that we were to be allowed our own clothing. This was not confirmed, though undoubtedly the Cardinal was of the firm belief that it was to happen. This would have been a huge development. However, following a meeting between the Cardinal and Thatcher, the NIO announced that a new form of prison clothing was to be introduced – 'civilian-style' clothing. It would still be a prison uniform but not of the black denim sort. There would be a choice of several colours of jumpers, shirts, and trousers. Prisoners on protest would also be permitted one extra visit per month. This in no way came anywhere near meeting our demands. For all intents and purposes the Cardinal had been hoodwinked.

Looking back on it, the Brits were never going to respond to appeals by the Cardinal (and others) for humanitarian gestures and nor were they going to acquiesce to demands from street protests or from international pressure. Their policy of criminalisation was an integral part of their comprehensive counter-insurgency strategy – and they were intent on forcing it home, regardless of what others thought. It was in this context that the decision was taken to commence a hunger strike. Fifteen years later I interviewed Brendan Hughes (who, as camp OC, made the decision for a hunger strike) for my doctoral thesis. He revealed just how personally he took the whole protest and the pressure he felt to achieve a result. He accepted that his approach to the situation may possibly have been egotistical or even chauvinistic:

> By 1980 I reckoned we had done enough. I felt that we had asked people to go as far as we could ask anyone to go. That was when the decision to hunger strike was made. I was advised against it but didn't think there was any other way we could go.
>
> I felt pressure from others to decide upon a hunger strike, very much so. Something I did which was very possibly wrong was that I took it personally, the whole blanket thing and I probably had no right to do that but I did. It was a personal thing for me to get the thing over with, to end it, be it hunger strike or whatever. People had left, OCs had left and to me a lot of the people there were kids. Now they weren't kids. I was only 5-10 years older than most of them, but to me they needed this. Maybe that's egotistical or chauvinistic or whatever but I felt this personal need to get the status back.
>
> The loneliest time of my life was walking back from a visit on the day Danny Morrison came and told me that there was nothing coming of the O'Fiaich talks. Thatcher had shut them down. The Cardinal was so shattered he couldn't come and tell me himself. I thought, 'Jesus, where do you go from here?'. That was the loneliest walk I ever had because I knew the only option left was hunger strike. The decision was made and I remember sitting talking to Bobby (Sands) about what strategy we would use. For a while it was like a big black hole and no light at the end of the tunnel until the decision to hunger strike was made and then a bit of light appeared. I don't know if that was the same for anyone else but for me I felt, 'Here goes, this is going to end it'.[65]

[65] Laurence McKeown (2001), *Out of Time*, Belfast: Beyond the Pale, p. 73.

That decision to initiate a hunger strike was not arrived at easily and only came after four years of intense protest. It was advised against by the leadership on the outside who conceded, however, that they had no other option to offer. Each prisoner then had to weigh up whether or not they should or could volunteer to join a hunger strike. I began to consider seriously my own willingness to participate in a hunger strike but I think I knew my position already. I knew I would volunteer. I believed in the strategy; believed it was going to take pressure of that nature to make the Brits move. As such, I felt I should be prepared to be on it. I knew that if we embarked upon a hunger strike it was a do-or-die effort. All that had taken place over the previous four years was at stake. It had to succeed.

I was still in H4 when I put my name forward for the hunger strike. Leo Green was the Block OC. He spoke to me about the seriousness of what was being proposed and asked if I was sure I wanted to go ahead with it. I said I was.

Not all blanketmen were in favour of a hunger strike. Some were certain that men would die on it and therefore felt it was preferable to continue indefinitely with the protest rather than take this step. That view was very much a minority one, however. By 1980, everyone wanted an end to the protest, one way or the other. We had endured four long, hard, brutal years. Years waiting, depending on others, hoping they could somehow resolve our situation. Now it was down to us to do it. A hunger strike would bring it all to an end and we never doubted that it would be a successful end. It had to be.

Eventually, seven prisoners were chosen to take part in the hunger strike: Brendan Hughes, Leo Green, Tommy McKearney, Tom McFeeley, John Nixon, Seán McKenna and Raymond McCartney. The decision for seven was influenced to some degree by the historical significance in republican terms of the seven signatories to the 1916 Proclamation. However, on a more practical level, it was also a large enough number to provide for a good geographical spread. Five of the six northern counties were represented, Fermanagh being the only exception.

On 10 October 1980, Sinn Féin announced that a hunger strike would commence on 27 October and we, the prisoners, released the following statement:

We, the Republican Prisoners of War in the H-Blocks, Long Kesh, demand as a right, political recognition and that we be accorded the status of political prisoners. We claim this right as captured combatants in the continuing struggle for national liberation and self-determination.

We refute most strongly the tag of 'criminal' with which the British have attempted to label us and our struggle, and we point to a divisive partitionist institution of the six counties as the sole criminal aspect of the present struggle.

All of us were arrested under repressive laws, interrogated and often tortured in RUC barracks and processed through special non-jury courts where we were sentenced to lengthy terms of imprisonment. After this, men were put in the H-Blocks and were expected to bow the knee before the British administration and wear their criminal uniform. Attempts to criminalise us were designed to depoliticise the Irish national struggle.

We don't have to recite again the widespread, almost total forms of punishment, degradation and deprivation we have been subject to. All have failed to break our resistance.

For the past four years, we have endured brutality in deplorable conditions – we have been stripped naked and robbed of our individuality, yet we refuse to be broken. Further repression only serves to strengthen our resolve and that of our female comrades enduring the same hardship in Armagh jail.

During this period many individuals, religious figures, political organisations and sections of the media, have condemned the way in which we have been treated. Yet, despite appeals for a resolution of the H-Block protest, the British government has remained intransigent and displayed vindictive arrogance in dealing with the problem. They refuse to treat this issue in a realistic manner, which is just another reflection of their attitude to the entire Irish question.

Bearing in mind the serious implications of our final step, not only for us but for our people, we wish to make it clear that every channel has now been exhausted and not wishing to break faith with those from whom we have inherited our principles, we now commit ourselves to a hunger strike.

We call on the Irish people to lend us their support for our just demands and we are confident that this support will be very much in evidence in the coming days.

We call on all solidarity and support groups to intensify their efforts and we also look forward with full confidence to the support of our exiled countrymen in America and Australia and throughout the world.

We declare that political status is ours of right and we declare that from Monday 27 October, 1980, a hunger strike by a number of men representing H-Blocks 3, 4 and 5 will commence.

> Our widely recognised resistance has carried us through four years of immense suffering and it shall carry us through to the bitter climax of death, if necessary.

In the years prior to the hunger strike, we had all written the occasional smuggled letter (comms) to the outside calling on people to support our demands. With the announcement of the hunger strike a major letter-writing campaign was put into action: to GAA and other clubs, schools and teachers, factories, Trade Unions, journalists, artists, singers, musicians, film stars and just about anyone we could think of. And not just in Ireland but abroad too: England, Europe, the USA, Canada and Australia. Some of us in the wing would write up a draft letter that others could copy or adapt, depending on who they were sending it to.

The letters were written on prison toilet roll, or on cigarette papers, and smuggled out on our visits with family or friends. We'd request that the letters be forwarded to those they were addressed to, or else given to someone in Sinn Féin so that they could be photocopied and enlarged, as the letters were very small in their original form. The writing was miniscule. There was often a competition between prisoners to see how many words they could get onto a single cigarette paper, while still being legible. That is, legible to us writing them, but maybe not so for those reading them!

I still have a few samples of such letters; one I wrote to be published in the *Mid-Ulster Observer* in 1980 just after the first hunger strike started, and another one, from 1981, which I signed under the name of another prisoner, Seamus McElhone from South Derry, who was in my wing at the time.[66] Some of us wrote more letters than others and rather than have our own name signed on each of them we'd use the names of other prisoners. I found the comms amongst a number of items that my mother had retained from the protest. Her possession of them shows that they were never forwarded (unless a photocopy was forwarded) to their destinations but it's good to have them for posterity. I'm amazed that not only did we know at the time that there was such an entity as 'BBC Radio Derby' (the one that the Seamus letter was addressed to) but that we also had the address of the station! And I'm also delighted today when I meet

---

[66] See photographs.

someone who tells me they received one of those letters all those years ago, whether from me or some other prisoner.

Although the guards captured an occasional comm there was a virtual river of communication in and out of the Blocks, as well as between Blocks. Bobby Sands could, in theory, send out a comm to the Army Council in the morning and get an answer back that afternoon, so sophisticated was the communication process – operationalised almost in its entirety by women: wives, partners, sisters and others who volunteered to assist in facilitating the communication network.

With the announcement of the hunger strike several dozen prisoners, possibly up to 40, who had left the blanket protest, returned. This was a morale boost to us and they were welcomed back. Probably as a direct result of the increased numbers H6 was reopened and our wing was moved there. This time the regime in H6 was different from what we had previously experienced in 1979. Parkinson was no longer there and gone also were the miniature bowls we once associated with him – which may confirm my suspicions that he had personally purchased them.

I ended up sharing a cell with Anthony McIntyre while in H6 and it was through Anthony that I met Deirdre McManus. Deirdre was a friend of Anne Marie Quinn who was a prisoner in Armagh Jail. Anthony, at the time, was writing to Anne Marie and Deirdre would visit both of them and help exchange comms between them. Given that the NIO now allowed us an extra visit each month Bobby Sands asked us all to 'donate' that visit for the purpose of communications. Anthony suggested that I send out a visit for Deirdre and that way not only would it assist his personal communication with Anne Marie but our (Republican Movement) communication network in general. I agreed, and Deirdre arrived up on a visit. It was the first time during the entire protest that I had a visit with someone who was neither family nor a close friend. Imagine, the first time I'd had a visit with a young woman and I'd been on the no-wash protest for over two and a half years! I felt very awkward. But something obviously worked. Years later we became partners and went on to have two daughters, Caoilfhionn, born in September 1996 – a gift for my 40th birthday! – and Órlaith, born in 1998.

Given that the hunger strike began on 27 October, those on it were going to be in a critical state in the run-up to Christmas. On 1 December, they were joined by three women prisoners in Armagh Jail – Mairéad Farrell, Mary Doyle, and Mairéad Nugent. There had been much debate about women prisoners joining the hunger strike for some weeks before the men commenced their fast and very mixed views were expressed. These ranged from, how it would be a great idea to have women on hunger strike – as it would rally even more support by touching a very emotional chord – to those who were totally opposed to the suggestion of women on hunger strike. No doubt some of the latter opinions were flavoured by a dose of sexism but I'm sure they also reflected a genuine sense of caring. One big practical issue that was raised, however, was that, according to prison rules, women prisoners were already permitted to wear their own clothes – whereas we weren't – so it would be easier for the British government to make some minor concessions on our five demands (regarding the definition of prison work, for example) if a woman on hunger strike reached a critical stage before any men did, thus dividing the situation in the women's Armagh Prison from ours in the H-Blocks. The 'compromise' reached was that the three women join the hunger strike some weeks after the men commenced it.

As the hunger strike progressed, the mood in the Blocks began to change. The guards were now really unsure of just what was going to happen. Our hopes were high. Our confidence was high. We felt that we were in the final phase of our struggle. This was it: the last battle.

On 15 December, 30 additional blanketmen joined the hunger strike. Anthony and I were among the 30. Adding the extra numbers to the hunger strike at that stage was mainly about getting publicity. By that time, the original seven had been on hunger strike for 50 days and one of them, Seán McKenna, was deteriorating fast.

On the night of Thursday 18 December, shortly after lock-up (8.30 p.m.), I heard the grilles at the top of the wing being opened and then footsteps approaching. The footsteps stopped outside my door and a key was inserted into the lock. My cell door opened and Bobby Sands stepped in. He was out of breath and appeared excited or agitated. He was looking for Pat 'Beag' – Pat McGeown – who was OC of H6 at the time, but the guards had brought him to me by mistake. Bobby said, "It's over, the *stailc's criochnaithe* (the hunger strike's ended). It's OK, the boys are OK." He appeared exhausted, as no doubt he was with all the responsibilities he shouldered throughout that period, and with the number of people he had to visit that night to carry the news about the end of the fast. We asked him what the craic was but he just repeated, "It's over," and asked which cell Pat Beag was in. He left then, and spent a few minutes with Pat.

Other men in the wing were shouting out, asking what was going on. It was unusual for a cell door to be opened at night and it often was an ominous sign. I shouted out in Irish that it was Bobby and that the *stailc* was over. There was some cheering. When Bobby left the wing Pat Beag got up to his door to speak. He said Bobby would arrange to meet with all the Block OCs the next day to update them on developments.

There was much discussion out the windows the rest of the night. Speculation was rife as to how exactly the *stailc* had ended and what we had achieved. There was a reluctance to become too excited. Years of protest had made us cynical about the Brits and the manoeuvres they would make. This feeling was strengthened by radio reports later that night saying simply that republicans had 'called off the hunger strike'. No reference was made to a 'negotiated end' or compromise. Unease began to grow. However, we also realised that the Brits would not want to publicly concede defeat so we considered the possibility that what was playing out on the airwaves was simply an exercise in media manipulation.[67]

The following morning Pat Beag was taken to see Bobby in H3. With his departure the speculation again began in earnest. The administration was facilitating the meeting of Block OCs so we guessed something definite in terms of our demands must have been thrashed out. We were aware that previously Bobby had been allowed up to the prison hospital to see the hunger strikers any time he wanted – he just had to request a van and it was there. He regularly met and spoke with Governors about the situation. This reality contradicted the many NIO statements at the time proclaiming a policy of not

---

[67] The women on hunger strike in Armagh Prison did not end their fast until the morning of 19 December and only following a visit with Danny Morrison, Publicity Director for Sinn Féin, confirming for them that the hunger strike in the H-Blocks had ended.

recognising prisoners' self-appointed leaders. We were expecting a clear outcome from the meeting.

When Pat Beag returned from H3 he confirmed that all the Block OCs had been in attendance. Bobby told them about a document the Brits had presented to the hunger strikers the previous evening and upon examination of this it was considered to fulfil our five demands. The document was to be further discussed and details thrashed out, but on the basis of what was on offer the hunger strike had been called off as Seán McKenna was in a critical state by that time. Bobby had been called to the hospital and informed of that development. He had then gone around the Blocks informing the lads – as we knew from his visit to us the previous evening – and then later that night he had revisited the hospital for a talk with the hunger strikers.

It was then that the first doubts about our situation began to emerge. In recounting this chain of events to us, Pat Beag had made no reference to specifics, no talk about what was going to happen immediately. We were still on the blanket. We were still on the no-wash protest. We were still putting shit on the walls. Pat Beag was having difficulty in explaining that. A blanketman returned later that day from a visit and told us of a victory march being organised for West Belfast that following Sunday. Victory? I wasn't so sure.

My growing sense of unease was added to the following morning. Our cell door opened early though it wasn't yet time for breakfast. A tall broad-shouldered man in a suit took one step inside and said, "This is a copy of the statement made by the Secretary of State yesterday in the House of Commons". He dropped a leaflet onto the floor and then stepped out again. The guard with him turned to us before closing the door and said, "If youse can wash shortly we'll get youse moved over to a clean wing and see about getting you some furniture." The words on the tip of my tongue were, "Fuck you and your clean wing and your furniture". But they were left unspoken.

That was the first morning of what I consider to be my worst period of imprisonment; worst because of the uncertainty surrounding the ending of the hunger strike and not knowing what exactly had been agreed upon or what was going to happen now. Worse still was the air of confidence that the guards now had. Their demeanour didn't give the impression that we had won something substantial, if anything at all.

Pat Beag attended several more meetings over the next couple of days. With the feedback from each one the position became clearer – if you read between the lines. Some who were doing that reading began to put these questions directly to Pat. He didn't have answers to them. In fact, he was in an impossible position of agreeing with the inference in the questions but having to give answers which suggested a more positive outlook. Dialogue was ongoing, he said, between Bobby and the No.1 Governor and NIO officials.

At this stage, given what I saw happening, coupled with what we were hearing on the radio, I began to view the situation as very bleak though I was still very reluctant to openly voice that opinion or even accept that it was indeed our situation. That ominous feeling was further strengthened when the administration ended meetings between Bobby and the Block OCs. Some of the guards now began to openly voice their opinion to us that, "Youse got nothing". This, in particular, made us feel very demoralised. Our struggle through the blanket and no-wash protest, culminating in the hunger strike was, on a day-to-day practical level, more waged against individual guards than Thatcher or the British government or the NIO. The guard in the wing was the personification of the enemy – and a much more personalised one. The hunger strike which was to defeat him had apparently not achieved its purpose. And he was now gloating about that.

All the hopes which had been built for an end to the protest and victory for our demands were now dashed. It was about more than the 53 days of the hunger strike that we had waited and hoped for victory. It was about more than the four years of protest, the four years of being confined to a cell, no books, no exercise, no TV, magazines, washing facilities, clothes, adequate food and the many other smaller but no less important aspects of life we normally take for granted. It was about more than four years of daily, casual brutality. The hunger strike was meant to end all of it. Our hopes had been pinned on it. The victory would not only have been the change in our material living conditions but also an important psychological victory over the guards. And it hadn't happened.

On the night of 18 December 1980, Bobby Sands returned to his wing in H3 after his second visit to the hunger strikers that night. He had with him the 30-page document that the prison authorities had given to the hunger strikers. According to those in the wing with him, he regarded the document as something that could have formed the foundation of talks and negotiations *if* the hunger strike had still been ongoing but now that it had ended there was no pressure on the British government to progress any such negotiations. However, Bobby was still open to looking at all options to facilitate a forward step, even if he was also, by that time, already firmly of the view that another hunger strike was most likely inevitable.

Some of our lads, strangely enough, still thought that things were OK and that soon the whole situation would be resolved. Maybe it was just that blind hope again – or an unwavering faith. I felt anger at what the Brits had done but also realised that they had played a very shrewd game. By presenting those on hunger strike with a document which appeared to cater for a resolution to our demands, and agreeing to thrash out the details later, they had created a moral dilemma. Should you delay agreement in order to secure the details of the document (but in doing so risk the life of a comrade who was deteriorating quickly and could die at any moment), or should you trust in the sincerity of the immediate offer and save a comrade.

The 'victory march' went ahead up the Falls Road on Sunday 21 December (republicans can always put a spin on defeat) and this added to our confusion as we were still sitting in our cells with no clear idea of what was happening. And it was more than confusion: it was a mixture of anger, frustration, and, in some cases, despair. As far at the British government was concerned, the hunger strike was over and they had conceded nothing. Their (understandable) belief was that republicans 'had played their last card' – as Margaret Thatcher was reported to have said. They, the Brits, had held their nerve and the prisoners had shown that they would not hunger strike to the death.

The Brits probably never imagined for one moment that we would embark upon a second hunger strike. So why should they bother to make any concessions now? The hunger strike was over. The protest was probably over too, or else destined to slowly fizzle out in disillusionment and dissent amongst the prisoners. The government and the prison authorities could live easily with that. They had won.

Danny Morrison, writing in 2011, recalls that period and how the Republican Movement on the outside responded to the abrupt and unexpected ending of the hunger strike:

> Although it is now well-known that Brendan Hughes ended the hunger strike unilaterally, without consulting his O/C Bobby Sands, we on the outside finessed the sequence of events for the sake of morale and at a midnight press conference merged the secret arrival of a British government document (promising a more enlightened prison regime: falsely, as it turned out) with the ending of the hunger strike.
>
> It was either that or admit – which to the republican base was inconceivable – that Brendan had ended the strike without getting a thing.
>
> Bobby – who turned out to be right – did not believe the British had any intention of working the unsecured promises contained in the document. But we begged him to put them to the test and that if the administration made things impossible then it could be claimed that the Brits were reneging.
>
> Had the British taken the opportunity to resolve the prison crisis at that juncture history certainly would have been different. Instead, the British crowed victory in their briefings to the press and the prison administration felt smug, unbridled and under no obligation.
>
> This bitter experience was to sear itself in the minds of the prisoners who were determined that there would never be a repeat of that scenario.
>
> Tragically, the stage was set for 1981.[68]

It's interesting, in itself, that it was 31 years from the ending of the 1980 hunger strike before a prominent member of the leadership of the Republican Movement at that time could accurately state what exactly happened on the evening of 18 December 1980, though I can fully concur with the reasons for doing so. "It was either that or admit – which to the republican base was inconceivable – that Brendan had ended the strike without getting a thing."

In the days and weeks following the ending of the hunger strike, Bobby contacted all the Block OCs to get feedback on the mood of the prisoners. He had already received comms from several individual prisoners seeking clarification on the situation and some threatening to go on hunger strike themselves immediately. There was confusion and anger but there was also a fear; a fear that maybe this was it, that this was the end to over four years of intense protest with absolutely nothing to show for it. Some blanketmen did think that; thought that we would just have to concede defeat. A large number of those who had returned to the protest for the duration of the hunger strike had

[68] Danny Morrison, 'The Tragedy of 1980', *Andersonstown News*, 3 Jan 2011.

already begun to leave, realising that the situation was no different from the time, several months previous, when they'd returned. That didn't concern me so much. I had been glad to see them return as it had bolstered our numbers for a while, but at the end of the day it wasn't simply about numbers on the protest that was going to win our demands but the resolve to see our struggle through to a successful conclusion. I knew that was how the majority of men felt. We had been through too much to accept that we had gained nothing.

Bobby set about strategising. Before embarking on a hunger strike he wanted to explore all options first. He knew better than anyone that a new hunger strike would certainly end in death as this time the British government would need to get their 'pound of flesh'[69] and see that we were serious about dying.

He decided that two wings, his own wing in H3 and another one in H5, would go off the no-wash protest. They would ask for clean accommodation and furniture. They would also seek to get pyjamas or football outfits to wear – anything other than the prison uniform. Ten men in each wing would also say that they were prepared to do prison work but that it should be of a vocational nature or as orderlies in the wing maintaining their own accommodation, giving out meals etc. Séanna Walsh, Camp Vice-OC, was in contact with Bobby at the time and he summed up Bobby's thinking about the tactic:

> In the immediate aftermath of the first hunger strike Bobby was adamant that there was no other way but another hunger strike. But after the initial few days Bobby began to believe that he might be able to salvage enough to allow us to create an acceptable ambience to do our wack. Most important of all was the issue of access to our own clothes, so the idea was hatched whereby instead of us agreeing to conform for 30 days after which we would be entitled to our own clothes (this was a device by which the administration tried to make us eat dirt and to allow them to claim outright victory), Bobby was working on a scheme whereby all protest would end on a given date. Due to our physical state after four years of blanket protest we would 'go on the sick' but use toilets and washing facilities and be issued with prison pyjamas and bedroom slippers. After 30 days we would get our own clothes (so many

[69] It's interesting that the phrase comes from William Shakespeare's play, *The Merchant of Venice*. The character Portia says this line on the insistence of Shylock, the Jew, for the payment of Antonio's flesh, which is a central point of the play.

> each day) and take up orderly duties in the wings, and we'd go on to develop it from there. Bobby really believed at one stage that this would work and thus avoid the tragedy which was to be an inevitable consequence of a second hunger strike.[70]

On a pre-arranged date, the two wings went ahead with the instructions. Men washed and shaved and had haircuts and were moved into a clean wing. Hilditch, the No. 1 Governor of the prison, who had been on holidays, cut short his break and returned to personally take over the situation. Hilditch was a born-again Christian and out-and-out unionist. Besides his general hostility towards republicans he also had a very personal connection to the situation. His Deputy Governor Myles had been shot dead by the IRA in 1978.

Hilditch arrived back in the prison and immediately assumed control. Prior to his arrival, other Assistant Governors and senior prison staff seemed to be willing to explore with Bobby how things could move forward. It was a totally new situation for everyone. With Hilditch's return, all that ended. He made it very clear to Bobby that there would be no changes whatsoever to the prison regime which all other prisoners experienced. There would be no concessions or 'wiggle room'. There would be total conformity – the wearing of prison uniform and doing prison work – and then we would have the same entitlements (exercise, shop facilities, access to education, etc.) that any conforming prisoner had.

Bobby had tried his best. He had explored every option. Maybe the NIO and prison authorities took that as a sign of weakness, the fact that he was willing to discuss potential options that would remove us from a state of protest into some form of conformity within the context of the prison rules and in line with what had been at least hinted at in the document given to him on that night of 18 December.

While writing this memoir, and thinking back to that particular moment, I thought there were many similarities to when Martin McGuinness resigned as Deputy First Minister from the Stormont Assembly in January 2017. Martin had, in my opinion, up to that point, bent over backwards to keep the Assembly up and running with the participation of Sinn Féin but eventually he had to acknowledge that all his efforts were in vain. The DUP were not prepared to play their part and indeed had become increasingly arrogant in their displays of

---

[70] *Nor Meekly Serve My Time*, p. 145.

non-cooperation. Arlene Foster's comment, "If you feed a crocodile it will keep coming back for more," was probably the most contemptuous indicator of how she and the DUP regarded Sinn Féin and their electorate. I think the DUP mistook good manners for weakness; mistook an attempt to find a solution as a willingness to accept anything. They learned the hard way. Martin resigned, and the Assembly collapsed. I don't think the DUP ever envisaged that. So too, in regards to the H-Blocks and blanket protest. I think the NIO and the prison authorities, in their arrogance, regarded Bobby's willingness to explore alternative options, as a weakness. I don't believe they ever envisaged the second hunger strike. They too were soon to receive a rude awakening.

With diplomacy exhausted, Bobby gave the order for those in the two wings that had washed to smash up their cells. They did that, the guards ran in, beat them, and dragged them two at a time to another wing that was in the process of being washed. The following day both wings were moved to H6 where I was.

Thus ended a period of confusion and of hopes raised only to be dashed. We now knew exactly where we stood. Bobby circulated a comm shortly afterwards announcing that there would be a new hunger strike. He outlined the various attempts he had made to try and resolve the deadlock and detailed the manner in which we had been arrogantly rebuked at every turn. It may sound strange to the outsider but I was delighted that we would be embarking on a second hunger strike. We weren't beaten. The H-Blocks would never become Britain's 'Breakers Yard'. We, the blanketmen, were once more back on the offensive.

With the announcement of another hunger strike, however, came the cold realisation that this time men would definitely die, and I knew that Bobby would be the first among them as he said he would be leading the *stailc*. When he asked for volunteers I put my name forward immediately. I had already considered all the arguments prior to the first hunger strike and given that one factor in the selection of men for the first *stailc* had been geographical spread, it appeared at one stage that I could very possibly be a candidate, if such a factor was still being considered. I had, therefore, already considered the possibilities very strongly and assessed my own commitment. I felt I could go through with it and felt I wanted to do it. I believed, prior to the 1980 hunger

strike, that the blanket and no-wash protest had peaked and that it required a hunger strike to bring things to a head. I felt no differently in the lead up to the second hunger strike.

Bobby's comm also proposed that we would end the no-wash protest on 2 March 1981, the day after he would commence his hunger strike. I was opposed to that. I thought that this would come across as a weakening of our position and that it would seem as if we were 'selling out' Bobby just as soon as he began his fast. We debated it out the door and I was very emotional in my protest against ending it and the majority view expressed in our wing was similar. This differed from other wings and Blocks who, I later discovered, thought it was a good idea.

Bobby's reason for ending the no-wash protest was that it had outlived its usefulness and was actually confusing the situation in peoples' minds on the outside. The NIO and prison authorities were regularly able to say that if we gave up our protest we would be moved to clean accommodation and get furniture and access to other facilities which, of course for us, was not the issue at all. Ending the no-wash protest would get rid of that confusion but more importantly (and I don't know if Bobby had this in mind at the time) it would move us to a position from where it would be easier to further advance if the hunger strike did not produce the desired results. We had learned from what happened at the end of the first hunger strike where we had been left still smearing our shite on the walls. No one wanted to contemplate that at the end of this hunger strike we'd still not have achieved our demands but it was best to plan for all possible outcomes. However it would eventually work out, the no-wash protest was over and, one way or another, the blanket protest would end with the ending of the hunger strike – however that end looked.

That understanding came later, however. What won me over to accepting the proposal at the time was that it was Bobby who was putting it forward and it was also him who was leading the hunger strike. There was therefore no argument against it. I have often looked back on it and taken lessons from it. It taught me to look outside of my immediate conditions and circumstances and resist getting emotionally tied to particular tactics or to carry on with a particular course of action for no other reason than it's familiarity.

As we moved towards the commencement of the second hunger strike, a fuller picture began to emerge of what exactly had happened on 18 December, the ending of the first hunger strike. Word began to circulate slowly around the Blocks from those who were in Bobby's wing that night. When he had first arrived back from the prison hospital he had stated openly that there would be another hunger strike. It also came out that he'd had a blazing row with Brendan Hughes when he had met him in the prison hospital – Brendan having called off the hunger strike and instructed the prison guards to feed Seán McKenna.

In the interview I had with Brendan in later years he had this to say about those final days before the end of the 1980 hunger strike:

> Round about fifty days into the strike an approach was made to us by civil servants. We were all there. Seán McKenna was there in a wheelchair. They put this proposal to us and I remember talking to Tom McFeeley about it and him saying that it was a Portlaoise-type agreement.[71] I asked him what that was like and he said it was OK. We sort of agreed on that but we wanted someone from the outside to write it down and we were holding off for that. The hunger strike could have been called off then except that the prison authorities would not agree to an outside party coming in and putting their names to it.
>
> Over the next couple of days that was the way it was lying. Sean was getting worse by this stage and one day they came in to take him out to the outside hospital and as they were wheeling him up the corridor I shouted, "Feed him". I had been going in to see him the days previously. He had been going in and out of coma and I promised him I wouldn't let him die. I held his hand and promised him and that's why I shouted up the wing and even then I wasn't even sure if he was going to survive or not and once I had made that decision it was a case of going back and trying to grab that Portlaoise-type agreement and we all know what happened after that. We didn't get it.[72]

Whilst there is a humanity in what Brendan did – not letting Seán die – he had no authority to do it. Neither did he have any authority to promise Seán days earlier that he wouldn't let him die. If he, or any other individual on the hunger strike, had wanted to come off it then he could do so. It was a voluntary choice to begin or end your hunger strike. But he didn't have the authority to call off the hunger strike itself. Only Bobby Sands could do that. Bobby Sands was the Camp OC, not Brendan Hughes. But I don't think that's how Brendan saw it. I suspect that when he started his hunger strike on 27 October, and made Bobby the OC, Brendan believed that the hunger strike would be successful and following its conclusion he would simply return to his position as OC. And there were others in the Blocks who probably saw it that way also. They perhaps still

---

[71] Reference to the agreement arrived at in Portlaoise Prison in the South of Ireland between IRA prisoners and the prison authorities following a hunger strike in 1977.

[72] Laurence McKeown (2001), *Out of Time*, Belfast: Beyond the Pale, p. 75.

regarded Brendan as the OC, given the high regard in which he was held at that time, and maybe regarded Bobby as no more than a stand-in during the period when Brendan was incapacitated. Raymond McCartney, who was on the hunger strike in 1980, confirms that 'confusion':

> If there was a fault it was that when we went on hunger strike we should have been removed totally and absolutely from any decision in relation to it because people weren't sure just who the OC of the camp was, the 'Dark' (Brendan Hughes) or Bobby.[73]

Bobby had always been Brendan's subordinate, if a trusted one at that. It was safe to make Bobby OC as he knew Brendan's thoughts. And it was safe to make him OC as he would stand down again in deference to Brendan once the hunger strike ended successfully. But it all went pear-shaped. When Brendan and Bobby met that evening of 18 December, 1980, in the prison hospital apparently Bobby said to him, "Dark, you fucked up". I'm sure Brendan Hughes was shocked at that: shocked that Bobby would not simply go along with something that he, Brendan, had decided upon and try to make the best of a bad lot, shocked that the student was challenging the tutor, the apprentice challenging the master craftsman.

For me, that is the most significant moment in Bobby's life; not his election later as an MP or his eventual death on hunger strike, but that moment, as brief as it was, when he transformed from the boy to become the man, from being the led to becoming, in all meanings of the term, the leader. When Bobby had originally been appointed OC back in October of 1980, I thought it a strange choice. Bobby, to me at the time, seemed to be too much 'one of the lads'. He was like us, the ordinary volunteer, the regular prisoner – even if one with great literary and creative talents. For me, leadership figures were something different. They had a charisma that set them apart from the ordinary. Brendan Hughes held that charisma for me – at the time. And that was an important lesson for me to learn; that it is not about how someone 'appears' in the world, and at a particular time, but how they actually handle situations and, most importantly, what they do once the chips are down. Bobby was that person, that leader. He got it: totally. And he didn't let ego get in the way. That was proven most

---

[73] Laurence McKeown (2001), *Out of Time*, Belfast: Beyond the Pale, p. 76.

vividly when he died on 5 May 1981: principles, beliefs, and values overcoming the power of ego.

Nothing is ever straightforward and hindsight is a very exact science. It's not about being judgemental. But there are always lessons to be learned. We all can, and do, make mistakes; the important thing is to learn from them. But I don't think Brendan Hughes was able to live with the decision he made on 18 December 1980. I believe his ego was dented and rather than learn from the experience he subsequently, in later years, shifted 'blame' onto others. In his mind, he was the one who was right; it was others who had let him down. And he began to express that resentment in public utterances, increasingly becoming more vociferous in his public attacks against those in the republican leadership, those who he had once been very close to, no one more so than Gerry Adams. His involvement in the now totally discredited Boston College Tapes project, where he divulged information about his IRA activities in the early 1970s, identifying and naming others as IRA volunteers and comrades, took things to a new low.

Brendan Hughes was an IRA volunteer: a very active, successful, well-liked and resourceful one who held the rank of OC of the Belfast Brigade before his arrest in 1974. As a volunteer, Brendan, better than anyone else, understood only too well that anyone who acquires access to otherwise unknown information on individuals or actions, as a direct result of their membership of the IRA, and who then later divulges that information to those who are hostile to the IRA (be it British Crown forces, the media, academia, or otherwise) is going against the IRA's code of conduct and discipline. During the course of the conflict, any IRA volunteer found guilty of such disclosures was executed. At the time Brendan made the allegations in his interviews to the Boston College project, the conflict was over. And by the time his allegations were made public he was dead. Speaking to a former blanketman and IRA volunteer who had been very much opposed to the Good Friday Agreement and who was totally opposed to the decommissioning of arms – to the point where he resigned from the IRA – he, nevertheless, said, "If you've something to say, then say it when you're alive and then either back it up or let others challenge you on it. Don't say it but demand that it be kept secret until you're dead whilst those you name and accuse are still alive."

We all have an ego – it's what drives us – but when we become egotistical that's something else, and the history of revolutionary struggle, be it in Ireland or internationally, teaches us that so many revolutions and organisations have foundered due to personal ego taking precedence over collective leadership and responsibility.

# 10
# Hunger and Politics

INITIALLY ONLY FOUR PRISONERS were to be on the hunger strike and they would not all start their fast at the one time. Bobby Sands would begin on 1 March, to be followed two weeks later by Francis Hughes, then one week after that by Raymond McCreesh and Patsy O'Hara.

Shortly before Bobby went on hunger strike I got the chance to see him at Sunday Mass. His wing had moved from H3 to H6 after they had smashed up the furniture following the unsuccessful attempt to explore whatever options were on the table following the conclusion of the 1980 hunger strike. He was busy talking with others so I only got a few brief words with him. He looked OK. Thin, but then Bobby was always thin. He looked relaxed. It can sound like a cliché but he did look like someone who had made a critical decision about his life and was happy with that decision. A look that reflected contentment or inner calm. A look that he was ready to face what was now to come his way.

I also met Francis Hughes in H6 for the first and last time. His wing had also been moved there following the smashing of the furniture. There were a few others from South Derry whom I already knew well and they introduced me to Francie. He was full of concern because he had just been told that week that he would not begin the hunger strike until *two* weeks after Bobby, instead of one week as had been originally decided. He worried that people outside, supporters in his local area, might think he was letting them down because he was to begin the *stailc* a week later than he had told them. Other than that, he was in the very best of form and looked it too. At the end of Mass we simply shook hands and said, "All the best".

During February, those who had been on the first *stailc* were moved out of the hospital and back into the Blocks. Brendan Hughes and

'Nixy' (John Nixon, Armagh) came to our wing and the first chance we got to see them was at Mass the following Sunday. Everyone was up around them asking how they were. Nixy was very lively; Brendan much less so, but then it wasn't in his nature to be lively. I remember looking across at him from the far side of the canteen and wondering just what was going through his head. A few months earlier he had been OC of the Blocks and about to go on a hunger strike which might have ended a four year stalemate. Now Bobby, who had taken over from him as OC, was also about to begin a hunger strike – again to end that stalemate, one way or the other.

When Bobby began his hunger strike on 1 March there was little media attention given to it. Funny how the 'great and the good' had disappeared; all those who had previously called on us to talk, to enter into dialogue, to reach compromise, to resolve the stalemate. Not one of them uttered a word of condemnation at how the British government had handled the ending of the 1980 hunger strike and their refusal to consider any reforms to the prison regime. We realised we had an uphill battle before us to mobilise support but we also knew that support was out there in our local communities and further afield.

The ending of the no-wash protest on 2 March did, however, receive some media coverage. Bishop Daly of Derry welcomed the development and called upon the government to respond to this gesture from the prisoners. He did, however, discourage the tactic of hunger strike itself.

That morning Pat Beag informed the guards that we intended to wash and wanted to move to clean accommodation with furniture. Within a short time we were moved over to D wing which had just been cleaned. The move across went very quickly and very smoothly. There was no mirror search; just a lot of guards looking very glum. I think it suddenly dawned on them that times had changed whatever the outcome would eventually be. We were once again dictating events. We would now be coming out of our cells, even if only for short periods to wash, brush out, and slop out. Things were changing. Things would never be the same again.

We got new mattresses and blankets before dinner time and sheets came a few days later. It was some time before we got furniture. The guards had to work much harder now, no longer could they sit with their feet up in their office. We all had to get slopped out. Everyone had to be washed and we all wanted a haircut immediately. For blanketmen, like myself, who hadn't been force-washed, it was three years since we had last bathed.

Because the guards in H6 were fairly flexible, and the lads were disciplined in not lingering in the showers too long, everyone in our wing was able to get a shower that day. I was amongst the last and that was after eight o'clock that night.

There was a pair of hand shears and disposable razors available for cutting our beards off. I took great pleasure in removing the straggling wisps of hair I had hanging from below my chin. I had little or no moustache and looked like an Amish person!

The shower was brilliant; the water was warm and the soap was lovely. There was no shampoo but I washed my hair with the 'buttermilk' soap which the prison supplied. Although the soap was held in low regard – given that it was prison issue and had no scent – I later discovered that it was the best soap to use specifically *because* it contained no scent or artificial colouring. Even though water hadn't touched my skin for three years the soap didn't feel harsh or irritating. I never thought it could be otherwise but three days later when I had soap and shampoo sent in by my family I used 'Imperial Leather' and it felt as if I'd washed in acid. My face burned and remained dry, red, and sore for at least two days.

When the last person had been showered, the guards left the wing and the buzz of conversation was everywhere – at the doors, at the windows, at the pipes, or within the cells to a cellmate. I felt warm and clean in newly-washed blankets. I felt the mattress and the dry floor beneath me. I felt the freshness of my recently-washed skin. I felt good.

The next day we had great laughs as we met one another on the wing. Some people were almost unrecognisable. This was particularly the case when we got our hair cut some days later. We were lucky in that Joe Clarke, from Ballymurphy, a hairdresser by trade, was in the other wing across the Block from us and was allowed over to cut our hair as soon as he'd finished in his own wing. Fortunately for me, he cut my hair before his wing was moved back to H5. When it was asked if anyone in *our* wing could cut hair, Harry Cavanagh said he could. However, some of the samples of Harry's work turned out looking much worse than what the guards inflicted upon prisoners during the time of the forced washings and haircuts! My cell-mate, Anthony McIntyre, was one of his victims so I saw his handiwork close-up. No one really cared, though. Certainly not Harry, who proclaimed out the door that night, "I said I could cut hair – I never said I could style it!"

Strangely, I can't recall how my family reacted when they saw me washed and shaved and with my hair cut. I do recall, however, what the guard escorting me said as we walked to the visit. I'd seen him various times over the course of the protest, so he'd been around for a few years, though I'd never had any dealings with him. He commented upon how shocked he was when he first went down the wings shortly after we ended the no-wash protest. He said, "It was like you were individual people. Before that you just all looked the same." He seemed genuinely taken aback by what he saw. It was as if, for the first time, he had actually seen us as human.

Being off the no-wash protest meant it was easier to access medical and dental facilities. Prior to this we had to wash to get dental treatment or treatment in the prison hospital so we would refuse to voluntarily do so, unless in the most dire circumstances. Some men had endured a lot of pain over the years as a result of the absence of such care. Several blanketmen had comms stuck inside their nasal cavities that they had been unable to retrieve. In some cases they had been there for months, if not years. Usually, when a comm was stuck up your nose, it would eventually loosen and either fall out, or more likely, fall down your throat when you were asleep, only to be discovered when you were rubbing a shite on the wall. That happened to me once. I thought initially it was just a hard piece of food that hadn't been fully digested, possibly a pea, but upon closer inspection realised it was a small comm. I'd hidden it when going on a visit a couple of weeks earlier. Although there was the fear that to reveal to the prison authorities that you had a hidden comm would mean ending up on the Boards, men were also concerned about potential health hazards, so a number of them went out to see the doctor to get them removed. In at least one case, a man had to be taken to an outside hospital to have it extracted. My recollection is that no one was actually charged for having a comm in their nasal cavity. Maybe there was no specific clause in the prison rulebook that stated explicitly that you were prohibited from shoving items up your nose!

Whilst the routine of our daily lives on the protest was changing – and improving – it was against a backdrop of Bobby's physical decline. I'm not sure if the others had joined him on the *stailc* by the time a comm came in from the IRA leadership on the outside, the Army Council, stating that in the event of Bobby, or the three other hunger strikers, dying, no one would replace them. I don't know if it was written to test our resolve and commitment to the *stailc* or if it was seriously intended that the hunger strike tactic should be limited in use, but it certainly provoked a response. I was one of those at the door "biting the angle-iron off" in rage at such a suggestion. My view was that if Bobby died and no one replaced him, it would be immediately obvious to the Brits that they had only to weather the storm of four deaths and the entire issue of the H-Blocks would be resolved. It was crucial to show the Brits this was not the thinking among the prisoners. We had to show that there was determination to achieve our demands and that the determination would not falter if faced with the reality of people dying. Many others expressed a similar viewpoint and the consensus in our wing, amongst those who offered an opinion, was that there should be replacements for those who died. Some withheld their views on the basis that they themselves were not prepared to go on hunger strike. I didn't think that a valid reason for not arguing the merits of a particular strategy but I was happy with the outcome. There would be replacements.

As weeks passed, the media continued to give little attention to the hunger strike other than announcements when Frank, Raymond, and Patsy joined it. We didn't know if that was deliberate or whether it just wasn't newsworthy enough during that period. Being fairly cynical about the media we mostly opted for the former. However, that situation, and our hopes, suddenly changed when Bobby was put forward as a candidate in the by-election for the Westminster constituency of Fermanagh/South Tyrone. The by-election followed the death of sitting Member of Parliament, Frank Maguire who, ironically, had been a strong supporter of our demands and had visited us in the prison a number of times. After much discussion and wrangling with other potential nationalist candidates, Bobby was eventually given a clear run as the sole (nationalist) candidate. The election was held on 9 April, by which time Bobby had been on hunger strike for forty days.

When we heard that Bobby would be standing in the by-election we viewed it merely as an exercise that would attract some publicity. Not knowing the Fermanagh/South Tyrone area or its history of voting, I never thought for one moment that Bobby had a chance of winning the seat. At least that was my initial feeling. As the date of

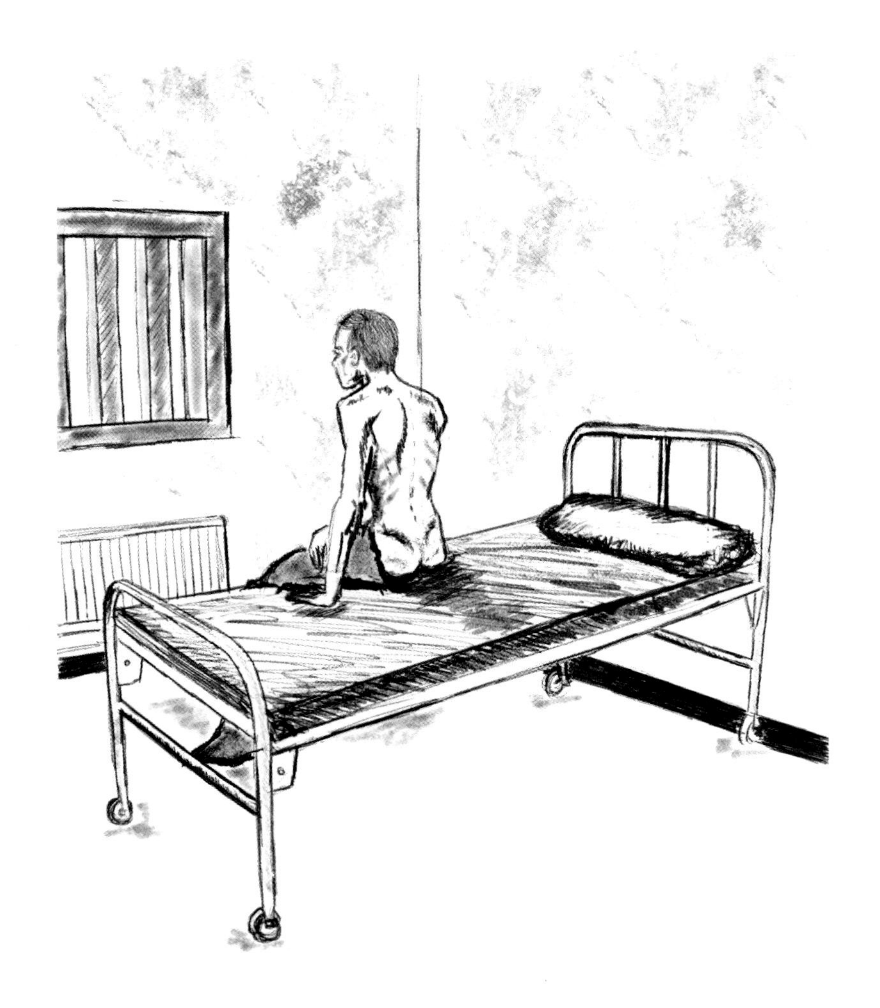

the election drew nearer, however, we were getting reports from the outside that Bobby was in a strong position and had a good chance of winning. However, Fr Faul at Mass one Sunday said that: "The people will give the Provos their money, their cars, their houses but never their votes". We hoped he was wrong.

We wrote comms to everyone and anyone in the Fermanagh/South Tyrone area calling on them to support Bobby. The letters were smuggled out and some weeks there could be over 50 of them going out from our wing alone. This increased as the election drew closer.

On the day when the election result was to be announced, we were instructed by our OC not to cheer or shout out if Bobby won. Doing so would alert the guards to the fact that we had access to a radio. We, in H6 didn't cheer, but other Blocks did. Obviously the ill-disciplined ones! It was difficult to suppress our excitement. In *H3*, the feature film Brian Campbell and I wrote, we try to capture that moment when the prisoners attempt to silently celebrate, gently slapping one another on the back or lightly hitting walls. Until, that is, the character 'Madra' can no longer contain himself and he lets out a loud yell, immediately followed by everyone else in the wing. That was what we all wanted to do at the time.

When the guards came back onto the wing that evening with the tea they told us Harry West, the unionist candidate, had won. One of them, a Scotsman, went to great lengths to try to convince us of this. It really sickened him when men stood with a broad grin on their faces and said with confidence, "No way. We know the people of Fermanagh/South Tyrone. We know the support there is for us." Another guard, the following day, tried to argue with a prisoner returning from a visit, insisting that Bobby hadn't won. This, despite the fact that the prisoner had been discussing the election victory for almost half an hour with his family, and within earshot of the guard.

We made up for our silence of the previous day. We were ecstatic. We sang and shouted. We rubbed it into the guards with great delight. Our hopes for the success of the *stailc* mushroomed. From a very gloomy beginning, we now felt we had moved into a new situation. Bobby was now an MP, elected with over 30,000 votes. What clearer sign could there be that people regarded him – and by extension, all of us – as political prisoners than by voting for him as their parliamentary representative? We felt this would cause the Brits all sorts of problems and put them in a dilemma as to how to treat an MP who they were condemning as a criminal. We believed that the contradictions would be extremely difficult for them to overcome. It was, without doubt, the happiest day I experienced throughout the entire blanket protest.

Once again, however, we underestimated the Brits' capacity to blatantly change the rules to suit themselves. They simply enacted a Bill which barred prisoners from standing in future elections. When they did that, it indicated how they were going to deal with Bobby's election. They were going to simply ignore it, ignore the fact that over 30,000 people had voted for him,[74] and let him die. And if they let

[74] More votes than Margaret Thatcher ever got in an election.

Bobby, an MP, die, then how much more readily would they let the others – Frank, Raymond, and Patsy – die?

It taught me a lot about the Brits and politics, and about power and the misuse of it. It taught me a lot about the façade of democracy – in whatever country – which often merely cloaks unjust and deep-seated systems of privilege and power in the hands of a few. My hopes from a few days prior were quickly dampened.

Over the following weeks we continued to receive word of Bobby's deterioration. In the meantime, our wing had moved from H6 to H3 and we were now adjacent to the wing that Bobby had previously left and which Brendan 'Bik' McFarlane, now the Blocks OC, was in.

We waited for the inevitable, even though we still clung to some hope, for something, for anything. On the morning of 5 May 1981 we slopped out, and washed and brushed our cells as usual. We noticed no real change in routine. The guards were perhaps a bit slower in opening the doors, or a bit more subdued, but there was really nothing significantly out of the ordinary. At lunchtime, Fr Toner arrived on the wing and visited Brendan Hughes who was in the end cell at the top of the wing. The dinner dishes had already been collected and the wing was quiet. We then heard Fr Toner's voice, a cell door slamming shut, then footsteps leaving the wing. Moments later Brendan Hughes shouted through the side of his cell door, "Bobby's dead". It was as sudden as that. There were no questions to be asked. We had all expected it sooner rather than later yet it still came as a shock. I simultaneously felt both sorrow and rage. There wasn't a sound to be heard in the wing. Few even spoke in their cells and when they did it was isolated, disjointed comments rather than dialogue.

His death was somehow unreal to us because we were isolated from what was going on. Those outside had up-to-the- minute radio and TV reports on it; we had to rely on information from visits and the few news items we could hear on our smuggled radios.

Bobby's death prompted violent outbreaks of rioting throughout the north of Ireland. Several days later his funeral attracted an estimated crowd of 100,000 people. Protests were waged outside British embassies in many parts of the world. In the USA there were marches in New York, Boston, Chicago and San Francisco. The state of Rhode Island declared a day of mourning. The New York state legislature passed a resolution of sympathy condemning the British government.

The New Jersey state legislature passed a resolution honouring Bobby's 'courage and commitment'. The Longshoremen's Union blacked all British ships on the day of the funeral and wouldn't load or unload cargo. Ted Kennedy and other US senators sent a letter to the British prime minister protesting at her 'inflexible posture which must lead inevitably to more senseless violence and death'. The New York Daily News said: 'He was a rare one, a young man who thought enough of the place where he lived to want to die for it'. The New York Times remarked that: 'Despite proximity and a common language the British have persistently misjudged the depth of Irish nationalism'. From Poland, Lech Walesa sent sympathy on behalf of the Solidarity movement. The Portuguese parliament observed a minute's silence. In France, protests took place, thousands marching behind a huge portrait of Bobby Sands; a street in Le Mans was named Bobby Sands Street. Le Monde wrote: 'His memory and recognition of the meaning of his sacrifice are heavy with an emotion that several times this century has aroused the passions of the world against Britain.' There were protests, in Switzerland, West Germany, Belgium, Holland, Greece and Italy, where the President of the Italian Senate expressed condolences to the Sands family. In Milan, 5,000 students marched, burning the Union Jack. In Tehran, the street in which the British Embassy was located was renamed Bobby Sands Street.

There were demonstrations in Australia, and in Oslo, Norway, demonstrators threw a balloon filled with tomato sauce at the Queen of England who was there on an official visit. The Indian parliament in New Delhi observed a minute's silence. The Hindustan Times observed that Thatcher had, 'allowed a member of the House of Commons, a colleague in fact, to die of starvation. Never had such an incident occurred in a civilised country.'

Bobby Sands's death on hunger strike was followed by that of Frank Hughes on 12 May and Raymond McCreesh and Patsy O'Hara on 21 May. Four prisoners, four comrades, four friends, dead in a period of 14 days. They were replaced by Joe McDonnell, Martin Hurson, Kieran Doherty, and Kevin Lynch.

It's difficult to describe the feelings in the Blocks, or to put into words the depth of strength and determination we felt. The protest had been going on for four and a half years. It had shaped our thinking and built our solidarity. We had adopted the consciousness of an army at war and our battle was with every manifestation of the system and its administrators, especially with the guard who opened and closed our doors. If we gave in now, that guard would have a grin on his face and would rub it into us for the rest of our time in prison. And we knew that a lot of us still had a lot of time to do. No way were we going to allow these people to make that life a misery. We were steeled for the battle.

Brendan 'Bik' McFarlane, had taken over as Camp OC once Bobby began his fast. Bik had got his nickname from a famous Biscuit company MacFarlane Lang: 'MacFarlane Lang' biscuits (or bikkies). Bik had been arrested in 1975 and later sentenced to life imprisonment but given that he was imprisoned before 1 March 1976 he was entitled to political status, so was initially held in the Cages of Long Kesh. However, on 31 March 1978 he attempted to escape, along with Larry Marley and Pat 'Beag' McGeown. The three of them were taken to the Boards and on 11 April were moved to the H-Blocks. They were subsequently charged with attempting to escape and sentenced the following year.

One Sunday morning at Mass, at the end of May or early June, Bik informed me that I would be joining the *stailc* on Monday 29 June. Prior to then, prisoners only joined the hunger strike to replace someone who had died but it had been decided to increase the number of men on hunger strike at any one time, to eight, rather than four, as had been the case up until then. Over a period of four weeks new men started the hunger strike on a Monday morning – Tom McElwee, Paddy Quinn, Mickey Devine, and then myself, the last of that group. After that, others joined the fast when someone died.

I had written to Bik a few weeks earlier inquiring how men were selected and if he had my name amongst those on the short-list. It wasn't a case of bravery or ego; I simply felt I could go through with it. I wasn't married and was serving life, and I felt I had a responsibility to those around me and to the struggle. I wasn't unique in that sense as I knew my views and reasoning were shared by a large number of others.

Several days after Bik had informed me that I'd be joining the *stailc* I received a comm from the Army Council. It read simply, "Comrade, you have put your name forward for the hunger strike. Do you know that this means you will most likely be dead within two months? That means, comrade, that you will be no more. Reconsider carefully your decision. AC." Those may not be the exact words, but it was as blunt as that. I hadn't expected the comm and the words did startle me at first. Seeing my 'death' written in black and white appeared very stark, but it didn't cause me to rethink my position. My earlier examination of the situation had been done seriously and responsibly. I was ready to go ahead.

I can't recall much about the first visit I had with my family when it was decided I was going on hunger strike. That may seem strange but as I had already prepared my family for such an eventuality during the first hunger strike, I suppose the shock was, therefore, somewhat mitigated. Nevertheless, I'm sure the strain was powerful. I only discovered later, once I had begun the *stailc*, that my mother had suffered a mild heart attack in 1978. I hadn't been aware of it as she had ensured I wasn't told, no doubt trying to save me from worrying. I was angry that I hadn't been told, though I understood the motivation behind it. Admittedly, I know also that had I been told, it probably would not have altered my decision to go on hunger strike. From the little I can recall from that first visit I spent most of it trying to inject a light-hearted tone to the discussion and reminding them that I wasn't yet on the fast and anything could happen between now and then, or even during the *stailc*.

At the time, a General Election was being held in the South of Ireland (on 11 June) and nine prisoners, eight from the H-Blocks and one from Armagh Gaol, were put forward as candidates: Kieran Doherty in Cavan/Monaghan; Paddy Agnew in Louth; Joe McDonnell in Sligo/Leitrim; Martin Hurson in Longford/Westmeath; Seán McKenna in Kerry North; Kevin Lynch in Waterford; Tony O'Hara (brother of Patsy O'Hara) in Dublin West; Tom McAllister in Clare, and; Mairéad Farrell in Cork North Central.

Kieran Doherty and Paddy Agnew were both elected to Dáil Éireann. All of the other candidates polled very well, with some of them narrowly missing election. It was another massive morale boost to us and our campaign.

Paddy Agnew was in my wing at the time and he got a lot of slegging at having been elected a TD (Teachta Dála – Member of Parliament). Paddy was a bit of raker! Several days later the OC told him to request to see the Governor and to say that he, Paddy, was required in Leinster House, Dublin, the seat of Parliament. I think Paddy initially thought the OC was 'winding him up' – and there was undoubtedly a degree of mischievousness involved – but Paddy duly did as he was told. When he appeared in front of the Governor in his office and stated his request, the Governor dismissed him immediately and told the guards to take him back to the wing. When Paddy returned to the wing I could hear him being thrown around and slapped as he refused to bend over the mirror. One of the guards made some flippant remark about him being elected a TD, telling him that his election would make no difference to how they would treat him. Imagine, a newly-elected Member of the Irish Parliament being beaten and verbally abused because he had the audacity to make a request to attend Parliament. I wonder how the British would react if something similar happened to one of their elected citizens?

I still shared a cell with Anthony McIntyre at the time. As 29 June drew closer there wasn't a lot said about my going on hunger strike. We both knew the seriousness of it and after that there wasn't much to be said. We didn't want to envisage that in two months or less I would be dead, not least because we didn't want to think that several more friends would die in the intervening period or that our demands would still not have been granted. So, in many ways our chat revolved around the same topics as were common in the Blocks: our visits, our families, our adventures while outside, and the friends we had come to know since being imprisoned. Plus, of course, a degree of the usual backstabbing of others in the wing! What sticks in my memory clearly, is that Anthony didn't eat his breakfast the day before I started my hunger strike. Whether that was because he genuinely didn't want it or because he wanted to afford me the extra meal before my impending fast, I don't know. But I took great pleasure in pouring the two bowls of cornflakes into one and eating the heap. Since the ending of the no-wash protest, and particularly since our move to H3, the grub had improved a great deal. We were now getting more than the previously common 5-6 spoonfuls of cornflakes and the milk didn't seem to be watered. I looked forward to, and thoroughly enjoyed, breakfast time. I still do today.

# 11

# Stealing from the Dying

ON 29 JUNE I STARTED MY HUNGER STRIKE as planned. At that stage Joe McDonnell, Martin Hurson, Kieran Doherty, Kevin Lynch, Paddy Quinn, Tom McElwee, and Mickey Devine were on it. On the day I began the hunger strike I weighed ten stone and eight pounds; about two stone underweight for my height (six feet, two inches). My heart, lungs, and blood pressure were checked and I was generally in good shape. I had never been in hospital or suffered any serious illness in the past so I wasn't too concerned in that regard. I was asked to read and sign a form which stated that I was aware of what I was doing and that doctors would not intervene medically unless I so requested.

I was moved that morning across to D wing – Bik's wing. A couple of the lads, Denis Cummings and Phil Rooney, were assigned to look after me – that is, brush my cell out and get me anything I wanted (which was pretty minimal, to be honest, as there was nothing to get!). They also took down the details of my weight and blood pressure each morning when I returned from the doctor. These were sent to the Sinn Féin centre outside and a record was also held in the wing. Tom McElwee and Paddy Quinn (who had already been on the hunger strike for some time) were on the wing also, but were moved a short time later to the prison hospital. Tom looked fairly well but Paddy, even at that relatively early stage, was showing the effects of his fast.

Coldness was what I felt first: my feet especially. The heating in the Block was off for the summer and when I complained about this I was told the boiler was being repaired. I got extra blankets. At one time I had seven of them covering me and some of these were doubled over making it about ten or eleven layers of clothing over me. Only then did I feel warm enough, though my feet always remained cold.

* * *

I started to smoke when I was about ten years of age and thereafter spent many years trying to scrape up enough money for twenty fags – or, as was more often the case, ten. During the blanket protest when weeks could pass without a smoke my commitment to the weed never weakened – until 1980. For some inexplicable reason I began to believe that I was being dictated to by this habit (as opposed to wanting to smoke) and simply stopped it there and then. To those who believed that I would sacrifice an arm and a leg for a smoke, this came as a major shock; and I think a few may have suspected that I had obtained some secret supply of snout and the best way to hide this from the lads was to say I had stopped using it! I continued to smuggle tobacco back from visits though, as I enjoyed getting one over on the guards. A visit didn't seem truly worthwhile if I didn't return from it with snout, plus there would be other items in the *beart* such as pens, cigarette papers, and articles in Irish that I wanted.

The next time I smoked I was just 3-4 days into the hunger strike. It wasn't a case of feeling I needed a cigarette, more a case of something to do, something to taste, even. Besides that, it was still an illicit activity so there was the act of rebellion connected with smoking. Indeed, this was the most satisfying aspect of a smoke during the protest and may be the reason why a lot of ex-blanketmen, myself included, gave up smoking in later years: no more fun with it.

I went out on a visit on the fifth day into my fast and as usual brought back the snout. The wing I had just moved into apparently wasn't the best for bringing back snout so that night the OC, Pat Mullan from Tyrone, got up to lecture the lads about how they must do better and pointed to me as a means to embarrass them: "...a hunger striker is even bringing back snout for the wing!". I was all chuffed about this until Bik got up to the door and gave me a lecture about what I had done, telling me it was dangerous with me on the *stailc* and not to do it again. There never seemed to be a problem with a tobacco supply after that. Though, then again, maybe I was specifically catered for. The most I would have smoked anyhow was 4-5 cigarettes a day. I had the luxury too of real cigarette papers not the 'bog-roll jobs' (tobacco rolled in prison-issue toilet paper) everyone else had to smoke. Having said that, the bog-roll jobs were a powerful smoke, like steel claws gripping your lungs when you inhaled deeply.

The presence of hunger strikers on a wing would encourage heightened sensitivity among other prisoners. While Paddy, Tom, and I were still in D wing of H3 a couple of lads had got their food handed in to them and discovered that there was only half a fish on each plate. The orderlies had obviously been short for themselves so just halved the blanketmen's grub, a not unusual occurrence. The two lads kicked up a racket and the guards were at their door to find out what was going on. The rest of the wing also started to shout over to find out what was happening. Bik then got to the door and asked what the craic was. When he found out it was a row over half a fish he told the lads to let the issue drop. He was raging that there was a row about small portions of food while there were three of us on hunger strike on the wing. But the lads were right to complain and our presence should not have hindered them in demanding what was rightfully theirs. In reversed roles the three of us would have complained too.

The guards would let me out to wash once everyone else had finished. Apart from that, the only time I was out of the cell was for my daily visit to the doctor and for Mass on Sunday. The lads would all be around me, eager to find out how I was keeping. Their comments were always positive though no doubt they noticed the effects even by then. Mostly this would be apparent in my slower pace of movement. I also had to be careful rising, ensuring that I didn't get up too quickly or I would get dizzy.

The Assistant Governor who did his rounds of the Block each day would look into my cell. He would ask if I had any complaints or requests. I wouldn't have, except for the heating to be switched on. Most of the Governors would confine themselves to these formalities though an odd one would make a comment. AG McMullan asked me one morning what date my birthday was on. I said, "19 September". He replied, "You'll not be seeing your next one then," gave a laugh and walked out. I was raging with myself for giving him the opening. I should have realised what was coming but after I had silently cursed him for a while and got it out of my system, I realised just how insignificant and powerless he must feel that his only way to assert any authority, was to try and annoy someone on the *stailc*. So I just dropped him and the incident from my thoughts.

Apart from isolated remarks such as that, I didn't experience too much verbal abuse from the guards. I think by that stage they realised they were living through a very tense and dangerous period and, as no one was telling them anything, they felt very vulnerable. They had done the administration's bidding down through the years and now realised they could be quickly dropped in the shit when no longer of assistance. The world of the H-Blocks that they had become so comfortable with, didn't seem so permanent any more, and they had no control over what change may come about.

I had been on hunger strike for a week when the Irish Commission for Justice and Peace (ICJP) arrived in the camp on Saturday 4 July and wanted to meet with all the hunger strikers. They were there to try and broker a resolution to the hunger strike – or so it appeared. I was taken, along with Bik, to the hospital about noon to meet them. Mickey Devine ('Red Mick') was already in the prison hospital canteen when I arrived. He had been brought over from H5. Those on hunger strike in the hospital were still locked up in their cells.

I first met Mickey while on remand in C wing, Crumlin Road Prison, Belfast. Patsy O'Hara was also there at the time. Although we both ended up, at least initially, in H-Block 5, I never saw Mickey after that as he was in a different wing from me and our paths never crossed, not even on visits. While we waited on the others to join us we had a yarn about our individual wings and particular characters I knew from my time in H5. It was small talk; talk to fill a space before we could learn what the ICJP was going to offer.

At 2.00 p.m. the lads in the hospital were unlocked and came down to the canteen: Paddy Quinn, Tom McElwee, Kieran Doherty, Kevin Lynch and Martin Hurson. A few minutes after that Joe McDonnell was brought in on a wheelchair. But for knowing that Joe was the last one to arrive I wouldn't have recognised the figure in the chair. He was slouched over, his head resting on his shoulder, his lips were cracked and saliva trickled from the corner of his mouth which seemed to be twisted. I had remembered him as 'Fat Joe' and this person before me resembled a third of the Fat Joe I knew. I learned an important lesson that day. Such was Joe's level of physical impairment, I found I was looking on him as if he was in some way mentally impaired. That was not the case. Joe was very lucid and when I heard his voice, though it was low, the character of Joe came through clearly. He was strong. He was interested to hear what was going on, what Bik thought of this 'crowd' (the ICJP), and he was concerned that everyone was getting a cigarette or drink of the spring water that was available to us. His hearing was affected and often he would ask for something to be repeated but Big Doc stayed beside him and ensured he was getting everything that was being said. However, he was too weak to stay for the meeting with the ICJP and returned to his cell.

They arrived shortly after this and introduced themselves: Bishop Mahoney (President), Hugh Logue (SDLP[75] politician), Fr Oliver Crilly, Jerome Connolly (Secretary), and Brian Gallagher (Chair, and a solicitor). Prior to their arrival, Bik had been informed by the prison authorities that he could not attend the meeting. We requested of the ICJP that Bik be allowed to join us but they said they had no authority over this and had been told he wouldn't be allowed. However, they informed us they would be meeting with him later. There was nothing striking about them, except for Hugh Logue whose language and manner I noted to be much more forward than the others. I asked Tom McElwee if he had caught his name when they had introduced themselves and he said he hadn't. I said he sounded like a politician. Tom agreed saying, "I was just thinking that myself." The other notable thing about him was that he smoked small cigars, so we helped ourselves to a few of those.

The day's discussions went over a lot of ground, toing and froing. They described their meetings with the NIO and what had been 'agreed upon'. They seemed happy with their achievements and felt they consisted of the 'basis' of our five demands. They kept repeating the term, 'basis'. Bishop Mahoney sat in the middle and said very little. Fr Oliver Crilly sat on his immediate right and did a lot of the speaking. We directed our questions at Fr Crilly as he was Tom McElwee's cousin, had visited the jail a few times, and we thought that he probably had a grasp of the situation. Logue sat on Mahoney's left hand side with Brian Gallagher between them. Gallagher and the other member of their delegation, Jerome Connolly, rarely spoke. Discussion went on for 2-3 hours. All of it was fairly amicable. We reiterated our five demands but said we would discuss with anyone how these could be implemented. Talks ended with us shaking hands all round and them promising to return the next day. They left, Bik re-

---

[75] Social Democratic and Labour Party based in the north of Ireland.

joined us, and all of us then discussed the meeting before Bik and I returned to H3 and 'Red Mick' to H5. We told the lads that night out the door what had taken place and discussed the general situation. What did we make of this group? Why had they suddenly arrived now? What agenda were they working to? What tie-in/authority did they have from the Southern government, the Church, the SDLP? We had by then discovered Hugh Logue was a member of the SDLP.

The following morning, Sunday 5 June, I was again taken to the hospital to meet with the other hunger strikers. I didn't know what to expect and certainly wasn't expecting Danny Morrison of Sinn Féin to be there.[76] He was banned by the NIO from visiting the Camp and as this was a Sunday morning when no normal visits took place, all sorts of rules had been set aside to allow him in. The first thing he said to us was that the guard who opened the front gate for him had exclaimed, "Bastard!". Danny had, of course, assumed the insult had been directed at him but then learned that it was aimed at Maggie Thatcher who, the guard must have thought, had conceded to our demands given this extremely unusual, previously-prohibited visit.

Danny told us about the Republican Movement's contact with the ICJP and also mentioned other contacts that were ongoing with the British Foreign Office. We told him that we had heard nothing so far to make us believe there was a resolution to the *stailc* in sight. The ICJP would, however, be returning that day. We split up after that and Danny went to see Bik who still wasn't permitted to be with us during our meeting. I was happy with what had taken place. It seemed there was movement. Why else would the NIO agree to Danny's visit?

The ICJP delegation arrived back that afternoon. A few moments were passed in exchanging small talk and then we got down to business. From the start Bishop Mahoney played the dominant role. He gave a breakdown of their negotiations, saying what they had 'achieved' and what was on offer to us. This was no different from the previous day when we had been told we would be allowed to wear our own clothes, work would be looked at in a constructive manner, and better facilities for association would be introduced. Logue came in to back this up by saying that what they had achieved was the basis

[76] Sinn Féin is the political party of the Irish Republican Movement. Danny Morrison, at that time, was its Director of Publicity and had been centrally involved in Bobby Sands's election to the Westminster Parliament.

of our five demands and in fact they had even gone further and got us a sixth demand. I looked at Logue a bit incredulously and said, "Go ahead, tell us what this sixth demand is". He said, "A recognition of the Gaelic culture and Irish language, and as a goodwill gesture we have been given permission to present you with this Bible written entirely in Irish." It appeared that this was a big deal to him and I don't think that he was too pleased with the response he got – total disinterest in his Irish Bible. If at any time during the protest we had conformed and gone to the other Blocks we would have had access to literature in Irish.

We asked a number of questions and attempted to involve Oliver Crilly in the conversation, without success. It was obvious he had been 'nobbled' by Mahoney and/or others. His whole demeanour portrayed a reluctance to involve himself in discussion; a significant contrast to the day before. At the end of a period of frustrating dialogue about the status of what was on offer, Big Tom (McElwee), who was sitting directly across from Oliver Crilly, put it straight to him; "What's being said is that our own clothes are on offer and that's the heap, isn't it?" Crilly didn't respond for a moment, then looked up at Tom and said, "Yes". At this point Logue burst in saying, "It would be criminally irresponsible to say that is the only thing on offer. We have outlined what is in fact the basis of your five demands and have indeed included a sixth." I thought then, and still do today, that his choice of words (directed at another member of his own delegation) 'criminally irresponsible', was somewhat ironic, given the nature of what we were discussing.

Oliver Crilly didn't reply, obviously aware that he had spoken out of turn and against what the rest of the delegation had planned to say. But whatever the reason, it was clear that he couldn't bring himself to lie to us or exaggerate the offer that was on the table. Perhaps it was because of the family connection – Tom being his cousin – or perhaps he was just overcome by the faces of men across the table from him, some of whom would most likely be dead within a few days. In my opinion, he was the only one to act with total honesty and integrity.

Logue (who that day had decided to leave his cigars out in the car) was, in my opinion, prepared to push through any duplicitous deal. Being a member of the ICJP delegation which negotiated an end to the hunger strike, when everyone else had failed, would no doubt do his political future a world of good. Ultimately, Bishop Mahoney must take full responsibility for the role the ICJP played. He must have been fully aware of how the ICJP was being used by both the Dublin government and the NIO officials. It would be interesting to know what brief the Church had given him on his role. What he was clearly intent on doing was forcing through a package which would have been a sell-out of our demands. And, in my opinion, he must have known that.

The discussion continued for some time after that but it was very clear it was going nowhere. We had rejected outright what was on offer. Maybe they thought we would tire. I know they were certainly frustrated and angered that we had cut through the frills of their presentation and exposed the reality beneath. No doubt Mahoney was not accustomed to having (non-clerical) people speak back to him or assert their views or belief in themselves, in their comrades and in their commitment to a struggle. Logue was certainly not amused. Oliver Crilly looked sad, very sad, perhaps the only one to fully appreciate the gravity of what had been attempted and the tragic consequences that would undoubtedly follow.

Years later I wrote a poem (about Mickey Devine, who was present at the meeting that day and who later died on hunger strike). I refer to the ICJP in the poem:

> Two days later we realised they consisted of
> a small degree of sincerity
> a large amount of naivety, and
> had loyalty to political and ecclesiastical masters
> rather than to the dying.[77]

The ICJP stayed in the news on the Monday and Tuesday, 6 and 7 July. On Wednesday morning, 8 July, Joe McDonnell died after 61 days on hunger strike. Then the recriminations began. The ICJP claimed publicly that the NIO had promised them such and such. The NIO said they hadn't. And the British government, to back up this position, pointed out that no junior minister could have promised anything of the sort. The whole episode of finger-pointing became very messy and unseemly. It only served to further expose the disingenuousness of the offer that was made to us, as limited as it was.

We now know, from David Beresford's book, *Ten Men Dead*, that on Monday 6 July two of the commissioners from the ICJP, Fr Crilly and

---

[77] Laurence McKeown (2018), *Threads*, Clare, Ireland: Salmon Poetry

Hugh Logue, secretly met with Gerry Adams in West Belfast at Gerry's request. The reason for the meeting was to inform the commissioners that the Republican Movement was in direct (secret) talks with the British Foreign Office concerning the hunger strike and that what the Government was offering in those talks was more than what was being offered to the Commission. Gerry advanced his view that:

> [T]he authorities were merely using the ICJP as an intelligence feed, as a cross-check to construct a strategy to win, or at least settle, the dispute. The commissioners were stunned by the disclosure. They returned to the Greenan Lodge Hotel to tell their colleagues.[78]

This was possibly the last serious attempt that the Church or the Dublin government made to intervene in the stalemate. After that their public pronouncements became more weighted against the hunger strike, calling on us to end it, effectively falling into line with Thatcher's mantra that 'no government could be seen to concede to such pressure'. I think it was at this stage I began to realise we were very much on our own and that our actions were having a wider political effect than we had first imagined. We were exposing the hypocrisy of so-called Nationalist politicians and cutting through their rhetoric. We were posing a threat to the status quo, both political and clerical, by demonstrating that we were no longer prepared to bend the knee and accept moral control from 'our betters'. We were thinking for ourselves and acting in our own best interests. And for this, we had to be stopped. Soon Fr Faul stepped up his anti-hunger strike campaign of vilification of the Republican Movement and its leadership. He had learned, obviously to his horror, that he had previously been wrong. The Nationalist people would indeed not only give the Provos their houses and their cars but also their votes.

* * *

On the morning of 13 July, just five days after Joe McDonnell's death, I was out with the doctor for my usual daily check-up. I inquired how Martin (Hurson) was keeping. Dr Ross (the Chief Medical Officer in the prison) was on the Block that morning. He looked up from what he was writing and said, "Martin's dead. He died early this morning." I was stunned. Martin had been nowhere near crisis stage. I knew he had been sick for a while but by then that was considered more or less

[78] David Beresford (1987), *Ten Men Dead*, London: Grafton Books, p. 297.

an inevitability for anyone on hunger strike. It hadn't occurred to me that he could be near death. The MOs with the doctor said nothing. Ross himself just stared at his desk and rolled a pen about in his fingers. I walked back into the wing, stopping at the ablutions area when I heard Bik's voice. I shouted over to him and as he walked towards me I said, "*Fuair Mairtín bas*" (Martin has died). Bik said "What!" and as I went to repeat what I had said, a tall guard, who I'd never seen on the wing before, grabbed me by the shoulder and said, "Come on you, you're not out here for association". As he spoke he tried to push me down the wing.

The guard must have momentarily taken leave of his senses as instantly all the lads who had been washing (Dennis Cummings, Marty McManus, Jake Jackson and a couple of others besides Bik), dressed only in their towels, came running out of the ablutions area. Emotions were already heightened in the Blocks and it would only have taken a spark to ignite it. Laying a hand on a hunger striker was like taking a flame-thrower to the situation. Seeing the lads racing out, the guard immediately took his hand off my shoulder. By this time Bik was in front of him shouting, "If you ever lay your hands on a hunger striker again..." Some of the other lads were not so much interested in providing advice; they were intent on showing the guard that he had crossed a line, big time. At that point, Gilmore, the Class Officer in the wing, appeared and asked Bik what was happening, slowly manoeuvring himself between Bik and the other guard. For a few moments everything hung in the balance. Gilmore kept reassuring Bik that it would never happen again and gave a personal guarantee. The other lads just stood and stared at the big guard. Gradually the tension eased. Bik called me and the lads back in to the ablutions area and we all had a few words together. We reckoned the guards had learnt an important lesson from it and it was unlikely there would be a recurrence.

For a few moments the news which prompted the incident was forgotten, but it soon returned to us. The lads asked what had happened and I told them the little I knew. All were shocked. Word was shouted over to the other wing and I walked back to my cell wondering just what had brought such sudden death to Martin. I began to realise that there were no reliable patterns in a hunger strike. Each journey was unique.

I was happy in the wing and the lads looked after me well but I wanted to be in the hospital with the others on hunger strike. I had been pushing for this since about the 20th day, but I wasn't moved until about the 30th day. I arrived in the hospital in the morning and that afternoon had a yarn with Tom McElwee and Paddy Quinn in the yard. It was good to see them again. As before, Tom looked OK whereas Paddy's condition had deteriorated rapidly. Big Doc and Kevin Lynch were confined to bed by that stage and, as their families were with them, I didn't want to disturb them by going in to see them. Pat McGeown, Red Mick, and Matt Devlin were also there.

The strange thing about being in the prison hospital was that we were no longer regarded as being on protest, or being 'non-conforming' prisoners. In the hospital, it was the norm to wear pyjamas and a dressing gown – as is the case in any ordinary hospital – so we couldn't be accused of refusing to wear the prison uniform. Similarly, because we were in hospital, we were regarded as unfit for work so therefore could not be charged with refusing to work. We were no longer 'non-conforming' prisoners despite the fact that we were on hunger strike. As prisoners in the hospital wing we could get a radio, newspapers and books. We could get out each evening to the canteen for association and during the day out to the exercise yard. We could also smoke, though the cigarettes were stored at the top of the wing and we had to ask a guard when we wanted one. The guard would also give us a light as we were not allowed to have lighters. It put a whole new interpretation on the saying, 'dying for a smoke'. In this instance, when you were dying, on hunger strike, you were allowed to smoke.

In the Blocks I had been showering but in the hospital I thought I'd rest in a warm bath. It was only then I discovered just how much weight I'd lost and from where. The flesh around my hips had totally disappeared. When I lowered myself into the bath it felt as if my hip bones themselves were resting on the bottom of the bath and were bound to cut through my flesh. That was even when resting on a rubber mat. One of the MOs had told me to be careful and not to run the bath too hot as I would feel the effects of it. Being none too fond of cold baths, however, I made sure the water was fairly warm, if not hot. I almost collapsed. I was lying back in the bath when suddenly I felt really faint. I tried to pull myself up and I thought for a moment I wasn't going to make it. I did eventually get myself up into a slouched-over position. I was sweating heavily and felt really dizzy. I reached down and pulled the plug out of the bath then sat in the empty bath long after the water had drained from it. When I had cooled down and felt more clear-headed I got out of the bath, slowly, dried myself, then shuffled back to my cell and into bed. I was exhausted.

The routine in the hospital throughout the period of the hunger strike remained very much as normal. There were no significant adjustments made because we were hunger strikers except when practical difficulties arose. We were locked in our cells most of the time, apart from the exercise period and association in the evenings. Most guards adopted a clinical and distant approach to us and simply went about their duties as if our circumstances and ailments were something they were accustomed to seeing every day. It's possible they had been schooled in this approach. Some, however, did show their hostility towards us. It would come out in minor ways, such as constantly locking grilles and doors even when they knew we would be going back in or out in a few moments. On one such occasion when I asked the guard – Gerry Cardswell – why the grille on the canteen was locked when the (wooden) door immediately inside the grille was also locked, he remarked to me "Never forget, Laurence, you might be in hospital but you are still in prison".

Similar acts of pettiness were demonstrated in relation to use of the exercise yard. It had been agreed with the Governor that we could take chairs and pillows out to the yard. This was common-sense as only in the early days of hunger strike could anyone walk in the yard and even then only for a few laps. In later days we would only want to sit down in the yard. To do so we needed chairs and as these were of the hard plastic type, pillows were needed as the bones of our hips would be pressing through the skin. Although an arrangement had been reached over the use of chairs and pillows some guards would continually challenge this. Their argument was that the yard was for exercising, so no one should be allowed to go out with the intention of simply sitting. There was no point in trying to reason with such people. We would just send for the Governor or PO to direct the guard to open the grille and let us out.

My day would begin with the cell door being opened to see if I had any requests – for letters, welfare, the Governor, and so on. The PO of the hospital later did his rounds asking if there were any complaints or requests. I slopped out and my urine was chemically checked. I was then weighed and my blood pressure taken. All of this was

documented. I was locked up again until after 10 o'clock when we went to the yard, if the doctor had done his rounds. His examination consisted of asking how I was feeling, as there wasn't much else he could do. If it was Dr Ross, he would engage in some small talk, sometimes about working on his family's farm on his days off or about his fishing trips. He was generally pleasant to talk to though I learned from Paddy Quinn after the hunger strike that he thought Ross was playing mind-games with him. I did notice that he could become excited or agitated and a few times I saw him being very abrupt with the MOs. Years later, when I had cause to see him in my capacity as Block OC post-hunger strike (to raise some issue like heating in the Block or the provision of medical treatment), we ended up, to my surprise, having a very heated row. He became suddenly extremely agitated and ordered the MOs to take me out of his surgery. It was behaviour that did not fit with my earlier experience of him and was a total over-reaction to the issue I was raising. In hindsight, I think he was under pressure. It wasn't very long afterwards that he took his own life. I often wondered what impact the hunger strike had on him or what, if anything, from that era possibly contributed to his suicide.

Another doctor in the prison hospital during the hunger strike was Dr John Hopper. He was also a qualified dentist and it was as a dentist that he was employed in the jail. He was an excellent dentist and when the hunger strike ended he had loads of former blanketmen who urgently needed dental treatment. To his credit, he accomplished that very quickly and very competently. At the time of the hunger strike he would occasionally come down the wing during his dinner break for a chat with one of us and he got on particularly well with Red Mick. His visits were not in his official capacity but because he had an interest in what was happening. In fact, according to prison rules, he should not have been visiting us at all.

The other regular doctor in the prison was Dr Emmerson. He was despised by blanketmen. At the time of the forced washings he was the doctor who signed forms that (incorrectly) stated that men had head lice and required haircuts and bathing – diagnoses that were used to justify the ensuing violence. He 'examined' the men from about fifteen feet away, after they had been dragged up to him by the guards. He also witnessed the bruises, cuts and scrapes on prisoners two days later, following the forced washings, but he passed no comment. For his role in this we nicknamed him 'Mengele' after the doctor who experimented on prisoners in the Nazi concentration camps. We were talking about Emmerson one night in the prison hospital and Paul Lennon, an MO, heard us refer to him as Mengele. The following day Emmerson was the doctor on duty and when he was examining me Paul said, dead innocently,

"What was that name, Laurence, you said you called Dr Emmerson?" He probably thought I would be embarrassed but I replied, "Mengele", and when Paul asked, "Why Mengele?" I explained. Paul stopped talking and looked at Emmerson. Emmerson commented that he had often heard names shouted at him when he was going in and out of the Blocks but couldn't make out what exactly was being said. I didn't tell him of our speculation that he was, in fact, a vet, or someone who, instead of being deregistered for malpractice, had been offered the job at Long Kesh, thus ensuring his allegiance and loyalty to the administration.

The Assistant Governor in charge of the prison hospital was called McCartney. We believed he was specially appointed to the post during the hunger strike period because he had an amiable manner and would be pleasant when meeting families and other visitors. There was obviously significant attention on the jail and the prison hospital, in particular, and we believed they needed someone who could look after that public-facing aspect well. Then again, maybe that's giving the prison authorities too much credit and his appointment may have simply been by chance. In any case, I found him to be polite and accommodating where he could be. He didn't recite prison rules in robot-like fashion but tried to adapt them to the unique circumstances and events. He would grant extra visits or 'special' visits as they were called. No doubt he had the authority of the NIO to do this but, irrespective, I don't think it would have been in his nature to limit us to only one visit per week (especially in the latter stages of a person's hunger strike), which was our strict entitlement according to prison rules.

He came in one morning to tell me three letters had arrived for me which I would receive soon but that there were two others he wouldn't be giving me. He explained that the two he was withholding did not come from 'friends'. They were wishing me a 'slow and painful death' and were what he called 'poison pen letters'. I was going to argue to be shown them just out of curiosity but then I let it drop. Why annoy myself? He said the sentiments expressed in one of the other letters were "none too favourable towards prison staff". He gave a broad smile at this, but added that I would be getting it anyhow as it was not his intention to hold back mail which came from family and friends. Later when I did get the letter and read how the guards were described as 'dirty Loyalist scum bastards' I was more than a little embarrassed!

After several weeks on the *stailc* my sight became greatly impaired. Simultaneously, my sense of smell grew much more acute. I found it particularly difficult to tolerate the smell of the floor polish that the orderlies used in the wing. When I pointed this out to the hospital orderlies they limited its use or on occasions didn't use it at all. Air fresheners had to go as the 'fumes' from them were overpowering. One morning Paul, the MO, brought me in a jug of water, the first jug of the day. As I reached for it I detected the scent of 'Old Spice' after-shave lotion. As I raised the glass to my mouth it smelt as though the glass was full of the lotion. I was almost sick with the smell. I inquired of Paul if he was wearing after-shave. He said he wasn't and he couldn't believe that I could smell anything, as he couldn't, but added that he had used after-shave the previous day but had showered and washed his hands several times since then.

Water itself, I discovered, has its own smell and taste, undetectable in normal circumstances. And it's not a pleasant smell. Drinking so much of it became very tiresome, but I knew it was best to drink at least six pints a day. So I staggered it. One pint early in the morning, one before lunchtime, another in the afternoon, one in the evening, one before lock-up that night, then the last before going to sleep. The last two pints were the most difficult to get down in the latter weeks of the *stailc*. But I was lucky; the water was staying down. I watched others being continuously sick, throwing up the water, along with green bile from their stomachs. It's an agonising sight to watch someone bent over a kidney dish, his chest and stomach heaving every few minutes. It was also physically exhausting for them.

Sparkling spring water was introduced during Bobby's fast at a time when he found it impossible to drink tap water. He could drink the sparkling variety more easily. After that they bought case-loads of it. There were times I preferred it and other times I preferred the ordinary tap water. I developed a routine whereby I drank tap water in the morning and spring water in late evening. That change made the last two pints a bit easier to drink. The taste was different.

We also took salt, which was easy once you knew how. When I first began the fast I put the salt into a cup of water to drink. I was sick with the first mouthful and after that I could only sip it in very small amounts. Though I caught on within a few days that if I wet the tip of my finger, dipped it in the salt, then put that in my mouth rather than put the salt in the water, that it was fine. I probably took far more salt than was needed but it helped flavour my mouth, if nothing else.

I couldn't detect the smell of my own body decaying, although for others who entered my cell, especially in the latter part of my fast, it was clearly overpowering (as much as they tried to hide it). It's a specific type of smell. Not a smell of body odour, nor the smell of rotting animal flesh; it was a smell of live but decaying flesh, even if that sounds like a contradiction.

While in the prison hospital we were still not allowed to have cigarettes left in for us in a parcel but visitors could carry a packet of 20 each in with them, then leave them at the desk at the top of the wing on their way out. If there were three visitors this meant 60 cigarettes per visit. In this way, a store of cigarettes built up and there was always enough. It seems this system had been introduced to resolve a contentious issue. It could be publicly embarrassing that dying men on hunger strike were denied even the simplest pleasure of a cigarette, but that's exactly how it had been initially when Bobby was on hunger strike. One guard – Gerry Cardswell – had apparently taken great pleasure then in enforcing the no-smoking rule whenever he was on the wing. On a daily basis he would search Bobby Sands's cell hoping to find the tobacco which he was sure Bobby had secretly hidden away. One day, in the latter stages of Bobby's *stailc*, Cardswell discovered a half-ounce in Bobby's bed. He came out into the wing highly pleased with himself, holding up the 'contraband' and shouting that he had captured 'Sands's snout'. Bobby Hagan, one of the prison orderlies, went up to Cardswell and said, "I suppose you're really pleased with yourself? Taking snout from a dying man! Well, I can assure you of this, I'll be giving Bobby Sands a half-ounce of snout before I go off here tonight." Other MOs who had listened to the goings-on took no part in it. Most of them were probably embarrassed by the incident.

Bobby Hagan was a middle-aged Protestant man from County Down. We heard he was sentenced for tax evasion. It might even have been Bobby Hagan himself who had told us that. Ironically, he discovered that he had once worked with Bobby Sands for a few weeks in East Belfast, but it wasn't this which prompted his defence of Bobby in relation to the tobacco. It was basic solidarity which exists between practically all prisoners despite any other differing views they might have. Besides that, there was empathy for a dying man. In this instance, Bobby Hagan put up a direct challenge to the guard. He could easily have been charged with an offence against the 'good order and discipline' of the prison with a resultant loss in remission and other privileges. He could have lost his job as an orderly in the hospital, a job that was seen as a 'cushy number'. He acted, however, without thought for himself and without regard to the potential consequences of his actions. That was how Bobby Hagan treated all the *stailceoiri* throughout the hunger strike. He was always there to assist us in or out of bed, fetch water, newspapers, or anything else that was requested. When I got to the stage where I could barely stand unaided, Bobby Hagan would help me walk by placing his arm around my waist and my arm around his shoulder. We'd shuffle up and down the wing for a short time like that. When writing *Nor Meekly Serve My Time* years later I tried to locate Bobby, without success. I've always hoped, though, that if he ever did come across the book he'd read how much we appreciated his care and how he was remembered with great fondness and respect.

One day a few of us were sitting in the hospital exercise yard. Paul Lennon, the MO, was with us. Out of the blue Paul said to me, "Keep an eye on your cigarettes". I asked him what he meant. He simply repeated what he had said. I knew this had to mean that someone was either stealing them or tampering with them in some way but I couldn't work out who or why. I knew the orderlies weren't involved because they were forever offering us tobacco.

That night when I asked a guard for one of our cigarettes during association time I inquired how many cigarettes we had left. The guard said there was one half-empty pack of Embassy. I thought it strange as I had assumed there would be more but thought I could be mistaken. What Paul had told me, however, made me suspicious. The next morning I told Paul we were almost out of cigarettes and he gave us a 20-box of Benson and Hedges. Fr Toner was in to say Mass and I asked him if he would bring in 60 Embassy Regal. He said he would have them in by lunchtime. That afternoon Pat McGeown, Matt Devlin, and myself each had visits. Each group of visitors left 60 cigarettes. This totalled 240 cigarettes, plus the 20 Paul had given us that morning.

Just before lock-up that night I again asked the guard on duty to check how many cigarettes we had left. He said we had two 20 packets, one half full; about 30 cigarettes. At least 200 cigarettes had gone missing. I couldn't believe it. I knew they couldn't be anywhere else as they were all kept together in a drawer of the desk at the top of the wing. I called Paul and told him I wanted to see the PO or SO. An SO arrived and I told him what had happened, or what I believed had happened – that someone had stolen 200 cigarettes from us. I know I was fairly agitated and probably incoherent at times as I simply couldn't comprehend how someone would go and steal cigarettes from people who were dying and had nothing else to enjoy but a smoke. Even if one of the guards had been stuck for a smoke they could have taken a packet to tide themselves over and then replaced it later. If they had asked, they would have been given a packet no problem, but stealing them and stealing so many?

The SO, who was new to the hospital, listened to what I had to say, asked some questions, attempted to say that possibly we had smoked more than we thought – 200 more in one afternoon? Paul spoke up to say the cigarettes had been in the drawer earlier. He confirmed that our visitors and Fr Toner had left 60 cigarettes each. He pointed out that there would be a record of it written in the wing ledger. The SO, clearly embarrassed by what was being implied, said he would look into it in the morning.

What happened next was simply a cover-up. Another wing ledger was introduced in which a record would be kept of how many cigarettes each individual *stailceoir* smoked each day. This in no way tackled the immediate issue of the theft, but it no doubt sent a warning to the guards. There were no further thefts, at least to the best of my knowledge.

Although I had no way of proving it I strongly suspect that the guard who had stolen the cigarettes was Gerry Cardswell, the same one who had been harassing Bobby Sands. He had been on duty that afternoon and was the only one whose behaviour towards us was openly vindictive. He had also previously come into my cell one morning in the hospital, smoking, held up the cigarette in his hand and said to me, "This is one of your cigarettes, Laurence." I had replied, "No problem. Enjoy."

* * *

It was during the hunger strike, while I was in the prison hospital, that I saw my father for the first time since my arrest five years earlier.[79] It was an emotional and particularly uncomfortable visit. Like his brother Joe, he suffered from claustrophobia, and that was the reason he gave for not visiting previously, but I believe it was more to

---

[79] See photographs, showing the prison hospital logbook which registered my father as having visited.

do with his inability to come to terms with the path I had chosen in life, and, perhaps, fear about how he would respond to seeing me in captivity. My father's view of life (and the republican struggle) was so different to mine. I know that in many ways I had been a disappointment to him. I had not lived the life he had hoped for me. Earlier I mentioned that at age twelve I had moved to St Malachy's Grammar School after completing my primary school education, and how the size and strict formality of the school was a challenge to me. It was a different world entirely from what I had experienced at Farinflough and I wasn't having any of it. I began to mitch school and although I had never been in Belfast before, I discovered, and then hung out at, the Central Library and at the old Smithfield market with all its bric-a-brac, antiques, and the soft porn magazines on open display. To be honest, I think I looked at more publications in Smithfield than I did in the Central Library. It was very unfortunate that in 1974 the market was destroyed by IRA incendiary bombs – not because of the porn magazines but for the overall nature of the place, and all the colourful characters it attracted.

When I say 'mitch' school I mean full-time mitching. I didn't attend any classes at all. Some days I'd arrive home early with a story that first-years had been excused from some classes. I don't know how I envisaged it was all going to end, but end it surely did. The Principal of St Malachy's eventually wrote to my parents inquiring as to why I hadn't attended school for three weeks. My father was livid. He took me into the school the following Monday morning and sat with me as I got a lecture from the Principal. I was then taken to my class, a class in Latin. I stayed until the end of the class and then headed into the city centre again. My father discovered me that Friday afternoon standing outside the Central Library as he drove past. I don't know if he was on the lookout for me or just happened to be passing. I was smoking. I was twelve years old.

It was my mother who decided that if I wasn't happy at St Malachy's then I should go to the local secondary school instead. My parents approached the headmaster there, Paddy O'Kane, and I was enrolled. I loved school after that, but my father was still hugely disappointed in me. He felt I had thrown away a great opportunity for a good education; an opportunity that he never had as he was forced to leave school aged 14 to work delivering coal. It marked the beginning of a rift between he and I; the start of a widening gap in our perspectives on the world. A rift that was deepened in subsequent years: me joining the IRA aged 17, ending up 'on the run' shortly afterwards and away from home, then my arrest, sentencing, the blanket protest, and finally, hunger strike. I think that was all incomprehensible to him. He would have wished for me to have had a good career – something that was never an option for him when he was growing up. I could understand that. We never openly argued. While still at home I would silently listen to what he would say, even if I strongly disagreed, but then I would go and do what I believed I needed to do. That was the type of relationship I had with my father before my arrest and now I was seeing him for the first time in five years.

He came with a friend of his, a retired doctor. It wasn't that he was close to Dr Cosgrave – he had closer friends – but possibly he thought a doctor best suited to help him through the experience, or maybe he wanted the doctor to give him some idea of my physical condition. Dr Cosgrove had been a supporter of the Civil Rights Campaign and maybe my father thought that would appeal to me in some way.

The visit took place in the afternoon. It was sunny and I could watch the lads in the yard as I was sitting on the bed, while my Dad and Dr Cosgrove sat on chairs alongside one another with their backs to the windows. I didn't think my Dad looked much different to when I had last seen him. He was always a few stone over-weight and his complexion was never pale, his face not so much reddish as having a weather-beaten appearance. He always wore a cap which he now held in his hands and which he twisted tightly throughout the visit. He looked about the place nervously. He would look at me then look away again. Dr Cosgrave was very calm and did most of the talking, much of it about local events, happenings and such like. Conversation was punctuated with long and awkward pauses.

At one stage my Dad blurted out, "Do you know what you're doing? Do you know the effect it's having on your mother? It's breaking her heart." I said I knew what I was doing and yes, I did know the effect it was having on my mother. I said I didn't wish that and I hoped that she would be OK. He listened to me, then looked away, tossed his head, and continued to twist his cap in his hands. Dr Cosgrave went on talking as if nothing had disturbed the flow of conversation.

The half-hour seemed more like an hour and a half but eventually the guard, whose presence was always in my thoughts, called time. The goodbyes were as awkward as the conversation. I never thought about it until writing this memoir but looking back on it now, it's strange that my father was not accompanied by my mother. It was only when Gabrielle (who drew the illustrations for this book) was proofing an early draft of the memoir that she inquired why my mother and father did not visit together. I've no explanation for it. It may be that he wanted to be in the company of another male. It may even have been that my mother wanted him to go without her and in the company of a doctor in case he experienced panic attacks or other health issues. Or that she felt that she had to be absent so as to allow him, for his sake, to 'confront me' to reconsider my decision. Yet another query from the past that I'll never be able to answer.

Looking back on that era, I'm sure my experience – and that of my father – wasn't uncommon. It must have been difficult for fathers, in particular, to have their sons openly challenge them at such an early age. I don't believe my mother ever thought for one moment that decisions I made about my life were meant as a challenge to her. It wasn't about challenging parental authority but rather about (indirectly) challenging their political views and, more particularly, how they saw their place and way in the world. My father knew he was a 'second-class' citizen in the north of Ireland. He knew that because that's how he'd been treated and made to feel. He didn't rebel against it. That's not to lay any blame on him whatsoever. It's just the way it was. My parents' generation, and the generation before them, had kept their heads down. They didn't cause any trouble. My generation was no longer willing to accept that; was no longer willing to accept being walked upon; no longer willing to be regarded as inferior, the 'other', discriminated against, harassed, batoned off the streets, interned-without-trial, and, on occasions, murdered. Those days were long gone and I wonder if sometimes my father felt guilty that his generation had not done more. Or maybe he just felt confused or bewildered about it all. The world that he had grown up in had been turned upside down.

I felt sad when my father left the visit that day. Not agitated or frustrated, just sad. The relationship was the same; him wishing me to go in one direction and me committed to going in the opposite direction. But there was no malice in any of that. Just him wishing the best for me. He had worked all his life to keep a family and home together. Life was as simple as that. I could still vividly recall watching him from the window in our bedroom when I was aged about eight, as he walked up the lane to our house at Carngranny after returning home for Christmas following a stint working in England. He had got a job as a lorry driver with Farrans. There was no work to be had at home. And he was always a worker. In the small, battered brown suitcase he carried there were two comic annuals, one each for me and my brother, Eugene. I think one was the *Victor* and the other possibly the *Beano*. I don't know what he brought my sister Mary.

It wasn't just the visit with my father that was difficult. Most visits during that time were difficult and more than a bit unreal. A guard always stood inside the cell during the visits. The really zealous ones sat right against the end of the bed. A number of them were known to intervene on visits and pass some comment on what was being said. Although an occasional one showed embarrassment about being there and tried to be as unobtrusive as possible, others carried out their orders to the dotting of every 'i' and the stroking of every 't'.

John and Mary, two close friends, visited me in the hospital when I was about 50 days into the fast. Again, talk revolved around very mundane matters; how John was getting on at work, how fast the children were growing and the list of who was asking for me. No one was prepared to mention the elephant in the room. No reference to the hunger strike was made until they were about to leave when Mary suddenly burst out, "Do you know what you're doing? You're going to die. Do you know that?" She appeared angry with me but at the same time I could see the tears in her eyes. I knew it was Mary's way of expressing concern for me. I just said, "I'll be OK. Look after yourselves," and they left. On another visit with some republicans from my local area I was asked if I wanted a military funeral. It was asked in all seriousness though I regarded it as a bit ridiculous given the manner in which all the dead hunger strikers had been buried up until then. I simply said, "Yes". I think it meant something to the person who asked. I've no doubt he would've carried out the arrangements with great precision as "Laurny made me promise that I would look after things". Maybe he had asked me so as to reassure me that things would be looked after in that regard.

Although I was always glad to see my family and other visitors, visits were something to be endured rather than enjoyed. The conditions did not allow for privacy and the circumstances did not encourage carefree conversation. The look on their faces as visitors said goodbye always lingered with me long afterwards as did the feel of their tight embrace or grip of their handshake.

One afternoon the Assistant Governor came to tell me that Gerry Adams, Owen Carron, and Seamus Ruddy would be coming to visit us in about one hour's time.[80] This was something totally out of the blue. I had been lying on the bed but now I got up to pace the floor – an old habit of mine formed during the blanket protest. Five paces forward; five paces back. I took the visit to be a very positive sign. If Gerry Adams and Owen Carron were coming it must mean some approach had been made to them by the Brits. Gerry, as with Danny Morrison, was banned from visiting the prison. At the same time I didn't want to get too optimistic. I had experienced the fiasco of the ICJP intervention and knew the Brits would do anything. Nevertheless, I couldn't stop my spirits from soaring and imagining the possibility that there had been some significant breakthrough. Besides that, I was excited about meeting Gerry Adams. I had heard much talk about him from others who knew him from his time in the Cages.

We were unlocked shortly before the usual time and made our way to the canteen, all except Big Doc and Kevin Lynch. At this stage Kevin Lynch was critically ill. Big Doc was conscious but too weak to be moved out of bed. Those of us who did meet with Gerry, Owen, and Seamus – Pat Beag, Big Tom, Paddy, Red Mick, Matt and myself – were in good form, curious about what was happening and speculating on what could be behind it all. The fact that Seamus Ruddy, an IRSP spokesperson, was also coming with Gerry Adams and Owen Carron added to the speculation that a possible deal had been worked out with all parties involved. We didn't have too long to wait before they arrived into the hospital canteen. Bik was also present by now, arriving at around the same time. Everyone was introduced, though Bik and Pat were already known to Adams from their time spent together in the Cages. The rest of us soon became acquainted. It was explained to them that the other two lads were too weak to attend. They said they would look in on them once they had talked to us.

---

[80] Gerry Adams was then the Vice-President of Sinn Féin; Owen Carron had been Bobby Sands's election agent and went on to become elected himself for the same constituency in the by-election following Bobby's death; and Seamus Ruddy was a leading member of the Irish Republican Socialist Party.

The meeting came together fairly quickly. We gathered around a few tables and Gerry began by explaining events leading up to his visit and hence the reason for it. He outlined how Fr Faul had called the families together to talk about their relatives on hunger strike and had claimed that the hunger strikers were unaware of the true situation, that they did not have knowledge about feelings or events on the outside, and that Gerry Adams should personally visit the hunger strikers and make this known to them. Faul had said that he would see to it that Gerry be granted permission from the NIO to visit the jail. All of this was, of course, to put Gerry Adams and the leadership of the Republican Movement under moral pressure.

Fr Faul, better than anyone, had a very good insight into the feelings of the men in the Blocks. He was still coming in on Sundays to say Mass and on at least one occasion had a blazing row with Bik and others in H3 after he made a statement claiming that letters written by prisoners had in fact been produced in the Sinn Féin centre on the Falls Road. This particular row lasted about two hours and when he left the prison he spoke to the media saying that the prisoners had approached him and clearly shown that they were up-to-date with events on the outside, and he was now assured that statements released by them were in fact written in the Blocks and sent to the Republican Press Centre to be forwarded to the media. Despite this he did, however, continue to attempt to force a wedge between the families and the leadership of the Movement.

Gerry told us that when asked, he readily agreed to visit us and give us an appraisal of the situation and how he saw our position in relation to the possibility of the Brits conceding our demands. It was a grim picture. There were no ifs or buts. He said that there were no deals on the table, under the table, or anywhere else. Really he was spelling out for us what we in a sense knew but didn't like to think about. The Brits had already allowed six men to die and they would most likely allow more to die. Certainly there was no movement to indicate that they desired a speedy resolution to the protest. All three of them pointed out the great admiration the nationalist community felt for us and that nothing but respect would be shown to us if we decided to end the fast there and then. We said we didn't want to. We believed then, as firmly as when we first joined it, that our demands were just and should be granted. We had also lost too many comrades to stop now. Gerry again stressed that if we continued then most likely all around the table would be dead in a matter of weeks.

Once these serious points had been covered, we engaged in some light banter. A sort of gallows humour. Big Tom wanted to know why the IRA couldn't hit Charlie's wedding;[81] "about 500 pounds of blowy gear under the reception table" and a few other remarks along the same lines. There was laughter amongst the *stailceoiri* but I'm not so sure if the other three felt quite as comfortable sitting in company which was (in a light-hearted though no less serious way) debating the merits of wiping out most of the English Royal Family. It made us feel good anyway.

Soon it was time for them to leave. Gerry had told each of us about his meeting with our families and how they were keeping. He then said that they would go to see the other two lads, shook hands with us and left the canteen. They went into Kevin Lynch's cell first. There was nothing to be said or done there though Gerry spoke with Kevin's family. They then went to see Big Doc who was still lucid and who could speak. Gerry explained the reason for their visit just as he had done with us and told Kieran that if he continued on hunger strike he would be dead within a few days. Doc said he was very much aware of that but if our demands were not granted then that is what would happen. He knew what he was doing and what he believed in. On their way out of his cell Doc's parents met and spoke with Gerry, Bik, and the others. They asked what the situation was and Gerry told them what he had told us and Kieran. They just listened to this and nodded, more or less resigned to the fact that they would be watching their son die any day soon. On their way back up the wing Gerry, Owen and Seamus called into the canteen with us again. Owen was very visibly crying and no doubt all three had been deeply moved by the experience though it wasn't the time or place to sit and philosophise about it. We shook hands again and they departed.

I don't think there was much conversation between those of us left in the canteen. Gradually we drifted back to our cells. Our earlier high spirits had dropped sharply. Each of us understood the cold reality of the picture that had just been painted. The Brits were intent on crushing us. There would be no humanitarian gestures and appeals for goodwill would fall on deaf ears. We were on our own.

---

[81] British Prince Charles was getting married to Diana Spencer that summer.

# 12

# Sounds of Death

PAT BEAG AND I WERE SITTING in the corner of the hospital exercise yard. It was a mild day; warm but not sunny. We knew Paddy Quinn was going through a bad period, vomiting and unable to keep water down. We both knew how important it was to keep water down. Martin Hurson had died, in part, from dehydration. Suddenly, there was a loud sound from Paddy's cell. There was no warning of its approach. It came out of the blue – a very loud bellow. It was like the sound a cow makes at times, especially if distressed. It was very low, very deep, and long. An inhuman sound. Richard Green, the MO with us in the yard, looked up and said, "What was that?" "It's Paddy Quinn," I said. "What's he doing?" he asked. "Dying," I replied.

The roar was repeated a number of times and it had an unnerving effect on both Pat and myself. We could only guess at the pain Paddy was going through. The roar would subside for a while, then be followed by a high-pitched scream, then what sounded like giggling or chanting in a very high-pitched voice. There would be an interval of silence then it would start all over again, slowly building up to a very loud scream. We could hear the MOs in the cell with him trying to calm him. This went on for about half an hour and then it was time for us to come in from the yard again.

Paddy had been silent for a while, or at least not as loud, but shortly after I was locked up in my cell he started again. It began like a chant which was weird as he used to be slegged[82] about resembling a North American Indian, and that's the image that came to my mind when I heard the chant. As it grew progressively louder I tried to shut it out by wrapping the pillow around my ears but it was impossible to deafen

---

[82] Good-natured banter.

it. It was becoming much worse than earlier. There were less breaks in between the screams and now more deep sighs or moans, possibly as a result of his body becoming totally exhausted.

Soon after, I heard a woman's footsteps in the wing and then heard her calling Paddy's name in a soothing way: "It's alright Paddy. What's wrong son?" It was his mother. I remember thinking that she was remarkably calm throughout what must have been a totally horrifying and heart-breaking experience. I knew the effect it was having on me just listening to him but it must have been agonising for her watching him, knowing that he was not in control of his mind and frantically struggling with himself. At one stage his screams and yells built up to a very loud pitch and continued for some time, then they were muffled. I learned later that Paul Lennon, the MO, had noticed that Paddy was hyperventilating. This is the result of rapid deep breathing where you take in a lot of oxygen but carbon dioxide is lost from your blood. It produces dizziness at first and if not controlled can have very serious consequences. Normally, hospital wards would have proper equipment to cope with this but without these facilities Paul improvised by placing a brown paper bag over Paddy's face. The physiological effect it had was that Paddy breathed in again some of the carbon dioxide he had breathed out and this reduced his oxygen intake. By this stage, a number of MOs were holding Paddy down on the bed as he twisted and jumped about and Paul had to lie across him to keep the bag in place. In the middle of this, an Assistant Governor happened to be doing his rounds of the wing and he looked through the flap of the closed door. God only knows what he thought when he saw the scene in the cell but he didn't interfere.

Soon the improvised equipment took effect and Paddy's breathing began to slow and he became more restful. He still talked and muttered, mostly unintelligibly, but more quietly.

From my cell I could hear his moans subside then the sound of talking. I could still clearly hear his mother speaking to him. Just over and over again saying, "You'll be alright son. You'll be OK Paddy". I then heard what I took to be the trolley coming through the top grilles into the wing and a bit of a commotion outside Paddy's cell, followed by total silence. I realised what must have happened and this was confirmed about half an hour later when I was unlocked – his mother had authorised medical intervention and he had been removed to Musgrave Park Hospital.[83] My

---

[83] When a hunger striker lost consciousness 'power of attorney' shifted to his

only thought at the time was that I was glad Paddy, and his mother, had been spared any further suffering and I hoped the effects of whatever damage had already been caused would not be permanent. Months later, I learned from Paddy that he had been hallucinating throughout that time. He had seen people outside the window shooting at him, British soldiers and RUC men trying to get in the window. Then his friend Raymond McCreesh, who had died on hunger strike, had appeared at the door armed with a rifle, fighting off the Brits.

I heard the sound of that trolley in the wing again the following day – and the day after. Kevin Lynch died on 1 August and Kieran Doherty on 2 August. The trolley was used to remove their bodies. It was similar to those you'd see in any hospital – used for carrying bed linen. They were long and stood about three foot high but were very light as they were made from aluminium. Due to its lightness, when the trolley would be coming into the wing I could hear it rattle as it banged against the grilles. Going out of the wing it made little or no noise. The weight of a dead body dampened the sound. The trolley no longer rattled if it bumped against the grilles. It just made a dull sound. A thud. It's a sound that remains with me. Like hearing a particular song from the past can bring back vivid recollections of what you were doing at the time the song was popular, so too when I think of that sound. A dead sound. The sound of death.

There was an MO in the prison hospital called Billy Moore. He was in his late 20s, a friendly guy though he never said much. He was a 'born-again' Christian. Shortly after Big Doc's death he spoke to me one day while in my cell. He said he had chatted to Kieran often, and especially about death and an afterlife. He said, "Kieran was totally confident that what he was doing was right and that he would not be in any way penalised for his actions in an afterlife. He had no doubt, whatsoever." I could see that Billy was really challenged by that, and he added, "As a Christian, I know I don't have the degree of faith that Kieran had." He then walked out of my cell.

As I got up to slop out on the morning of 8 August, my mother's birthday, I sat for a moment on the edge of my bed. At this stage into the *stailc,* care had to be taken when getting out of bed. I would first rise up on my elbows, sit with my back against the pillows and the wall, and then slowly move up into a sitting position. I'd then put my

---

next-of-kin who could authorise medical intervention, if they so desired.

feet over the edge of the bed, resting there for a few minutes until my body and circulation grew accustomed to the new position. To rise quickly would very easily lead to a blackout, or at the very least, a feeling of faintness and nausea. I had learnt that from experience.

My door was open, as was the one into Tom McElwee's cell directly across from me. We exchanged '*Maidin mhaith*' – 'Good morning'. An MO was sitting with Tom as he was very weak by this stage but was able to sit up in bed and was still very lucid. The night before he had sat with us in the canteen for a while. He was in a wheelchair and had to be assisted when he wanted to move position in it. A lot of pillows were placed around him to soften the seat and mould it to the shape of his body to give the best support. Despite his physical condition he was in the best of form having had a visit from Dolores O'Neill, his fiancée from Armagh Prison that day. He described the visit and went on to talk about his family and how he hoped to see Benny, his brother (who was in H5) the following day. He had been pushing for ages to get a visit with him but the NIO had refused. He spoke of his hometown of Bellaghy (Co. Derry) and how he would love to live there again, to get married and invite all the neighbours to a big, outdoor reception. Everyone would be invited he said and this would show to the Protestants of the area that republicans meant them no harm and that the Ireland republicans wanted was one in which Protestants and Catholics were to be treated equally; not the way Catholics had traditionally been treated in the North.

After about an hour or so he had become very weak and said he would go back to his cell but would see us all the following morning. We bade him '*Oiche mhaith*' – 'Good night'.

As I looked across at him that following morning he appeared to be as well as could be expected under the circumstances. I shouted into him again on my way out for the regular morning check-up and weighing. When the doctor finished his rounds I went out to the yard with a couple of the other lads. Pat Beag was one of them and we sat on a couple of chairs. It was a brilliant morning, very sunny and I could feel the heat beam down on me. I love the sunshine and as it had been so long since I last felt its rays I sat there enjoying them. The next thing I knew I was being carried into the wing by one of the orderlies. He had caught me as I blacked out and began to topple off the chair – obviously the heat of the sun was too strong for me in that condition. He put me across his arms and walked in with me. I would have been about eight stone at the time. Just before we reached my cell I spotted Fr Toner walking down the wing. He spoke to me, joking that there was no better way to travel – a reference to me being carried. I fell asleep in my cell immediately, feeling totally drained.

Waking later, I reached out and switched on the radio, more so to get the right time than to listen to anything. The news at noon was just ending on Downtown and I caught the headlines "...this brings to nine the number of those who have died on hunger strike..." I knew then that Tom must have died. I discovered later that he had been sitting up smoking and talking to Fr Toner. At one point Toner went out of the cell for a few minutes. When he returned he found Tom dead. It had been as sudden as that, occurring just as I was being carried up the wing.

Tom's brother, Benny (Benedict), also a Blanketman, had been requesting a visit with Tom from the time Tom commenced his hunger strike. The prison authorities repeatedly refused the request. During the protest the two brothers were consistently refused joint visits with their family, meaning that the family had to make separate visits to see each of them. That was even the case when both of them were sharing the same wing in H6 in 1979 – the wing that I was also in. In David Beresford's book, Ten Men Dead, he recounts that on the morning of 8 August, Benny's cell door in H4 was opened and he was told to get ready for a visit with Tom and that when he arrived into the prison hospital he found Fr Toner waiting for him in the Circle. As the grille into the Circle was opened and Benny entered, Fr Toner walked over to him and said, "I've sad news for you. Thomas has died." Fr Toner told him that his family had already been told but would he, Benny, go in and see Tom, just to identify him for the record, and thus save his family from having to do that. Speaking to Benny when writing this memoir he disputes this version of events – particularly in regards to Fr Toner – though he accepts he is unclear of how things unfolded on the day. What is not in dispute, however, is that he was asked to identify Tom, rather than his parents or siblings having to do it.

I've often wondered at the rationale behind the decision to repeatedly deny Benny a visit with his brother, Tom, until a point where he was so critically ill that he was in danger of dying at any moment. There was no security issue involved. No risk. Tom was going nowhere; neither was Benny, other than to the prison hospital.

There was no difficulty with transport or time. It was nothing less than a crude demonstration of power; power for its own sake. The power of a bureaucrat. The power to grant or withhold permission for a visit. And that's what they did. Until it was too late.

Years later, I wrote this poem about Tom's death:

Tom

He was sitting up in bed
with a cigarette between his lips.
It was the morning of
the day the sun shone.
His voice was weak but clear
his one eye sharp in focus
and he smiled over at me.
That morning of
the day the sun shone.
At noon from the radio
I learnt he had died.
I remember it clearly
It was the day the sun shone.[84]

From the time I had been moved to the hospital, my progress through the fast, like those who went before me, was one of slowly weakening. After about 40 days my eyesight had become distorted. I initially had double vision which lasted a few days and then my sight became hazy. I found it very difficult to read and soon after this I stopped even trying. Similarly, watching TV became painful. Anything which was bright, such as the large light in the cell, was irritating, so I requested that it be switched off. Guards on night duty would switch it on hourly, however, to do a 'check', which usually meant any sleep was disturbed. My step became shorter and my pace grew slower.

The weakness in my body was paralleled in my mind. I found it difficult to maintain interest in conversation. I wasn't the only one who appeared to feel this way, and all dialogue between us on the *stailc* consisted of short comments interspersed with long periods of silence. It wasn't melancholy or depression, it was simply tiredness and a disinterest in most topics which I would normally be thinking about. I found that increasingly I had little, if anything, in common with those I met with other than the other hunger strikers. The distinction was between those on hunger strike and those not. Those

[84] Laurence McKeown (2018), *Threads*, Clare, Ireland: Salmon Poetry p. 57.

not on hunger strike lived a different life from me. Or maybe it was that they lived a life whereas I knew that mine would soon end. The things they seemed anxious about seemed ludicrous to me. It was difficult therefore to express any real interest in what was taking place around me or to engage in it in any way.

Throughout the course of the *stailc* I hadn't given too much thought to the actual process or moment of dying. I had, of course, thought of how people would feel about me dying; how my family would take it. And I thought of the things I would never do again and the people I would never see again. At the same time I realised that if I was dead I wouldn't be thinking or feeling at all. I would be dead. At this time I still held religious beliefs and, though by no means a committed Christian or Catholic, I still prayed. I was surprised that the prison chaplains, Tom Toner and John Murphy, hadn't attempted to talk me off the *stailc* by saying it was a sin against God or in other ways using religion against me. Perhaps they had gone over the merits of that with the previous hunger strikers, but at no time did they in any way attempt to dissuade me from what I was doing. I enjoyed their daily visits; they weren't religious occasions, more a bit of craic than anything else. Spud (Fr Murphy) spoke often of Francie Hughes and how he enjoyed debating with him. They would also bring Holy Communion with them each day which I received.

The food placed in the cell every day never tempted me – though as time went on the smell of it became obnoxious. It's difficult to describe the feeling of not eating. Some had told me that after three days I would lose interest in food. Well, I never encountered that nor did any of the other *stailceoiri* I spoke to. I think after a few days the stomach reduced in size and the body began to adapt to not using the digestive process, but I still had thoughts of food. During the blanket protest we often talked for hours about the enormous meals we would make ourselves once we got political status. These would be described in great detail and the smell of the dishes was almost palpable. This was at a time when prison routine made it possible to predict what meal we would get on which day up to three months away.

If you go for a considerable number of hours without food, or if you expect a meal then don't get it, you begin to think of food and what you are missing and that's when you start to feel hungry. A hunger strike is different. I knew I wasn't going to eat. It wasn't that

I was denied food or that I had missed a meal. I had decided I wasn't going to eat and I knew the reasons why I was doing that. The food sitting on my table therefore had no appeal to me and it wouldn't have mattered how delicious it was. The sense of hunger that would exist on other occasions didn't therefore arise. Of course there was a feeling of emptiness, but not hunger pangs. Often in the hospital when adverts for food would appear on the TV when we were out in the canteen in the evening for association we'd joke about it. "Would you beat that down your neck? Better fuckin' believe it!", and we would discuss it just as we had done prior to the fast.

The orderlies working in the hospital were very sensitive about food. They would be afraid to eat in front of us, though one evening Bobby Hagan walked into the canteen absent-mindedly munching away at a hamburger before he realised we were all there. He was overcome with embarrassment and really angry with himself even though we were all saying to him, "Go ahead Bobby, for Christ's sake. It doesn't annoy us". Every Thursday, steak and eggs were sent up from the kitchens for the orderlies who'd cook it when we were locked up. The smell of the steak frying was delicious and we would come out of the cells at half past five swearing to have one of those dinners as soon as we got status.

I received many letters and cards while in the hospital and was grateful for every one of them. Some of them were from people I hadn't heard from since going into prison. I knew people found it difficult to know what to say in them. Whether or not, for instance, they should refer to the brilliant holiday they just had. The most they could do was wish me all the best and say how they were thinking about me and praying for me. It didn't really matter though what they wrote: it was just nice to receive the letters and cards. I didn't write much myself and then only in the early stages of the fast. As time went on I couldn't motivate myself to put pen to paper. What would you write about anyhow?

At the beginning of the *stailc* my thoughts were very much focused on political events and what could have a bearing on the outcome of the fast. Later in the prison hospital I read the newspapers, listened to the news and current affairs programmes, and discussed the situation with the others on the *stailc*. But as time wore on I found (as did the other *stailceoiri*) that I became less interested in the news. It wasn't a case of losing hope, more a lack of enthusiasm, a settling down to just doing the fast; focusing energy, emotional and psychological, on the task at hand.

Time dragged by fairly slowly in the hospital but the nights were the longest. Despite this, I looked forward to locking up at 8.30 just to be on my own. While my sight was still good I did the odd crossword or I listened to the radio, but it was more a case of the radio providing background music than me actually listening to it. As time went on, though, I listened to the radio less and less. Strangely, during this time I experienced a change in my taste in music. Normally I enjoy most types of music with the exception of Irish Country and Western. I loathe it (apologies to all fans!). Yet during the latter part of the fast it was the only music I could listen to. The only explanation I can offer is that the genre is so boring and repetitive, you don't have to think about it; just switch it on and let it drone away.

Most of the time was spent reminiscing and day-dreaming. I had images of how the *stailc* would suddenly end with all our demands granted and the partying we would do afterwards. Now and again I thought of my death. I feared that it would be a painful one or one in which I had lost control of my senses for a time beforehand, as had happened with Martin Hurson. I wanted to stay lucid for as long as possible.

I thought of my family often and of how the hunger strike was affecting them. I knew my mother was the one bearing the brunt of the pressure. She was the one most in contact with me, the one who had visited me regularly since my imprisonment, and the one who felt most deeply for me. She was not a republican and I wondered how she now felt being to the fore in this form of republican struggle. She was the one who attended marches and appeared on platforms and on occasions even spoke at those gatherings. She was the one who appeared in photos and articles in the local press. For someone who avoided the public gaze, it must have been quite a challenge for her. I knew that her thoughts were with everyone on the *stailc* and especially so with their families. I regretted I hadn't more time and better circumstances to speak with her on the visits but also realised that I was often avoiding talk of what she meant to me as it would be too emotional for both of us.

I relived many exploits with old friends. In fact, because the years on the blanket involved recounting old stories of our youth, the images were familiar to me. I had nothing in common now with most of these people, having drifted apart over the years, but their earlier friendship was still dear to me. You could say, in a sense, that after 8.30 at night I wasn't really in the hospital but off in either bygone days or living in a future H-Block with political status and all the freedom of movement and pastimes that allowed for.

Sleep was not deep. I would sleep for a few hours, then suddenly find that I was wide awake staring at the ceiling. Bernadette, my first love from secondary school days, kept appearing in my dreams. I hadn't seen her in about ten years and couldn't recall a time I had ever been reminiscing about her with any great depth of feeling, but for the duration of the *stailc* I felt very, very close to her. I don't know if she was thinking of me at the time or what caused it.

Like the prison camp in general, the hospital wing was very, very quiet at night, and although I know it sounds like a cliché, I was often just listening to the silence. At such times I felt very close to the ones in the Blocks. I knew they would be thinking of us, asking for scéal about us, writing to whoever they could on our behalf and in some cases preparing to join the *stailc* themselves. The nights were long but I enjoyed the solitude.

Pat Finucane, the human-rights lawyer (whose brother Seamus, was on the blanket protest), came to see me one day to make my 'last will and testament'. It was a bit unreal, me, who did not even have a set of clothes, making a will. I'm not so sure how I felt about it – 'in the event of my death' – but I don't think I really took the whole process too seriously. It was all a bit abstract in a sense. I enjoyed the visit though. Pat was able to tell me what was taking place outside and give a general assessment of feelings in the community. He did a lot of work around the time of both hunger strikes and we much appreciated it. On 12 February, 1989, Pat Finucane was shot dead in his home in front of his wife and children. His killing was one of the most controversial during the conflict because the loyalists who killed him were working in collusion with British Intelligence and Security Services. A campaign by his wife and family for an independent inquiry into his killing continues to this day.

Apart from the occasion of Gerry Adams's visit and that of a Red Cross delegation (the content of which I remember little about as it was more or less a greatly reduced rehash of what took place with the ICJP) I met with Bik on a number of other occasions. One of these was following the intervention of Pat Beag's family and his removal from the *stailc*. Pat had been sick for a few days and I knew his condition had deteriorated rapidly. Pauline, his wife, was then allowed in to see him and when he became unconscious she authorised medical intervention. I was locked in my cell next to his and could just hear the noise of the trolley being wheeled in and out again. I guessed what had happened when all went quiet soon afterwards. Fr Murphy who had been present in the hospital that afternoon came and told me later that Pat had been moved to Musgrave Park Hospital.

I can't recall much that happened after that except that Matt Devlin and myself decided to get Bik up for a visit the following day. I was to request the visit. When Paddy Quinn's fast had ended I was relieved as I had listened to his painful roars and cries and it had occurred at a time when there was less focus on the families to intervene. In the meantime, however, Fr Faul had stepped up his moral crusade against the hunger strike and was encouraging families to end it by medically intervening once their relative went into a state of unconsciousness. I knew therefore that a lot would be made of the intervention of Pat's family and I knew that the Brits would regard it as a victory for them and a weakening of our position. I was concerned about the overall effect this would have on our strategy. I also wondered about my own family and what my mother would be thinking.

Bik arrived at the hospital. I don't think he was surprised at our request to see him as he figured we would want to discuss the overall situation. There had been a degree of reluctance in asking for him in case the administration saw it as a panic move on our part, but we knew such illusions would soon be dispelled.

We gathered together in the canteen and went over the whole situation. It's possible that the others then on hunger strike (but still held in the Blocks) were also present because I did see them at one time, but am not sure of exactly when it was. We all accepted that the Church and media were coming out strongly against the continuation of the *stailc* but that our support on the ground and internationally had not diminished. There were also others still prepared to join the fast at any time despite the numbers they had witnessed dying. The chat was good and we all agreed that whilst we had suffered a setback it was one that could be weathered and which didn't ultimately affect our overall position. Bik relayed a few messages from the lads in the Blocks. As usual there were witty remarks. Then we broke up and Bik and the others left.

I thought then, as I had done on a few occasions before, that Bik's role was a thankless one. I had some idea of how he must feel, sitting down to talk to men, not having any answers to questions they might raise and some of whom he might not see again. I knew we all understood the pressure he was under and I think we did our best to ensure we didn't add to it with a careless word. There was a close bond between all of us which allowed men to firmly argue their position even though the result of that would most likely mean the deaths of some of those across the table from them. It had been our experience throughout the Blanket and it was how we intended to continue.

As I grew progressively weaker and realised that death was something which faced me very soon, my thoughts were mostly about the manner in which I would die. I had already witnessed others dying and in different ways. I hoped it would be sudden, like Big Tom, and without sickness.

I thought about Tom's death a lot. It was the most vivid to me, having spoken together the previous night and having seen him again that morning, just hours, if not minutes, before he died. He had been relatively free from sickness throughout the *stailc* and my own health and rate of deterioration up until then had very much mirrored his. I therefore looked on Tom's death as the most likely example of how I would die. That is, I would be lucid right up to the very end then suffer a coronary attack or some other form of instantaneous death. That wasn't a morbid thought; it was relevant to my circumstances. I had witnessed other men suffering the pain of sickness, had listened to the torments of Paddy Quinn, and had heard of what Martin Hurson had endured in his final hours before dying. So the manner in which Tom died was therefore very much to be desired and I viewed it as pragmatically as that.

The actual fact of dying, of being no more, didn't occupy my mind a lot. There may have been a reluctance to dwell on that – actually dying – as that would have ruled out the thought that we might still win. I generally always think positively – I'm inclined by nature to be more of an optimist than a pessimist – and I always thought positively then. Or as positively as I could. I would, for instance, as long as it was possible, get up out of bed each day and walk about for a while or even sit in the armchair beside the bed. I could see the sense in it even if physically it took a great effort to do so. It kept the mind alert. It was important, psychologically. Once you were confined to your bed, either because you could no longer physically move out of it, or you just didn't want to move out of it, you were on the way out.

In the last days of my fast, death took on a more real appearance and was now an inevitability rather than a possibility, but by then I was almost totally exhausted and to even think such things in any deep sense or for any length of time takes a lot of concentration, so I didn't dwell on it. I think it must be like someone who has been on their feet for days without sleep and who is totally exhausted, then gets the chance to lie down and sleep but is awakened to be told the house is on fire. They don't want to know; they just want to lie and sleep. Danger means nothing to them. All that matters is the craving for rest and sleep. That's how I would describe the last days of the hunger strike; a state of total exhaustion – physical, emotional, and psychological – where all I wanted to do was close my eyes and sleep. I had reached a point where I accepted that I wasn't going to see a successful outcome to the *stailc*. I therefore fixed my mind on living out my last few days as peacefully as possible. Death now began to appear more as a release from a weak and decimated body.

From watching how others progressed on the fast, I noticed that about two, certainly no more than three, days before death, a hunger striker's bowels would open. I believe I first identified it in the case of Tom McElwee. Following it there was a marked deterioration in Tom's overall health and energy. It wasn't that the bowel movement itself was the actual cause of deterioration but was an indication that the person was in the very last stages of life. Then Red Mick told me one night in the canteen that he had diarrhoea most of the day. I already knew as one of the MOs had told me, so I didn't comment much other than to ask if he was OK, and he said he was. Both of us knew what it signalled. We had previously talked about this phenomenon. Mickey was already very weak by this stage, though because his features were less sharp he didn't appear as gaunt as others such as Big Doc, Kevin, or Tom had.

That was the last night we talked together. The following day Mickey didn't get out of bed and his family were allowed to stay in the hospital on a permanent basis. I could hear them going in and out of his cell for the few days he lingered on but didn't go in myself. Amongst the hunger strikers there were no goodbyes said, only, "See you". His death occurred silently. All that was heard was the trolley knocking against the wall with a dull thud as it manoeuvred through the doorway.

*Ten Men Dead* by David Beresford is an excellent book about the hunger strike though I thought his account of Mickey's life was unfair and unjust. He depicted Mickey as a sort of tragic figure and referred to him as a 'very untypical hunger striker'. I don't know what Beresford meant by 'untypical' as I don't regard any of the others who died as 'typical' hunger strikers. I think it unfortunate that he portrayed Mickey in such a way.

Regardless of our individual pasts, family histories, and the various routes we took that eventually led us to the H-Blocks, we became a 'family' in prison. The family of blanketmen. We didn't identify those on hunger strike as being either IRA volunteers or INLA volunteers. It didn't matter who they were, what organisation they belonged to, what part of the country they were from, what they were charged with, or how long they were serving. They were blanketmen. They were friends. They were brothers. They were, Bobby, Frank, Patsy, Raymond, Joe, Martin, Kevin, Kieran, Tom, and Mickey.

Reading Beresford's account prompted me to write this poem as a tribute to Mickey. H-Block prisoner. Blanketman. Hunger striker. Comrade.

Red Mick

The day I first met you
(to speak to that is)
you were slowly dying.
Not something which was immediately noticeable on your face
but then you had only begun to die and
that was why we were together in that room
because some thought they could stop that death
stop it by appealing to those they saw as the
weaker element in the fight.
Two days later we realised they consisted of
a small degree of sincerity
a large amount of naivety, and
had loyalty to political and ecclesiastical masters
rather than to the dying.
They will have taken away with them an image of you
distinguishable features most likely
just as others who knew you will define you in various ways.
As the child born on 20/5/54, who
grew up in Springtown and then the Bog, the
brother of Margaret, husband of Maggie
father of Mickey Junior and Louise

friend of Noel
associate of Eamonn.
Each will have their own story to tell.
But it was many years later that I read these details of your life
for they were unimportant at the time we first met
our world being very much of the present and future
and reminiscences were for later when sleep would not come.
Your end was not glorious
not as heroes die in Hollywood creations
and in chapter ten someone comments that really
you had very little to live for.
I dispute that
though I understand that it was spoken from another's world.
For I believe that in the H-Blocks you found something to love
and live for
a place to give what was yours to offer
and not be judged by societal norms,
exalting the few and damning the multitude.
And you loved and lived that so much
that you loved and lived it
to death.[85]

I began to prepare myself for death as I had joined the *stailc* a week after Mickey and was at that point the longest on it. Even when Matt Devlin's family authorised medical intervention, it didn't cause me any great concern. No doubt a degree of fatalism had set in.

When I had been on the fast over 60 days, the MOs started to give me a body rub each day to improve circulation and stop sores from forming on the skin of my back and hips where my body's weight was pressing down. I was also given a sheepskin rug to lie on, which greatly helped. Extreme luxury. Someone came in to visit me one day and I still don't know if he was a doctor or an NIO official. He was with a few others besides the prison doctor and he strutted around my bed asking a few questions about how I felt. Initially I was replying to his questions but as his manner was noticeably abrupt I began to look away and ignore him. He stopped at the end of the bed and in a loud clear voice told me what was happening to my body. "These purple marks on your chest and arms are blood vessels which have broken down and collapsed, your eyesight has been permanently damaged, your vital organs are under intense strain at this moment. There are a number of ways you will

[85] Laurence McKeown (2018), *Threads*, Clare, Ireland: Salmon Poetry p. 63.

possibly die: a brain tumour or a massive coronary attack, your kidneys or liver could collapse at any moment. Either way you can expect to die very shortly." He turned on his heel and walked out of my cell, apparently more upset at my impending death than I was.

Only in the last few days of my fast did they stop leaving food in my cell. I had complained to them before about the smell of it once it cooled but they said they were legally obliged to provide me with food. A different doctor came to visit me one day, accompanied by Paul Lennon, the MO. Paul pointed out to the doctor that I physically couldn't eat the food being left in my cell even if I *did* decide to eat. He added that he thought it actually cruel to put the food in my cell and suggested they stop doing so. The doctor agreed. At the time my cell door was locked during the night (as per normal practice with all prisoners) and Paul said that was both illogical and dangerous, given my state of health. The doctor agreed it should be left unlocked.

Although I saw Paul Lennon on a number of occasions after the hunger strike I never really had the opportunity to thank him for the kindnesses he showed us during that time. Or maybe I never took the opportunity? Maybe it's only now, looking back on those days, that I can more fully appreciate what he did. Why did *he*, and not others, behave in the way he did? Paul was a trained nurse and I'm sure that influenced him. Most other MOs were basic prison guards with six weeks first aid training. He was also a Catholic but then again, experience had shown that in such situations Catholics could be even more brutal, mean, or sadistic than their Protestant colleagues. It all comes down to how individuals, all of us, behave when we're put into challenging situations.

I was becoming increasingly sick, the first time during the *stailc* that I had experienced sickness. I don't know if it was because I wasn't consuming as much water; I was finding it almost impossible to drink any significant amount of it. I made a determined effort to increase the intake of it and thankfully the sickness got no worse, though it remained. What was worse were the hiccups which came after about 67 days. They remained with me almost constantly and just as a bout of them would stop and I was getting some relief, I would move in the bed and they would begin all over again. On top of this, I couldn't hear clearly and was having headaches.

When the bowel movement came, I knew I had not long left to live. It was on a Friday afternoon and the sensation was no different from feeling the need to go to the toilet in normal circumstances. However, it became excruciatingly painful. It had been more than nine weeks since I last had a bowel movement. The MOs gave me suppositories which helped, to a degree. Nevertheless, I still spent about an hour in the toilet and was exhausted – totally drained – by the time I was finished. I was already in a very weak condition by then but this spent my last reserves of strength. Bobby Hagan assisted me back down to my cell, almost carrying me, and got me into bed. I didn't get out of bed again. I knew that I had now no more than two or three days left to live, if that.

Some hunger strikers' families had been with them for a long period of time before their deaths. They would sleep in an empty cell in the prison wing and one of them would always be with their relative on hunger strike. In Big Doc's case his family had come in when he was 50 days or so on hunger strike because he took very ill at that time. However, he picked up again and lived for almost three more weeks, during which time his family were always with him. After this, families were not allowed in until it was very apparent the *stailceoir* was going to die or, as in the case of Big Tom, they didn't get the chance to come in at all because he died so suddenly.

A Doctor Bell came to see me when I was 68 days on hunger strike. He asked me a few questions about how I felt. Again, Paul Lennon, the MO who accompanied him, intervened and suggested that my family be allowed in. He said that medically it could not be said that I was on the point of death, yet everyone knew that I could die at any minute given the length of time I had been on hunger strike and the pattern of those who had already died. Dr Bell seemed to consider it for a few moments then nodded his head that he would give permission for my family to come into the hospital. They came that night.

My recollection of this period of the *stailc* is not clear in terms of the order in which events occurred. I remember Mary, my sister, coming in with my mother. Mary was in a distressed state and asked me if I intended continuing with the fast. I said I did and she began sobbing loudly. My mother sat beside her looking over to me in an expressionless manner. I knew that out of them, despite being the most calm, she would bear not only the burden of her own sorrow but the weight of comforting others. I talked about some neighbours and friends and generally tried to make some conversation to show that I was lucid. I knew it distressed them when I was sick, particularly when they saw how much the hiccups

drained me. My Dad came in to see me but just stood in the corner of the cell for a while and went out again. He was unable to speak. Eugene, my brother, also visited and appeared to be handling it OK. On the Saturday I was dozing in and out of sleep. I kept dreaming that I was in some place totally surrounded by blackness and that I felt very, very tired and wanted to sleep but kept saying to myself, "You mustn't sleep, you mustn't sleep or you're a goner". It seemed like the last fight to hold onto life. The ego not wanting to succumb.

Members of my family kept a constant vigil at my bedside. When I would wake they would ask me if I was OK and pass me a drink of water if I asked. I don't know when exactly I began to lose consciousness but the last time I recall coherently talking to anyone was on the Saturday. My mother was at my bedside on her own. She had never asked me at any time since joining the hunger strike, or even when I had first told her that I would volunteer, not to do so. And she didn't ask me now. She had never discouraged me in any way and had worked wherever and whenever possible with anyone who wanted to help our protest. We had never discussed the likely consequences of my going on hunger strike, both knowing what could happen, and we had left it at that. So much went unsaid between us. I knew that when she was out of my cell she was across the wing in an empty cell on her knees praying and when she would return to me she would still have that calm face even though I knew she must be feeling her sorrow intensely. That evening I said to her, "I'm sorry all this came about for you". She leaned across to me and whispered, "You know what you have to do and I know what I have to do". I didn't understand at the time what she meant but I think I do now, years later. If I was to die suddenly then that was how it was intended to be. It would be God's will. But if my life ended up in her hands and the decision was hers, then she would give me life as she would see it. Later that evening I became delirious and then slipped into unconsciousness. Early on Sunday morning, the 70th day of my fast, my mother authorised medical intervention.

*Photo:* Paddy Hillyard

Wall mural recording the deaths of Bobby Sands, Ray McCreesh, Frances Hughes, Patsy O'Hara, Joe McDonnell, Martin Hurson, Kevin Lynch, Kieran Doherty, Tom McElvee and Micky Devine, and showing 'Larry' McKeown on day 69 of the *stailc*

# 13
# Ending It

I AWOKE FROM UNCONSCIOUSNESS to the sound of a female voice. I heard my name spoken: *Laurence*. The female voice was telling me I was in the Intensive Care Unit of the Royal Victoria Hospital, Belfast. The voice was that of a nurse. I was practically blind and could only make out a vague human form. It hurt to open my eyes in the bright light so I kept them closed. I felt her hand on my upper arm; a gentle touch. A female voice speaking my name and a gentle female touch on my body. It had been many years since I had last experienced such. She was telling me they were going to slowly turn me over onto my other side. I imagine they were wary of me lying for too long in one position, with the possibility of bones breaking through flesh. They had no lambskin rugs for me like they had back in the prison hospital. She asked me if I was ok and I said yes, but that I needed to urinate. She immediately went and got the appropriate dish and assisted me to urinate into it. I thanked her and then just lay with my eyes closed.

I was aware that I was alive. I was neither happy to be alive nor sad to be alive. I just knew I existed. I couldn't have cared less what that existence looked like. I was empty. I was totally exhausted; physically, certainly, but psychologically and emotionally too. It was as if I had used every bit of energy in me to pursue the hunger strike, and that energy was finally depleted.

I could vaguely make out the dark outline of figures beyond the end of my bed and could hear English voices. They were British soldiers who were guarding me; probably uneasy given we were on the staunchly republican Falls Road.

Not long after I had first asked the nurse for assistance to urinate, I felt the need to urinate again. I decided I'd say nothing and just sit with it as I was embarrassed to ask the nurse for assistance again. But as the minutes passed by the need intensified. Eventually I called the nurse and said to her, "I'm very sorry but I need to urinate again." She gave a short laugh and said, "Laurence, there are two intravenous drips going into you; one in each arm. We'd be concerned if you *didn't* feel the need to urinate."

The following morning I was moved to the security ward of Musgrave Park Hospital, Belfast. The ward was used to house prisoners who required medical treatment. I was placed in a small single room at the top of the ward. I was still rigged up to the intravenous drips. I learned from a nurse there, Audrey, that one was glucose and the other contained vitamins and minerals. She loosely wrapped a cable around my right wrist that had an alarm button attached to it. She told me to press the button whenever I needed her, even for the simplest thing.

I had a visit from my mother on the afternoon of the day I arrived in Musgrave Park Hospital. I now know that she felt apprehensive about that visit. Like many visits over the period of the protest and hunger strike the one thing that wasn't spoken about was what was really happening – or, in this case, what had just taken place. I don't recall much about the visit other than that I didn't want her to feel bad. All of our parents, wives, partners, and children were in the same boat. They wanted so much for us to achieve our demands but they weren't IRA or INLA volunteers. They were our families. And they watched as one after the other died without, increasingly in their view, any hope of success. Coupled with Church and media pressure on them to intervene when their loved one lost consciousness, they acted to save them – even if it was against their loved one's wish. That's what my own mother did. Thankfully, I had the maturity to recognise that for what it was – love.

> When next we met,
> the scars of that battle were etched deeply upon your face.
> Hustled in and out again
> we got no chance to say the things we wanted to
> and I wondered
> if you'd left still unsure
> of how I felt
> towards you.
> You who were blameless.[85]

---

[85] Laurence McKeown (2018), *Threads*, Clare, Ireland: Salmon Poetry, p. 32.

I've wondered in later years, if I would have felt differently – about my mother and myself – if mine had been the first instance where a mother or wife intervened, or if another hunger striker had died after me. But it wasn't the first instance and no one else did die so it's all just conjecture, like so many other things about the past.

I don't recall much of those first few days in the security ward of Musgrave Park Hospital. There isn't really much to recall. I existed. I was on a drip (eventually just one). I went to the toilet in a bedpan, assisted by Audrey or whichever nurse was on duty at the time. On the second day in Musgrave they started to feed me small amounts of chicken, blended into a watery paste. When it was established that my digestive system could handle semi-solid food they removed the remaining intravenous drip from my arm. Soon, I could make it out of bed to go to the toilet myself, although the nurses discouraged this. I was obviously extremely weak and they were concerned that I might collapse with the effort and hurt myself. But the embarrassment and indignity of having to be assisted to go to the toilet in a bedpan far outweighed any fear of falling.

The one thing I do vividly remember from those days, however, was this sound that I first seemed to sense rather than hear. The ward was quiet but there was this sound, as if in the distance. It was like a song going round in my head that I was familiar with but I couldn't recall who the singer was or what the lyrics were. I don't know how long the sound had been going on before I became aware of it, but suddenly I realised what it was. It wasn't in my head at all; it was in my ears. It was the sound of children laughing and playing. Unknown to me, the ward adjacent to the security ward was the children's ward. They must have occasionally been in a particular part of the ward, possibly a play area, which is when I heard them. It had been at least five years since I'd heard the laughter of children. I was slowly becoming aware of the sensory deprivation of the years on protest. The female voice and touch on my arm in the Royal Victoria Hospital, and now the laughter of children in Musgrave Park, reminded me that there was a world outside of the one I had existed in for the past five years but which I'd shut out so as to survive; so as to cope with the conditions I existed in.

Three days after arriving in the security ward I was moved out of the single room into a large four-bed room. Paddy Quinn, Pat McGeown and Matt Devlin who had both been on hunger strike were there. It was a strange situation; a bit like the realisation in the Royal Victoria Hospital that I was still alive. There was neither a happiness nor sadness at meeting one another. The mood was sombre. The last time we had been together had been several weeks earlier in the prison hospital in the H-Blocks. Now we were no longer there nor on hunger strike, but we were conscious that others still were. The hunger strike was still ongoing. It was like we were in the centre of some major event; involved, but at that point in time dislocated from it. Soon after, Paddy Quinn, Pat McGeown and Matt Devlin were moved back to the Blocks and not long afterwards Bernard Fox and Liam McCloskey were admitted to the hospital. Bernard's family had intervened when he went unconscious; Liam came off the hunger strike of his own accord after his family told him that they would not let him die and would authorise medical intervention in the event of him losing consciousness.

Shortly after moving into the big ward I noticed that Audrey, the nurse, was no longer around. I discovered from one of the others that she had been moved to another ward. Apparently the Charge Nurse on the ward, a man called Archie, thought she was too friendly with us and had her moved. Whether or not that is true I don't know but his behaviour towards us would make me believe it *was* true. He was always brutal when taking blood from me, leaving a bruise on my arm, something that never happened when other nurses took blood. Many years later he was dismissed from the ward following a physical altercation with an Assistant Prison Governor who had called at the ward for a regular inspection. The story I heard was that Archie was drunk, that he didn't like the manner of the Assistant Governor and refused to allow him onto 'his' ward. The Assistant Governor challenged this, ultimately ignored Archie's refusal, and moved to walk down the ward whereupon Archie tried to stop him. I heard the story from various sources – a republican prisoner who had been held in the security ward at the time and from a nurse who worked in the ward who would only confirm that Archie was no longer in charge and had been moved elsewhere. Years later I tried to discover if Audrey still worked in the hospital – to thank her for her care – but had no success. She was a wonderful nurse and she took great care of us.

I made regular six-monthly visits to the security ward over the remaining eleven years I was in prison, as nine months after the hunger strike I was diagnosed with ulcerative colitis which arose as a result of the fast.

Visiting conditions were better in the hospital than in the prison. The guards usually stayed outside the room and visitors came in and sat by your bedside. The room was comparatively large too; probably about 25ft x 20ft, much bigger than we had been used to over the previous five years. I was soon eating regular solid food – it's amazing how quickly the body can adapt – and it was then that I experienced intense perspiration. The security ward at Musgrave Park Hospital was constructed of portacabins joined together in a long line. There was a corridor with the individual rooms off to the right if you were walking down the corridor from the entrance. There were windows with small openings at the top and with metal grilles on the outside. My bed was positioned parallel with the outside wall and at night I lay close to the window with the top part open. The sweat poured off me. I wore pyjamas and had only one sheet covering me but I'd wake in the middle of the night and have to take the pyjamas off me as they were soaked through – as was the sheet I was lying on. I'd change into fresh pyjamas and put a new sheet on the bed and by morning they would be equally soaked. It settled down a bit after a week or so but even today I can experience a burst of perspiration if I eat after an extended period of not eating.

I weighed 105 pounds (47.7 kgs) at the end of the hunger strike. So, basically skin and bones. No fat. No muscle to speak of. I had blood taken and my blood pressure tested every day. For practically all of the time I was in the hospital I was confined to bed mostly, unless to go to the toilet. I'd initially walk there holding onto the wall to steady myself. Later I began to use the food trolley at the end of my bed like a Zimmer frame, though in this case the trolley had wheels at the bottom of each leg, which could be dangerous. One day I pushed the trolley too far in front of me and wasn't able to step forward quick enough to keep my balance, so ended up falling onto the floor. Thankfully I didn't do any damage to myself.

The first ones to have come off the hunger strike were held in the outside hospital for anything up to six weeks, but later the prison authorities began to return people to the prison much sooner. Whether or not that was to put pressure on those still on hunger strike it's hard to tell, but after only three weeks or so in Musgrave I was sent back to the H-Blocks. I was dressed in striped pyjamas and a dressing gown. When I arrived at the reception area of the prison I was told by a Medical Officer that I was being taken to the prison hospital. I told him I wasn't going there. There were people there on hunger strike and no way was I going to be placed amongst them and the awkwardness and discomfort that would cause for all of us. He went away and came back a short time later and said that they couldn't take me directly back to the Block at that time (it was over lunchtime), so I would have to go to the hospital in the meantime, but he assured me that they would then take me to H4 that afternoon. I insisted I'd only go to the hospital temporarily on that basis.

I arrived at the prison hospital and an MO helped me down the wing by taking my arm. It was eerie to be back in the space that held such recent memories. As I walked down the wing slowly I could hear the familiar sounds of someone in an advanced stage of hunger strike; the sighs and the retching of bile into a kidney dish. I was put into a cell at the bottom of the wing. I lay down on the bed as I was exhausted and tried not to think of where I was. But of course I couldn't stop such thoughts. The place had been my home for almost six weeks; six weeks during which I'd witnessed four comrades and friends die. Conversations I'd had with them, or the last words I'd had with them, were still very fresh in my mind.

When two o'clock came and lock-up was over I was taken to H4. Before leaving the hospital I was again asked if I was sure I wanted to go back to a Block rather than remain in the hospital. I think the person who asked was actually being genuine. I can't recall now who it was. I suppose it displayed just how disconnected they were to what was happening. How could they not be aware of the sensitivities involved?

I arrived at H4 and made my way into the Circle of the Block. Usually when a prisoner arrives onto a Block the guard on duty in the Circle calls out, "One on", and whoever is in charge of monitoring the total number of prisoners in the Block at any given time has to alter the number. The same happens when a prisoner leaves the Block for a visit or some other reason. As I walked into the Circle the guard called out, "Another failed hunger striker on." Given the problems with my eyesight, the journey from Musgrave Park Hospital in the back of an enclosed, blacked-out van, and the travel to and from the prison

hospital, I was by then extremely exhausted and worse still, very nauseous. To make my way to the corridor that led to the wing I couldn't just walk across the Circle. I was too weak. Instead I walked around the Circle with one hand holding onto the wall for support, then holding onto the bars of the grille until I got into the corridor, then holding onto the wall again until I reached the grilles into D wing, then the wall of the wing until I reached the first cell in the wing: cell 3. The door slammed shut behind me. Throughout that journey, various guards looked on in silence, opening and closing grilles behind me and finally closing the cell door behind me.

Someone called in to me from the cell next door to discover who I was. It turned out it was Raymond McCartney who had been on the first hunger strike. I answered and then heard my name being passed around the wing. Some men got up to their doors to shout down to me, to welcome me, but I was too weak, and by then too nauseous, to reply to them. I lay down on my bed and for the first time ever since I had entered prison, including the time spent on remand, I felt claustrophobic. It may have been the contrast to the three weeks spent in the large room in Musgrave Park hospital, but the cell I was in now seemed so small. Or maybe it was the fact of being back in a prison cell in the H-Blocks – the Blocks that I'd left almost three months previous. The Blocks I'd left to continue the battle in the prison hospital, a battle that was still ongoing. Ten comrades were dead and yet we still hadn't achieved our demands. It felt as if I could hardly breathe. I lay on the bed and closed my eyes and tried to fight back both the claustrophobia and the nausea.

Several days later, on 3 October, the hunger strike was called off. With other families stating that they would intervene if they had the opportunity to do so, and now with no real pressure on the British government to grant any concessions, the tactic of hunger strike had lost its momentum and its potential. No one wanted to end it – as we hadn't achieved our full demands – yet no one wanted it to continue. A statement was released outlining our reasons for calling an end to the hunger strike. It thanked all who had worked on our behalf and ended by saying:

> There were several reasons given by our comrades for going on hunger strike. One was because we had no choice and no other means of securing a principled solution to the four-year protest.
>
> Another, and of fundamental importance, was to advance the Irish people's right to liberty. We believe that the age old struggle for Irish self-determination and freedom has been immeasurably advanced by this hunger strike and therefore we claim a massive political victory. The hunger strikers, by their selflessness, have politicised a very substantial section of the Irish nation and exposed the shallow, unprincipled nature of the Irish partitionist bloc.
>
> Our comrades have lit with their very lives an eternal beacon which will inspire this nation and people to rise and crush oppression forever and this nation can be proud that it produced such a quality of manhood.

> We pay a special tribute to the families of our dead comrades. You have suffered greatly and with immense dignity. Your loved ones, our comrades and friends, were and would be very proud of you for standing by them. No tribute is too great.
>
> Also, we give a special mention to those families who could not watch their loved ones die in pain and agony. We prisoners understand the pressure you were under and stand by you.
>
> We thank the National H-Block/Armagh Committee, the H-Block movement, the nationalist people of Ireland, and all those who championed our cause abroad. We are indebted to you and ask you to continue your good work on our behalf.
>
> Lastly, we reaffirm our commitment to the achievement of the five demands by whatever means we believe necessary and expedient. We rule nothing out. Under no circumstances are we going to devalue the memory of our dead comrades by submitting ourselves to a dehumanising and degrading regime.

It was a strange moment. Not only had the hunger strike come to an end but so too had five years of intense protest. They had been difficult, brutal years and yet, in contrast to where we now stood, they had a clarity to them, a focus, a clear goal. We were now in uncharted waters.

I know I wasn't alone in the mixture of emotions I felt. Sadness at the loss of ten friends and comrades, anger at the British government, and, undoubtedly a sense of defeat – of having given our all but feeling that just hadn't been enough. There was a sense of relief too though; relief that no one else was going to die, coupled with a determination to move forward and build upon the sacrifice of those who had died. I believe it was many years later, however, before I truly experienced the grief of their passing. A photo, a sentence, a chance conversation with a relative; wife, brother, sister, daughter, or with a comrade, brought back the enormity of their passing.

# Epilogue

THE HUNGER STRIKE ENDED with only one of our five demands being met – the right to wear our own clothes. This new ruling applied to all prisoners, political or otherwise.

However, winning the right to wear our own clothes had great significance – on two counts. On a symbolic level, we had stated that we would never wear the prison uniform, and we hadn't. As the chorus of the H-Block song says, 'I'll wear no convict's uniform nor meekly serve my time'.[86] But besides the symbolic achievement, getting our own clothes also meant enormous changes on a practical level. While on the protest, the prison authorities refused us exercise or access to the canteen because we were not wearing the prison uniform. Now, with our own clothes, we could, for the first time in five years, get out of our cells, eat together in the canteen, be together in the yard for exercise, have association time together in the evenings and, being together, we could begin to strategise about how to achieve our outstanding demands. That said, we were still on protest. We refused to do prison work other than as orderlies in our own wings and thus continued to lose remission and other privileges such as access to the gym, football pitches, education classes, and shop facilities.

Bik McFarlane was still Camp OC. He called on everyone to sit tight and let the dust settle so that we could then plan on how best to move forward. Brendan Hughes, the former Camp OC, left the protest shortly afterwards. Others followed him, the thinking most likely being, 'If it's OK for Brendan Hughes to go, it must be OK for me'.

---

[86] The H-Block song was composed and sung by Francie Brolly, an Irish musician, teacher and Irish republican from Dungiven, County Derry. www.youtube.com/watch?v=U-k_7f4bInE

Richard O'Rawe who had been PRO during the hunger strike also left. Richard caused much controversy in later years by claiming in a book he published that there had been a deal on the table in July 1981, just before Joe McDonnell died, but that the IRA's Army Council had rejected it, thus leading to the death of six more prisoners. His claim was challenged by all others centrally involved at the time, both inside and outside the prison, and was ultimately discredited when confidential British government files were released after a 30-year embargo. Despite that, his claim led to much hurt amongst families, sowed doubt amongst many supporters, and was eagerly seized upon by hostile elements of the media and the political world in Ireland, both north and south.

It's ironic that we withstood all that the Brits and the prison regime threw at us. We held firm. And it cost us a lot. It cost us an awful lot. And yet it was 'one of our own' who in one short sentence sowed division, animosity, and doubt.

In general, I'm non-judgemental about those who left our protest over the years, at whatever stage and for whatever reason. We're all human and no one ever truly knows what's going on in the mind and world of others, even those who are close to us. But I also believe that if you've held a position of authority within the IRA, and have issued orders to other volunteers, or written statements on their behalf, lauding the great sacrifice they were making, then you have a responsibility to follow through in your own actions. If you walk away after being asked to give a little yourself, just a little, a very little in contrast to the ultimate sacrifice others have just made, then, in my view, you cheapen all that went before. You debase it. All the orders to fight the guards during the no-wash protest. All the shite on the wall. All the beatings. All the heartache that families endured. And the words. What of the words? The words that were written. The last words written of the last statement ever from the blanketmen; "Under no circumstances are we going to devalue the memory of our dead comrades by submitting ourselves to a dehumanising and degrading regime." Just a little was being asked. So very little. It seems, however, that for Brendan and Richard it was too much to ask of them.

For those who remained on the (no-work) protest, being out of our cells threw up many challenges for us. We now came into closer contact with the guards, many of whom had overseen the prison regime during the blanket protest and hunger strikes. There was an overt tension. We were also confronted with petty rules which the prison authorities imposed in their continued attempts to criminalise us and to hold onto their power. And although we had always said that we did not regard maintaining our own wings as doing prison work, we nevertheless felt uncomfortable with the manner in which that was being overseen. Prison guards could issue instructions to the 'orderlies' which made it appear as if those carrying out the orderly duties were obeying prison guards rather than an IRA OC.

Overall, there was confusion about just what would happen in the time ahead. Our life on a day-to-day basis for the previous five years had become a routine, which, if not desirable in terms of conditions and living standards, nevertheless offered a degree of security and comfort in its predictability. Now all that had ended. Those old patterns of life had gone forever and as yet no alternative had been put in their place. We were at sea, in uncharted waters.

When we emerged from our cells in October 1981 I don't think we fully comprehended the power we had. I certainly didn't. Five years of being physically confined to a 10ft by 8ft space and being treated harshly, often brutally, had left its imprint. Maybe it was just me personally being in a state of physical and psychological exhaustion that led me to feel that way. Maybe it was because throughout the protest I had envisaged that moment when the protest would end and imagined that we would immediately move into circumstances and conditions where we had all of our demands met. That hadn't happened. There had been a shift – a quite dramatic shift – but we were a long way from where we wanted to be and where we had hoped to be. It was a lesson to me that struggle rarely ends in complete or sudden success or even when it does, the outcome is not always as you once envisaged it would be. Participating in the struggle, in and of itself, changes our perceptions and often reshapes the original goals.

October 1981 was the end of prison struggle as we had previously understood it. There was never again going to be any type of physical protest, or length of protest, like the one we had just endured. There was never again, certainly in our lifetime in prison, going to be a hunger strike of the magnitude of 1981. Prison struggle had to be entirely rethought. The days of, "throw what you have at us; we can take it," were long gone. The days of physical confrontation were long gone. There's an old Irish saying, "*An duine nach bhfuil laidir, caithfidh sé/sí bheith glic.*" That is, "The person who isn't strong, has to be clever." We now realised we had to be clever. We had to use our heads, not our hearts.

Ernie O'Malley, an IRA revolutionary from the 1916 era, once wrote out from prison to a comrade, "The Irish have always made good rebels; not so good revolutionaries". In 1981 we had to stop being rebels and become revolutionaries. And we did. In subsequent years we used our intelligence, our discipline, our comradeship, and our camaraderie to totally frustrate all ongoing attempts by the prison authorities to suppress us and to continue to implement their policy of criminalisation; a policy they eventually, and quietly, dropped. Nowhere was that intelligence, discipline, and comradeship more evident than in the mass escape that occurred on 25 September, 1983, less than two years after the ending of the hunger strike. Not only was the escape a massive morale booster for all of us but it affirmed the new approach we had to prison struggle: "*An duine nach bhfuil laidir, caithfidh sé/sí a bheith glic*".

If the hunger strike killed the policy of criminalisation, the escape buried it six feet under. Prior to the escape, prison rules dictated that prisoners must do prison work. That meant taking prisoners to the workshops. After the escape, the workshops were closed and thus ended any talk about prison work. Obviously someone in the prison authorities or the NIO realised, with hindsight, that taking dozens of IRA prisoners out daily to workshops wasn't such a good idea as it facilitated the gathering of accurate and detailed intelligence on the layout of the prison and the routine of prison guards, all of which were crucial to the success of the escape. In an unpredicted way we had achieved our second demand – the right not to do prison work.

On a personal level, the years immediately post-hunger strike were about trying to return to full health, or at least to the greatest degree possible. For many weeks I still experienced an ongoing nausea. I was physically still very weak. To sit erect, on a chair for instance, and hold my head up straight, took a large degree of effort and it wasn't a position I could hold for any length of time. Each day I had to go out to the prison doctor in the medical room in the Block to be examined, have my weight taken, and blood pressure checked. Going out to the Circle I often had to wait in the airlock – the space between the wing and the corridor leading to the Circle – with grilles locked closed either side of me. I'd wait in that space to be called for the doctor. During the first few weeks I could never stand there but had to sit down on the ground after a few minutes as I got faint and nauseous. A guard ordered me one morning to stand up straight. I ignored him, not out of a sense of deliberate disobedience but simply because I couldn't stand up until I knew the grille was open and I could make my way directly to the Circle. He didn't push it.

I didn't go out to the exercise yard when the others went out but instead walked up and down the length of the wing, holding onto the wall when needing to, but trying as much as possible not to. Gradually I was able to stay on my feet for ten to fifteen minutes without feeling too bad. I kept going and eventually was able to go out to the yard. It was great to feel the fresh air on my face and breathe it into my lungs. It was late October, going into November. The air was crisp.

Walking as part of a group was difficult as I regularly bumped against those either side of me. My balance and coordination were still way off. Taking a corner was a challenge – and there are a lot of corners to take when walking around a small rectangular-shaped yard. I'd have to stop and in robotic fashion turn my body to proceed in the new direction, then do similar with the next corner, and the next. I sometimes saw the frustration on the faces of those walking with me, having to pause in their stride to give me time to find my coordination.

Seán McKenna, who had been on the first hunger strike and who was critically ill when it was called off, was in my wing and suffered the same lack of balance and coordination, even though by then it was over ten months from the time he had ended his fast. I sometimes walked with him, both of us regularly bumping into one another as we walked. It was clear from the conversations we had that the hunger strike had not only impacted upon Seán physically but also mentally. Talk could move from discussion about ordinary, everyday matters to the totally surreal – and often absurd. Seán never recovered. He was released from prison several years later and on 18 December 2008 – exactly 28 years from the ending of the hunger strike he had been on – Seán took his own life at his family home in Ravensdale, County Louth.

The hunger strike left me with permanent damage to my eyesight. It wasn't damage done to my actual eye but the death of brain cells that control the optic nerve. Unlike other parts of the body, brain cells do not regenerate. The condition is called nystagmus. Women who suffer from malnutrition during pregnancy often give birth to babies with nystagmus so the ailment is commonly associated with a lack of food. But I've learned to live with it. The dictionary defines it as:

> a vision condition in which the eyes make repetitive, uncontrolled movements. These movements often result in reduced vision and depth perception and can affect balance and coordination. These involuntary eye movements can occur from side to side, up and down, or in a circular pattern.

In my case, the movement of my eyes was, and still is, up and down. In those early days post-hunger strike, the movements were rapid and they greatly impacted my balance and coordination. It was actually easier to walk with my eyes closed than open, as with them closed it didn't feel like everything was moving around me. With my eyes open, it was like trying to find your balance on a small ship in the middle of a stormy ocean. The rapid eye movements also contributed to the nausea I felt, especially in the bright light of overhead fluorescent tubes. For several months I wore dark sunglasses. I had to get a doctor's permission to allow my parents to send them in to me. They helped reduce the glare of the cell lights.

The nausea gradually eased over subsequent months but the nystagmus continued to seriously affect my balance and coordination for many years to come. I worked at it, though, doing various eye exercises including relaxing the eye rather than trying to 'screw' it into a certain position whereby my vision became more 'fixed' or focused. I was determined to get back to as full a state of well-being as possible and gradually I was able to reduce the pace of the erratic eye movements, and the impact they had on me. I've learned to live with the condition. I read, I write, I drive. However, others have told me they can still occasionally see the rapid eye movements. Gabrielle, for instance, who I first met in 2005 to conduct an interview for her studies, recalls, "I remember handing you the consent form for my interview and you were moving your head quite visibly, and sometimes even moving the page, seemingly to accommodate the eye movements. Fast forward 15 years, it's much less obvious to me now than it was back then, although occasionally I see you strain hard to focus your eyes, when reading a menu, for example, and sometimes I can see the slight flickering of your eyes when I look into them."

As mentioned earlier, I also developed ulcerative colitis as a result of the hunger strike. I was diagnosed in 1982 and was treated for the condition for the remaining ten years I spent in prison. At one time I was on 16 tablets a day, had regular enemas, and bi-annual trips to Musgrave Park Hospital for an internal examination. One prison doctor during that period, however, told me that there was a theory about colitis developing as a reaction to dairy products. He was a friendly man and, maybe not surprisingly, therefore, didn't last too long in the prison. I recall the day he told me about his theory. I was in the medical room in the Block and there were two MOs with him. As he was talking to me they were making a lot of noise. The doctor stopped talking and said to me, "Hold on a second, Laurence". This was unique in itself as none of the other doctors ever addressed prisoners by their first names. I think they regarded us first and foremost as prisoners, not patients. He then called out to the MOs, "You might wish to listen here. You might learn something from it." I think his tone of voice probably sped up his departure from the prison.

In response to his information, I did briefly try to avoid dairy products but as we had no control over our own diet (the food being supplied to us by the prison) that didn't last long. The dairy we got was largely in the form of milk and as breakfast consisted of cereal, rather than a cooked meal, to avoid dairy would have meant going without breakfast entirely; so I took the cereal. However, the doctor's words always stayed with me and when I was eventually released I experimented. I substituted soya milk for dairy milk. Within a week the symptoms of the colitis disappeared. That was further confirmed several months later when I had to attend the Lagan Valley Hospital for a colonoscopy. The consultant said to me, post-examination, "It's rare that I'm in a position to tell anyone this but your condition has totally disappeared." It seems that the hunger strike, whatever it did to my intestines, had made me become lactose-intolerant, or, as my youngest daughter, Órlaith, once thought it was called, 'black toast intolerant'!

Nystagmus and ulcerative colitis aside, I physically survived the hunger strike. Ten others didn't. And others who did survive, including Pat McGeown and Matt Devlin, died while still relatively young. Paddy Quinn still suffers from kidney problems. The hunger strike took its toll in more ways than one and not just on those who participated in it, but those close to us.

Post-hunger strike, family visits were often with both my mother and father. It was good to see them together. I'm sure my mother was glad to have my father by her side after five years of visiting me either alone or with a neighbour or friend. And I know my father would have taken support from her and her familiarity with the process of entering and leaving the prison, just as he always took support from her.

About a year after the hunger strike they both travelled to the USA, to Washington.[87] My mother had always wanted to see the grave of her father who was buried there. During the blanket protest a couple in Florida, Vita and Tom Cox, had contacted her. They were following events in Ireland and were supportive of our prison protest. The correspondence grew into a close friendship and Vita and Tom invited them to the States, offering to meet them in Washington and to help them locate the grave.

On my first visit with them upon their return home I could see very clearly how much my mother had enjoyed the trip. Not only had she been able to fulfil a lifelong wish but she was greatly fortified by the love and admiration showered upon her. At one point in their trip they were taken to a concert. Before it commenced it was announced over the PA system that the parents of an Irish hunger striker were in the audience. There was an immediate and long standing ovation. Having for so many years lived with the fears and anxieties, the condemnations and rebukes, it must have warmed her heart so much to discover that there were other communities who admired what we had done.

> The happiest I ever saw you
> was on your return from the States a year later;
> a life-long dream fulfilled in the act of placing flowers
> on your father's grave.
> And the joy you experienced in your newly-discovered fame
> as the mother of a freedom fighter
> not a terrorist.
> Concerts stopping mid-way through to introduce you to the
> audience who
> rose and applauded.
> You leaned across to me and whispered, conspiratorially,
> of how you met a woman you believed to be a socialist,
> and I smiled at your earnestness.[88]

---

[87] See photographs.

[88] Laurence McKeown (2018), *Threads*, Clare, Ireland: Salmon Poetry, p. 32.

A few short months after her return from the States, my mother passed away. On the morning of 8 June, 1983, my father woke, got out of bed, made tea for both of them, and returned to the bedroom. My mother didn't rouse. It was only then he discovered that she was dead. She was aged 61, eight years older than my father.

I have no doubt that the hunger strike contributed to her early death. I've looked at photos of her taken in the late 1970s and those taken in 1982, just a few years later, and can clearly see the tragedy of those intervening years etched on her face. I know my father was devastated by her death, though as usual on visits, or, just more generally between men, those emotions were never discussed. It was only when I was released from prison and got to talking with Peggy McKeown, a neighbour from across the road, that I got some idea of the extent of the devastation my father felt at the loss of my mother. Peggy told me how he would visit occasionally, possibly when he felt particularly down, and cry openly for ages.

I'm grateful that I had that 21 months with my mother following the end of the hunger strike. I'm especially glad that she got to visit her father's grave. I had always known that he had gone off to America at some stage. I didn't know, and still don't know, why he left. I also somehow assumed that when he had left, my mother was an adult, or at least a teenager. It was only when writing this memoir, and checking details with my sister, Mary, and a cousin, Alice, that I discovered that my mother was aged only six when her father left home. He left behind a wife and three young children. He left a wife, who, perhaps unknown to them at the time, was also pregnant with their fourth child.

I've often wondered since then, what my mother's abiding memory of her father was. What image of him did that six-year old child hold as he left that day? Did she know her father was leaving, never to return? What thoughts did she have as she stood at his grave 55 years later? All the unanswered questions, and more besides, that I would have loved to have asked her had she lived.

I was given twelve hours parole to attend her funeral and my father, very thoughtful of him, got a local photographer, Michael McKay, to take a photo of all of us gathered for the funeral, and one of me.[89]

After her death, my father visited me in prison, sometimes on his own and at other times with a friend. The period between the end of

[89] See photographs.

the hunger strike and my mother's death had provided the space for him and I to reach some sort of rapprochement; an acceptance that we viewed the world differently. I know too, that he was trying to see that world more and more through my eyes. He was delighted when he learned that I was enrolled in the Open University and often inquired about my studies. I always recall, when growing up, that he had a phrase, "education's easily carried". And I know he was devastated when I left St Malachy's aged twelve, throwing away what he regarded as a golden opportunity.

My father died on 9 July 1988, just before his birthday on the 12th. The physical cause of his death was a heart attack but I know he was also heart-broken. At the time of his death I was on the IRA's Camp staff. We had initiated a campaign one year earlier to vastly improve conditions and one of our demands was for statutory 24-hour compassionate parole in the event of a death in the family. A number of prisoners had already been granted the 24 hours and we assumed that our demand had been accepted. However, when I applied for this parole to attend my father's funeral, I was offered only ten hours. This was two hours less than what I had been granted five years earlier when my mother died. I refused to accept it and demanded 24 hours. Later that same day I was called out to the Circle and an Assistant Governor, who I had never seen before, told me that I was now being offered 12 hours. I refused again and he said: "Well, that's all you're getting. You can take it or leave it".

That night I wrote a comm to my sister, Mary, to explain things from my perspective; why I was refusing the 12 hours. I knew my family would be wondering what was going on. They would know I'd been offered parole and refused it, and I was concerned that they might think it had something to do with my previous relationship with my father. I didn't want my actions to appear heartless and wanted to explain that, from my position, and in the context of what we were then struggling for in the prison, I could not accept anything other than twenty-four hours.

Just as I finished the comm there was a knock on my door. It was an old English guard who was always friendly. He shouted in to me, "Laurence, I'll open you up at six in the morning for a shower." I replied, "Nawh, it's ok, I'm not accepting the parole." He said, "Did no one tell you yet? You were granted the 24 hours."

I was elated. I returned to the comm and at the bottom of it wrote, 'Up the Ra!'

I learned later that there had been a very vigorous effort made by a number of people on the outside to get me released on parole. To the fore was Oliver Kearney, a close family friend from Antrim town who played a very prominent role in the protests for political status and later the 'McBride Principles' campaign.[90] Oliver was friends with the Church of Ireland Bishop of Derry and Raphoe, James Mehaffy, and it appears that it was a telephone call to the NIO from Bishop Mehaffy that finally swung it.

Why the NIO had initially offered me only the ten hours is anyone's guess. There was no logic to it, other than antagonism. Whatever the thinking behind it, they had to back down in the end.

One year later, over the summer of '89, I was temporarily released (along with many other life-sentence and long-term prisoners), for three days on ordinary parole. It came about following a very successful campaign waged by us to have life-sentence prisoners released permanently. It was the first parole of several which I got over the following three years before my eventual release from prison in 1992. It was tragic that my father didn't get to see me out, back at home, even if briefly. And I know that he would have been delighted to see me graduate from Queen's University in 1998 with a PhD. I'm not sure, though, what he would have made of the title of my doctoral thesis, *Unrepentant Fenian Bastards*.[91] I think though, by then, he would have winked, nodded his head, smiled wryly, and said, "That's our Laurence for you!" I would have loved for him to have seen that

[90] The MacBride Principles consisted of nine fair employment principles aimed at tackling discrimination against Catholics in the north of Ireland. They became a corporate code of conduct for US companies doing business in the North and the Congressional standard for all US aid to, or for economic dealings with, the North. The Principles were named after Irishman, Seán McBride, a former Chief of Staff of the Irish Republican Army (1936-1937), later, politician who served as Minister for External Affairs in the Dublin government, (1948-1951), and a founding member of Amnesty International.
https://www.irishtimes.com/news/the-nine-macbride-principles-1.32756

[91] The title comes from the refrain in a track – Fenians – by the New York rebel hip hop band, Seanchaí and the Unity Squad. The full title of the thesis is, *Unrepentant Fenian Bastards: The Social Construction of an Irish Republican Prisoner Community.*

I could pursue formal education and obtain academic qualifications in my own way and on my own terms, and that there was no contradiction whatsoever in doing that whilst also engaging in political struggle.

Leaving aside any physical damage brought on by the hunger strike, what about psychological or emotional scars? Maybe it's only others who know me who can more correctly assess that. But I do know the protest, the five years of it, left its mark, for either good or bad. I believe that to survive in those conditions, and to cope with the challenges they threw up, we had to cut ourselves off from others, family and friends. Our world was different from theirs and to engage too much with their world, and with them, was only going to cause us additional pain. It was better to sever those links as much as possible in order to engage with what needed to be done. That type of thinking was taken to a new level with the hunger strike. You have to really deeply shut yourself off from that world, or maybe it's more accurate to frame it as going deeper into your own world. And, once you've done that, I'm not sure you can ever fully return to where you were before. It's like becoming aware of some new piece of information. Once you have it, you cannot return to a previous state of 'not knowing'.

Despite this, I think I'm fairly grounded and laid back. Some close friends have remarked that if I was any more laid back I'd be fast asleep! I have never had nightmares about that time, or any other time, thankfully. And I don't carry any bitterness. To do so would be to hand power over to those who brutalised us. But I do know I can compartmentalise my emotions. I do it unconsciously. It's learned behaviour. At times, and to others, it may appear cold, clinical, brutal even – though I never intend it to be that way nor even think of it in that way. For me, it's as if it is the most logical thing to do; the most rational choice to make in whatever the situation.

Eckart Tolle writes in *The Power of Now* about 'acceptance'.[92] He's not advancing the proposal that we should 'accept our lot' and not attempt to change it, but rather speaks about accepting the reality of the conditions and circumstances we experience, rather than attempting to avoid that reality and 'wish' those conditions and circumstances to be otherwise. A bit like the phrase we had in the jail

---

[92] Eckhart Tolle (2001), *The Power of Now*, London: Hodder & Stoughton.

in later years, 'a concrete analysis of a concrete situation' (rather than appraising situations from a subjective position). Maybe that's why Tolle's perspective appeals to me so much. But I understand that approaching life situations and challenges from such a perspective could appear to others as hard or even selfish. Maybe it appears that way to them because there doesn't seem to be a conflicted emotional journey taking place that leads to the making of a decision from which actions then flow – when actually there always is. The emotions *are* there. It's just that they are not allowed to cloud or distract from what needs to be done. There's that distancing again. The use of the autonomous tense. Leaving the 'I' out of it. It becomes the 'not allowed' and the 'what needs to be done'. Let me rephrase it. The emotions *are* there. It's just that *I* do not allow them to cloud or distract *me* from what *I* need to do.

My former-wife, Mick, often said to me, "Laurny, I didn't ask you what you think. I asked you what you feel. I don't want an analysis of what has to be done – that will come later – I just want to know what and how you are feeling in this moment." Initially, I thought that absurd, or a luxury; an indulgence. If we're eventually going to end up with an analysis of what's happening and what needs to be done, and from that will flow decisions and then courses of action, why not just move immediately to that stage now? What's all this fuzzy-wuzzy stuff about emotions? Does it really matter? Or worse, are they going to cloud or distract from what I know I need to do?

I now believe it's not an 'either/or' situation; you can have both emotion and pragmatic analysis; we are emotional/sentient beings. However, as Tolle again writes, we can experience the emotion without *becoming* the emotion. And I know the emotions do exist, even if buried. Since my release 29 years ago I've spoken about the protest and hunger strike at numerous events and given countless interviews. Usually, I do so without any difficulty. At other times though, I can be in the midst of a sentence when a word, an image, a sound comes to mind, and I'm flooded with emotion. I either openly weep or have to pause mid-sentence and wait until I can compose myself again.

I've always had an affinity with native American people. I don't know why, but have had a sense of closeness to them from my earliest days. Maybe it was knowing how their land was taken from them and their people oppressed, murdered, and finally crushed and that bore such a similarity to Ireland and our experience of colonialism. In later life, however, I came to learn much more about their culture and sense of community. I believe we could take many lessons from them, especially in regards to the expression of emotions. One of their most powerful adages, for example, is that 'the bravest warriors are those who can cry most easily'.

I've often told others that adage. I've conveyed it at a time when they were becoming emotional about something and then embarrassed at being so. I probably need to repeat the story to myself more often.

I've found, though, in recent years that I can let my emotions rise more easily to the surface, or maybe it's the case that they force their way out more readily. In 2019, for instance, I was giving an interview in my home to Dr Roisín Higgins (Reader in Modern History, Teeside University, England) who is working on a new research project on *The Sensory History of Conflict*. The project aims to tell the story of the conflict differently – using memories of sight, sound, touch, taste and smell to recall personal experiences. Roisín told me that she had been really struck by some of the writings of Bobby Sands and the way in which he created a particularly vivid, imaginary, sensory world that was the complete opposite to his immediate surroundings. She had also heard some public comments I had made about the way in which senses were heightened during the hunger strike so she thought it would be a fascinating area of research to pursue.

We got to talking about the hunger strike and I told her about how my sense of smell heightened as simultaneously my eyesight deteriorated, and about the noise the trolley made as it moved through the prison grilles, and how I could distinguish the different sounds it made. How it rattled when there was nothing on it, how that rattle was dampened when piles of bed linen were on it. And how sometimes it made little noise at all – when a dead body was on it. Roisín was sitting directly across from me at my kitchen table and soon after I began to talk I also began to sob. She sat and waited until I composed myself and was ready to continue. Three times during the hour-long interview I broke down and eventually said to her, jokingly (or out of embarrassment), "My God, Róisín, what the hell are you doing to me?" She just smiled. I suppose I had (in the first interview she had conducted as part of the project) confirmed for her the significance of her research – the significance of sensory memory. But it also confirmed for me just how deep those memories and associated emotions run and how easily they can be triggered by an image or the recollection of a sound, smell, or touch.

I know it's a good thing that I'm letting go, even if I never consciously thought at any time that I was holding on. I know that suppressed emotions do eventually make their presence felt, often in the form of physical ailments. Emotions from a time when it was too much of a luxury to experience them, too much of an indulgence, too much of a risk. And yet it's a territory that I still unconsciously or subconsciously attempt to avoid. Even in writing this Epilogue, the concluding words of the memoir, it took Gabrielle to (gently) point out to me that I had covered in detail the physical effects of the hunger strike but had made no mention at all of the mental or emotional impact of those years. I returned to the text to correct that.

However, and not to revert to a 'defensive' position, I do believe that, overall, we (blanketmen) came through it fairly well. That's not to ignore those who didn't. I remember all too well Alec Comerford who I was on remand with and who later, on the blanket, suffered a mental breakdown. He died young, in 2000. Alec wasn't the only one; there were others. But given the conditions, the brutality, and the length of time the protest lasted, I think we did come through it better than could otherwise have been the case – even if we undoubtedly bear the scars. In many ways I put that down to the camaraderie we shared inside but also the immense love and support we got from families and communities on the outside. They were our backbone.

The H-Blocks eventually closed in July 2000 with the (early) release of all political prisoners following the signing of the Good Friday Agreement. Soon afterwards there was talk of demolishing the prison. One unionist referred to 'bull-dozing it into history' – as if such a thing was possible. At that time I worked for Coiste na nIarchimí (Committee of ex-prisoners), the umbrella organisation for former IRA prisoner groups across the north and the southern border counties. Mike Ritchie, the Director of Coiste, initiated a process under the British government's heritage legislation to have the prison preserved due to its historical value. While in prison, republicans sought to destroy the prison; when on the outside, we sought to preserve it! We won the case. The British government appealed the decision, and lost. I always think it somehow poetic that it was their

(British) legislation that facilitated the preservation of a site that they wanted so much to eradicate from public memory and consciousness.

A very lengthy process ensued after that. Unionists were totally opposed to the preservation and initially would not engage. However, when it became clear that there would be economic advantage to developing the huge 365-acre site, they began to come around. At the same time we (Coiste) accepted that the entire prison could not be preserved and agreed to the demolition of seven of the eight H-Blocks, leaving one (H6) remaining, the prison hospital, the chapel, the visiting area, and part of the exterior wall complete with watch-towers. We also wanted one of the Cages moved to that area. Besides the preservation of part of the prison we also proposed the construction of a new iconic Peace and Reconciliation centre at the site where the stories of all who had been impacted by the conflict, regardless of what side they were on, or none, could be stored.

Our aim in preserving the site of the former prison was not, as unionists claimed, to create 'a shrine to the hunger strikers', but as a lesson to future generations about how not to deal with socio-political issues and legitimate demands for reforms and civil rights. Unionists had opened the prison in 1972 to house those (all nationalists initially) who were interned without trial. When internment didn't work they then built the H-Blocks to try and criminalise those engaged in political struggle. We now know how that ended. The prison became a battlefield and there were countless deaths on the streets as well as those who died within the prison. Surely there's a lesson to be learned there.

As we began to move forward with our plans to preserve the prison we organised for the families of the hunger strikers to come together in the Felons Club, Falls Road, Belfast on Wednesday 4 June, 2005 to hear what we had in mind. We felt they should be the first to know. Two bus-loads arrived at the Felons, one of the buses driven by a former blanketman, Eamonn O'Donnell from Derry. Mike made a presentation and there were loads of questions, most of which we couldn't answer at the time as we had only started out on the process. Overall, there was a very warm and supportive response to our proposals.

We then travelled in the two buses to the H-Blocks. The NIO had facilitated our request to allow the families to visit the prison and especially the prison hospital. The prison was in a state of early dilapidation, given that heat and light had been cut from it once prisoners had been released. We had arranged for a Mass to be celebrated in the canteen of the prison hospital and for the two former chaplains, Fr Toner and Fr Murphy, to celebrate the Mass. My former-wife, Mick, had gone to the prison hospital earlier that morning and had lit candles and placed them between the concrete bars of the windows. She also placed Easter lilies there.

Some of those gathered there that day had been in the prison hospital when their relative died but many relatives, especially parents, had died in the intervening years. Others were family members who were too young at the time of the hunger strike to remember, or not even born before 1981. Alfie and Margaret Doherty (parents of Kieran) did not wish to attend. I met with them privately at their home beforehand and they applauded what we were doing but said that their memories of the (lengthy) time they had spent in the hospital with Kieran before he died were just too raw.

After the visit to the prison hospital we went to H-Block 4 to let people see around an actual Block. We walked down the wings and into the exercise yards, the canteens, and education rooms.

Apart from relatives of the hunger strikers and some former blanketmen being present on the day, I had also asked Éamonn O'Faogáin if he would accompany us. Éamonn was a traditional singer, teacher, and gaeilgeoir (now sadly deceased), and I wanted him to sing at the Mass in the prison hospital. His reply was, "Laurence, it would be the deepest honour for me". Éamonn had sang at the celebration of the birth of my daughter, Caoilfhionn. Her mother, Deirdre, and I did not have a traditional church christening or have her baptised but still wanted to mark the occasion, so we organised a private party for family and friends in Maddens Bar, Belfast, one Sunday afternoon. Éamonn was an amazing singer. A large, heavy man, his voice was so incongruous with his physical presence. It was so soft and melodic. So warm and with such depth. His voice totally reflected the nature of the man. A kind man. A gentle man. A gentleman.

On that day in Long Kesh, as we walked out of H-Block 4 into the front yard, Éamonn got us to pause a moment. I think he actually asked me for permission to do so. As we gathered around him he began to sing *We Shall Overcome* in Irish. The hair stood on the back of my head. There was not another sound to be heard.

> *Ó, go domhain i mo chroí, creidim go sároimid lá éigin.* (Oh, deep in my heart I do believe we shall overcome, some day.)

The front gates of the Block lay opened wide. The locks on the gates were already beginning to rust. Small plants were growing up through cracks in the tarmac and concrete. Yes, we *had* overcome.

Later that year, I took my daughters, Caoilfhionn, aged eight, and Órlaith, aged six, to visit the prison. It wasn't prompted by any attempt to indoctrinate them into a republican history but rather to confront their fears. We were living in Mullaghbawn, South Armagh, at the time and as I was taking them to school one morning – *Bunscoil an Iúir* in Newry – Caoilfhionn burst out crying. I pulled into the side of the road and asked her what was wrong. In between sobs she asked me if the soldiers were going to come and take me away to prison again. She was aware I *had* been in prison. At that time the British Army lookout posts were still on the top of mountains in South Armagh and it was that which prompted her sobs. I told her that, no, they wouldn't be taking me to prison again and that soon they would be leaving our land altogether. She settled down and we drove on, but I decided shortly afterwards to take them both to Long Kesh to see it for themselves. I believe in confronting fears. Often the fear is worse than the actual experience. Like waiting for a beating is usually worse than the beating itself. Your mind prepares for the worst and often exaggerates. I wanted them to see open gates and grilles, and empty watch-towers. I wanted them to see an abandoned site. I wanted them to see the small plants growing up through the tarmac and concrete that I had seen. I wanted them to see a *former* prison.

We visited the prison hospital and were photographed in the last cell I was in on hunger strike. Caoilfhionn and Órlaith were more delighted with getting their photo taken in this strange place rather than any consciousness of what the space meant for me. We then walked out into the exercise yard of the prison hospital, the yard that I had once fainted in. I asked Mick to stay at one end of the yard while I walked Caoilfhionn and Órlaith to the other end, and for her to have her camera ready. When the three of us got to the top of the yard we paused and chatted for a short while and then I casually asked them to run down to Mick to see who would get to her first. I knew they would regard this as a great game. A bit of fun. Some friendly competition. Although Órlaith was two years younger than Caoilfhionn, and smaller, I knew she was very athletic so both of them would be neck and neck in the race.

As they got close to Mick she took their photo. It's a photo of them laughing as they ran. Running without a care in the world. Running in the yard of a former prison that meant absolutely nothing to them. Running with all fears banished. (See photographs.)

Bobby (Sands) had once written, 'Let our revenge be the laughter of our children'. I think it an amazing quote, written as it was while he was naked, malnourished, barefoot in a cell whose walls were covered in his own excreta. They are not harsh words. There is no bitterness in them. No call for vengeance. Quite the opposite. There is hope for laughter. The laughter of children. The laughter of children of a new generation who thankfully would know nothing about internment, criminalisation, hunger strikes, and armed conflict.

As I stood at the top of the yard that day, listening to their squeals of delight as they ran, I hoped that Bobby too heard their laughter and that he had his revenge. I hoped that Frank, Raymond, Patsy, Joe, Martin, Kevin, Kieran, Tom, and Mickey heard that laughter too.

To conclude, I'm often asked if the blanket protest and hunger strike was a success, or not. My reply is always that it depends on how you look at it and in what context. Confining it to the prison, we had five demands and achieved only one of them – the right to wear our own clothes. One out of five could never be deemed a successful outcome to any endeavour. But our struggle in the prison was not confined to the prison nor was it essentially about prison policy. Our struggle was part of the wider republican struggle and in that sense the blanket protest and hunger strike were hugely successful.

Just how successful, was summed up in a conversation I had in later years with Brian Keenan, a very senior IRA volunteer. Brian was recounting how, in the late 1970s, the British security and intelligence services had pretty much got the upper hand in regards to the conflict. Mass arrests, ill-treatment and torture in the interrogation centres, and convictions in the Diplock Courts had all taken their toll. Aerial surveillance (by helicopters), land surveillance (through the use of hidden cameras and bugging devices), plus informers (or the general public) passing information to the British had impacted greatly. On top of that, he said, there was the 'hearts and minds' issue – a lot of people were becoming war-weary. And then he turned to me and said: "And who would have believed it? A group of naked prisoners turned all that around."

It's now well-documented that post-hunger strike the IRA was practically overwhelmed with people seeking to become volunteers. It's widely recognised too that political, financial, military, and moral support, not just nationally but internationally, flowed in bucket-loads to the IRA in the years that followed. The tide of the war shifted dramatically because hearts and minds had shifted – had *been* shifted.

It makes you wonder.

It makes you wonder, what would have happened if the British had sought merely to defeat the IRA rather than try to crush the very idea of Irish republicanism. What if their major, comprehensive counter-insurgency programme against the IRA launched in 1975, had not contained the criminalisation element? I would still have ended up in prison. So too would have Bobby Sands, Francis Hughes, Raymond McCreesh, Patsy O'Hara, Joe McDonnell, Martin Hurson, Kevin Lynch, Kieran Doherty, Tom McElwee, Mickey Devine and hundreds of other republican volunteers. We'd have been incarcerated in the Cages of Long Kesh where we would have worn our own clothes, not done prison work, and spent our time making handicrafts, parading, walking around the yard, struggling to learn Irish, reminiscing, and making the occasional batch of poitín.

There wouldn't have been a word either from us or about us. The world would not have known we even existed.

It makes you wonder.

It makes you wonder if, in such circumstances, the British could have been successful in their military campaign to defeat the IRA.

Today, in 2021, Irish republicanism is stronger, more vibrant, and more successful than it has ever been. It is also more comprehensive, broad and deep, inclusive, diverse, and mainstream.

If it hadn't been for the protests in the prisons, the deaths on hunger strike, the electoral successes achieved during that period, and the worldwide media attention that became focused on the conflict in the north of Ireland, would things have evolved as they did?

It makes you wonder. It certainly does make you wonder.